It has been a peculiar honour to be privileged to write this History and Memoir, of which I am very sensible. It has also been a work of love. It has been written so that our men, and our mothers and widows, may tell to their children of how their own kin fought, bled and even died, that our country should be unsullied; and our women remain unbesmirched by the wolves of Europe; and that Britain fought for her word, her honour and her friends; so that they may know, also, at first hand, of where and how our lads fought, and suffered and won.

If also, in some din, afterglow fashion, the strivings and the frolics, the horror and the fun of our past days is reflected for us, so that, in the comfort of our homes, as we turn the pages, we can again visualize the smoke of the battlefield, or the Mule Race at Ayette; hear the crack of rifle at the Sambre, and the purr and boom of guns at Ypres and Meteren, or the triumphant strains of a Band echoing through the streets of ruined Baupaume; scent the dank rot and filth of the Somme trenches, or the yellow gas fumes of Passchendaele; feel the pulse quicken with the thought of Zero hour, or with the warm glow of the companionship of good friends, huddled under the same blanket, in the straw of an old granary; and know that we strove manfully and unselfishly as one man towards the common end, with high hope, pride, godliness and happiness; the utmost mission of these pages will have been accomplished.

G. S. H.

4th August, 1921.

SKETCH MAP ILLUSTRATING OPERATIONS BY THE 33RD DIVISION
IN FRANCE AND FLANDERS
NOV. 1915 TO NOV. 1918.

Scale of Miles
0   5   10   20   30

G. S. H.

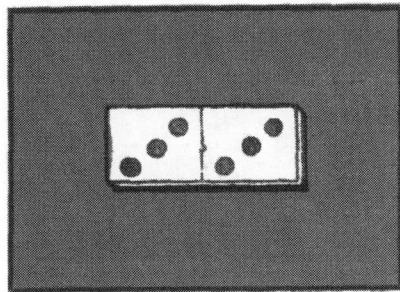

(From an Official Photograph.)

MAJOR-GENERAL SIR REGINALD PINNEY, K.C.B.,

WHO COMMANDED THE THIRTY-THIRD DIVISION
FROM OCTOBER, 1916, UNTIL FEBRUARY, 1919.

THE
THIRTY-THIRD
DIVISION
IN FRANCE AND FLANDERS

1915–1919

BY

LIEUTENANT-COLONEL GRAHAM SETON HUTCHINSON
D.S.O., M.C., F.R.G.S.

The Naval & Military Press Ltd

published in association with

FIREPOWER
The Royal Artillery Museum
Woolwich

Published by
The Naval & Military Press Ltd
Unit 10 Ridgewood Industrial Park,
Uckfield, East Sussex,
TN22 5QE England
Tel: +44 (0) 1825 749494
Fax: +44 (0) 1825 765701
www.naval–military-press.com

in association with

FIREPOWER
The Royal Artillery Museum, Woolwich
www.firepower.org.uk

In reprinting in facsimile from the original, any imperfections are inevitably reproduced and the quality may fall short of modern type and cartographic standards.

Printed and bound by Antony Rowe Ltd, Eastbourne

"They were a wall unto us both by night and day."

I. Samuel, xxv. 16.

TO THE FALLEN.

Come, where the great have trod
   You who pass by.
Palled by the blackened sod,
   Thin-wrapt, they lie.

Deep in the shades of Time
   Men of their blood,
Sworn to avenge a crime
   For freedom stood.

Sleep, under mound and tree
   Warrior of old,
True was thy bairn to thee
   Safe in the fold.

So, in the Thunder's wake
   Still may we tread
Paths that great men would take,
   Paths of the dead.

Come, where the great have trod—
   Sunshine is there.
Straight was their march to God—
   That be our care.

A.L.

CONTENTS.

ILLUSTRATIONS.

FIELD-MARSHAL LORD H. C. O. PLUMER, G.C.B., G.C.M.G., G.C.V.O.,
WHO COMMANDED THE SECOND ARMY.

A history of the 33rd Division
is a narrative of some of the most
important phases and of the most
thrilling incidents of the Great War —

The part played by the 33rd Div:
which the narrative describes is one on
which all who served with the Division
can look back with pride.

The history will conjure up
memories of brave deeds and service
gallantly and faithfully performed.

As Commander of the 2nd Army
with which the Division served for
some time I can bear testimony
to the value of their service —

5. Sept. 1920

F. M.

WHAT is to come we know not.   But we know
    That what has been was good—was good to show,
Better to hide, and best of all to bear.
We are the masters of the days that were :
We have lived, we have loved, we have suffered . . . Even so.

Shall we not take the ebb who had the flow?
Life was our friend.   Now, if it be our foe—
Dear, though it spoil, and break us!—need we care
                                    What is to come?

Let the great winds their worst and wildest blow,
Or the gold weather round us mellow slow :
We have fulfilled ourselves, and we can dare
And we can conquer, though we may not share
In the rich quiet of the afterglow
                                    What is to come.

                                    W. E. HENLEY.

NOTE.

VERY many volumes have already appeared upon the Great War from the pens of British, Allied, and enemy Commanders, and others. We have been, and are, satisfied with Lord Haig's official despatches as the only necessary reference. We claim for this narrative that it has the veracity to be expected of an account compiled in the field of operations in which we have actually participated.

Two years have already elapsed since the Armistice and we are fortunate, therefore, in having been able to view the actions and events, in which we have played our part, in a more correct perspective than would have been possible had the History of the 33rd Division been written whilst the heat of War conditions was still in our veins.

It has been a most difficult task to steer between the barren presentation of historical facts and the undoubtedly highly coloured story of gallantry, bloody victory and failure. The task of thus chronicling the events of 1915-1919 has not, therefore, been lightly approached. There is nothing told within these pages which has not actually occurred to us as a Division, or under our own observation. Much it is regretted has been omitted despite hard endeavour to procure facts. We wish it could have been otherwise, but in the turmoil of War and confusion of the battlefield many acts of collective and individual gallantry must essentially for ever remain obscured.

Having finished the work it will always be a disappointment to me that justice has not been done to the subject. There are others also who will be aggrieved that special mention, which they or their Units have, without doubt, merited, has been omitted, has escaped notice, or, in the heat of battle, has been overlooked, when the result of the whole has been subjected to the expert scrutiny of a Higher Command. We must mutually share our disappointment ; and some of us, perhaps, read again " Ole Lukoie's " little parable in " The Green Curve "—" The Point of View "—" Proportion, Gentlemen ! Proportion ! No ! it's not worth moving a flag."

I wish to record my appreciation of the generous and kindly assistance which has been rendered to me, particularly by Major-General Sir Reginald Pinney, K.C.B., who has revised much of the original manuscript, and correctly focussed the actions described. To Colonel C. G. Stewart, C.M.G., D.S.O., R.A. ; to Captain A. Clifton-Shelton, R.A.S.C., especially for his notes on the R.A.S.C. embodied in Chapter IX ; and to those officers and others who have given valuable assistance and advice, I am indeed very grateful.

CHAPTER I.

Organization of the 33rd Division—The La Bassée Front, Cuinchy and Cambrai—Evolution of Tactics, Trench Mortars, Mines, Raids—Brilliant attacks by 2nd Battalion Royal Welch Fusiliers, Glasgow Highlanders and 2nd Battalion Argyll and Sutherland Highlanders.

HEADQUARTERS, 33RD DIVISION—19TH NOVEMBER, 1915.

Commander	Major-General H. J. S. Landon, C.B.
Aide-de-Camp to Commander	Lieutenant C. Bushell, The Queens (Royal West Surrey Regiment).
Aide-de-Camp to Commander	Lieutenant A. H. W. Landon, Royal Canadian Regiment.

GENERAL STAFF BRANCH—

General Staff Officer, 1st Grade	Lieutenant-Colonel A. Symons, 13th Hussars.
General Staff Officer, 2nd Grade	Major G. de la P. B. Pakenham, D.S.O., Border Regiment.
General Staff Officer, 3rd Grade	Major E. L. Makin, Wiltshire Regiment.

ADJUTANT AND QUARTERMASTER-GENERAL'S BRANCH—

Assistant Adjutant and Quartermaster-General	Lieutenant-Colonel H. B. Des. V. Wilkinson, Durham Light Infantry.
Deputy Assistant Adjutant and Quartermaster-General	Captain A. H. Du Boulay, Royal Engineers.
Deputy Assistant Quartermaster-General ..	Major C. F. Alleyne, Army Service Corps.

ADMINISTRATIVE SERVICES AND DEPARTMENTS—

Assistant Director of Medical Services ..	Colonel T. Daly, Royal Army Medical Corps.
Deputy Assistant Director of Medical Services	Lieutenant-Colonel R. J. Blackham, C.I.E., Royal Army Medical Corps.
Assistant Director of Veterinary Services..	Major R. A. Plunkett, Army Veterinary Corps.
Deputy Assistant Director of Ordnance Services	Captain A. Gray, Army Ordnance Department.

SPECIAL APPOINTMENT—

Assistant Provost-Marshal	Captain J. M. Gordon Dill, 5th Lancers.

HEADQUARTERS, DIVISIONAL ARTILLERY—

Commander	Brigadier-General C. F. Blane.
Brigade-Major	Major P. Sheppard, D.S.O., Royal Field Artillery.
Staff Captain	Captain T. C. Usher, Royal Artillery.

I

THE THIRTY-THIRD DIVISION.

HEADQUARTERS, DIVISIONAL ENGINEERS—
Commander .. .. Lieutenant-Colonel F. E. G. Skey, Reserve of Officers.
Adjutant .. .. Lieutenant J. S. Baines, Royal Engineers.

HEADQUARTERS, 98TH INFANTRY BRIGADE—
Commander .. .. Brigadier-General E. P. Strickland, C.M.G., D.S.O.
Brigade-Major .. .. Major R. H. Hermon-Hodge, M.V.O., Reserve of Officers.

HEADQUARTERS, 99TH INFANTRY BRIGADE—
Commander .. .. Brigadier-General R. O. Kellett, Reserve of Officers.
Brigade-Major .. .. Captain R. R. G. Kane, D.S.O., Royal Munster Fusiliers.
Staff Captain .. .. Captain L. H. Andrews, Bedfordshire Regiment.

HEADQUARTERS, 100TH INFANTRY BRIGADE—
Commander .. .. Brigadier-General R. H. Twigg, C.B., Indian Army.
Brigade-Major .. .. Major G. J. P. Geiger, Royal Welch Fusiliers.
Staff Captain .. .. Captain V. Ward Brown, Middlesex Regiment.

The 33rd Division was constituted in December, 1914, but was broken into independent Brigades in April, 1915. It was reconstituted on 27th April, 1915, and having been inspected by Her Majesty the Queen, embarked for France on 13th November, 1915, under Major-General H. J. S. Landon, C.B. It was then composed of New Army Units as under :—

98TH INFANTRY BRIGADE—
    18th (Service) Battalion Royal Fusiliers (1st Public Schools).
    19th (Service) Battalion Royal Fusiliers (2nd Public Schools).
    20th (Service) Battalion Royal Fusiliers (3rd Public Schools).
    21st (Service) Battalion Royal Fusiliers (4th Public Schools).

99TH INFANTRY BRIGADE—
    17th (Service) Battalion Royal Fusiliers (Empire).
    22nd (Service) Battalion Royal Fusiliers (Kensington).
    23rd (Service) Battalion Royal Fusiliers (1st Sportsman's).
    24th (Service) Battalion Royal Fusiliers (2nd Sportsman's).

100TH INFANTRY BRIGADE—
    13th (Service) Battalion Essex Regiment (West Ham).
    16th (Service) Battalion Middlesex Regiment (Public Schools).
    17th (Service) Battalion Middlesex Regiment (1st Football).
    16th (Service) Battalion King's Royal Rifle Corps (Church Lads' Brigade).

PIONEER BATTALION—
    18th (Service) Battalion Middlesex Regiment (1st Public Works, Pioneers).

MAJOR-GENERAL H. J. S. LANDON, C.B., C.M.G.,
WHO COMMANDED THE THIRTY-THIRD DIVISION IN
FRANCE FROM NOVEMBER, 1915, TO OCTOBER, 1916.

ORGANIZATION OF THE 33rd DIVISION.

DIVISIONAL CAVALRY—
1 Squadron North Irish Horse.
33rd Divisional Cyclist Company.

DIVISIONAL ARTILLERY—
156th Field Artillery Brigade
162nd Field Artillery Brigade
166th Field Artillery Brigade   (Camberwell).
167th Field Artillery Brigade (Howitzer)
133rd Divisional Ammunition Column

DIVISIONAL ENGINEERS—
212th Field Company, Royal Engineers
222nd Field Company, Royal Engineers   (Tottenham).
226th Field Company, Royal Engineers

SIGNAL SERVICE—
33rd Divisional Signal Company (Tottenham).

DIVISIONAL ARMY SERVICE CORPS—
33rd Divisional Train (225th-228th Companies, Army Service Corps).

MEDICAL UNITS—
99th Field Ambulance.
100th Field Ambulance.
101st Field Ambulance.
33rd Divisional Ambulance Workshop.

VETERINARY UNIT—
43rd Mobile Veterinary Section.

Very shortly after arrival it was realised that in order to obtain that efficiency necessary to troops intended to take the field immediately, it would greatly strengthen them by bringing into their ranks and composition several of the old Regular and Territorial Regiments which had already borne the brunt of a hundred battles. It was thought, also, that the war-worn battalions of French's "Contemptible Little Army" would be enriched by infusing into their hearts, hungry for home and new companionship, the joyousness and freshness which the rank and file of the New Armies had already shown they carried in their packs as part of their equipment. The Division was therefore reconstituted, the 19th Brigade replacing the 99th Brigade, and three veteran Battalions of the 5th Brigade replacing three of the New Army.

3

In the New Year, 1916, the constitution of the Division, which took over the line at Cuinchy and Cambrin, was as under :—

ROYAL ARTILLERY—
    156th Brigade, Royal Field Artillery.
    162nd Brigade, Royal Field Artillery.
    166th Brigade, Royal Field Artillery.
    33rd Divisional Ammunition Column.

ROYAL ENGINEERS—
    33rd Divisional Signal Company.
    11th Field Company, Royal Engineers.
    212th Field Company, Royal Engineers.
    222nd Field Company, Royal Engineers.

19TH INFANTRY BRIGADE—
    2nd Battalion, Royal Welch Fusiliers.
    1st Battalion, Scottish Rifles (The Cameronians).
    5th-6th (Territorial) Battalion, Scottish Rifles.
    20th (Service) Battalion, Royal Fusiliers.

98TH INFANTRY BRIGADE—
    1st Battalion, Middlesex Regiment.
    2nd Battalion, Argyll and Sutherland Highlanders.
    4th (Special Reserve) Battalion, The King's (Liverpool) Regiment.
    4th (Territorial) Battalion, Suffolk Regiment.

100TH INFANTRY BRIGADE—
    1st Battalion, The Queen's (Royal West Surrey) Regiment.
    2nd Battalion, The Worcestershire Regiment.
    9th (Territorial) Battalion, Highland Light Infantry (Glasgow High-
        landers).
    16th (Service) Battalion, King's Royal Rifle Corps.
    16th (Service) Battalion, Middlesex Regiment (Pioneers).
    33rd Divisional Train, Army Service Corps.
    19th Field Ambulance, Royal Army Medical Corps.
    99th Field Ambulance, Royal Army Medical Corps.
    101st Field Ambulance, Royal Army Medical Corps.
    43rd Mobile Veterinary Section, Army Veterinary Corps.

It will be seen, therefore, that this reconstructed Division, which was to win such fame in battle, no less than in " stunts " behind the line, incorporated in its ranks, not only the peculiar fighting qualities of men from every district and town in the United Kingdom, but the experience and moral elevation won on the battlefields of Le Cateau, the Marne, the Aisne, Ypres, "Plug Street," Neuve Chapelle, La Bassée, and at Loos.

At this period the Machine Gun Corps had just received sanction; and three new Brigade Machine Gun Companies were completed in April, 1916. A large number of men from the old Regimental Machine Gun Sections were absorbed into the Companies and transferred to the Machine Gun Corps.

The reconstructed Division took over the line on the La Bassée front at the end of December, 1915, occupying the intricate trench system around the Canal, Cuinchy, "The Brickstacks" and Cambrin. Probably, in the history of warfare, there has never been any scene of operations of more absorbing interest, and in which there was so much scope for initiative and ingenuity for all arms of the service—and of all ranks of those arms—than this labyrinth of trenches, bastions, strong points, communication trenches, dug-outs, sap-heads, and mine-craters. The period spent in this sector was one of most valuable training.

It was a time when the antagonists had expended the full force of their power in the opening clash of war. The first round was over. After a ding-dong battle, both sides were exhausted. It was necessary for the opposing forces to take stock in their corners of the whole range of their knowledge of ringcraft. To their aid, therefore, they called in their seconds—the inventor, the chemist, the engineer, and the scientist. New engines of war had to be experimented with, new inventions tried, new tactics evolved, in order that the deadlock of trench warfare could be overcome.

It will well be remembered how the armchair critic of the press at this time filled its columns with statement and argument intended to convince a credible public that the German armies would be starved into submission by the ring of steel around them, and how our own relations and friends at home imagined, as indeed they did until the end of the war, that every man in France or Flanders, whether in the front line or at the base, was stuck in a trench, usually with his feet in water, armed with a long bayonet, ready to repel the advancing hordes of the enemy! If, in their conception, it was possible for the enemy to advance upon us, as apparently it was, it was never clear to us why these gullible people could not appreciate the fact that it was equally possible for ourselves, by the evolution of our tactical method, to advance upon them, and finally overwhelm the forces of Germany.

It came to pass, therefore, that from the sap head and the front line, the Mining Companies which were in the process of formation, on both sides, commenced to dig. Within a few weeks they had formed under No-Man's Land, and under the front trench system, a maze of galleries and mine shafts as intricate as the labyrinth of trenches and communications which existed on the surface.

Whilst the miners were throwing out their galleries and preparing demolitions on a grand scale in No-Man's Land, the infantry in the front and

5

support lines were testing bombs, grenades, and the new automatic small arms with which they had been supplied.

Of the many varieties of these weapons and forms of destruction, the most famous and durable were the Mills Bomb, the Lewis and Vickers Machine Guns, and the Stokes Mortar. We feel sure that if Sir Wilfred Stokes, when he so patriotically offered his wonderful drain-pipe to the British Government, had known what a volcano of unpopularity and lava-flow of oaths he would call down, not only upon his own head, but upon the heads of those unfortunates who were called upon to manipulate his weapon, he would have confined his inventive genius to something which irritated the Hun less, and, consequently, aroused in " Gerry " less anger in the shape of high explosives thrown back at the imagined location of this flatulent weapon.

" You ! 'Oo are you ? The b . . . trench mortars ! You ain't a-comin' 'ere, any'ow ! Crimes—here's the Jocks luggin' the gaff up for 'em !

" Hey ! Are you the gowks that wants tae play about wi' these tin-ribbed polonies ? "

" Hand 'em over, Jock ! "

" Stand by———FIRE ! " (Swish-swish !) " Duck, boys ! " (Crack-ss-ss-swish !) Into the dug-out ! (Phut !)

" 'Oo the 'ell's comin' dahn 'ere ? Blarsted wind up ! This ain't a Rowton 'ouse ! Tork abaht the overcrahding question ! Wot I ses is, damn them flamin' mortars ! "

In conjunction with these experiences with mine and mortar, it was decided that the " Grey Rats " on the other side of No-Man's Land must constantly be dug from their holes, and irritated by personal contact with the British soldier. A new tactical operation was therefore introduced, an operation, which, by the way, became an exceedingly popular one with our troops. This was known as " The Raid."

On reading the official communiqué that a successful raid had been carried out on a given sector resulting in the taking of a few prisoners, few realized what such an operation involved in the way of preparation ; the study of ground ; compilation and issue of maps, siting of mortar and machine guns ; digging of mine galleries ; cutting of wire ; placing of barrage ; getting up of bombs, gas cylinders, medical stores, signalling apparatus ; deductions by the intelligence branch of the General Staff from aeroplane photographs ; and not least, the rehearsal on similar ground behind the line by that body of troops selected to play their little part in the tactical operation.

The enemy on our front, particularly opposite the " Brick-stacks "—Cuinchy—had been most active, and had caused us a considerable number of casualties. Indeed, the " Brick-stacks " themselves had become a bye-word as a death-trap ; for not only had they been raked in their very foundations by the explosion of vast mines beneath them, but they were showered, both by day and by night, with minnenwerfer bombs, mortars, " flying pigs," and other metallic gifts of a generous enemy. Six brick-stacks were in our lines ;

6

four in those of the enemy ; and between them a narrow strip of No-Man's Land, not more than forty yards wide. Owing to the fact that the Brick-stacks in our lines were built on a high elevation, in full enemy view, and the base of those in the German lines protected from our observation by a similar rise in the ground, it was an impossible task for us to commence mining operations from our side, whilst, on the other hand, it was an easy matter for the Germans to commence such operations from theirs. They were not slow to utilise this tactical advantage. On three separate occasions in January the Brick-stacks and the trench systems surrounding them had been shaken and partially destroyed by a mighty upheaval of bricks and clods of earth, some of which must have weighed nearly a ton.

It was the misfortune of the 2nd Battalion Argyll and Sutherland Highlanders to garrison these strong points in our line on each of these three occasions. They had suffered heavily, and their anger was deeply aroused. It was discovered, however, that if one of our strong points on the south side of the La Bassée Road was projected a few yards further into the enemy's lines, that from this point excellent observation could be obtained, in enfilade, of the German operations behind their brick-stacks. A small mine was therefore blown opposite this point. From the chalk surrounding our lip of the crater an admirable view could then be obtained of the Hun miners entering and leaving their mine shafts behind a brick-stack in their lines. A periscope and telephone were fixed up here in connection with two machine guns in the hands of the Machine Gun Corps firing from the support line, and by this method we were over and over again successful in being able to interfere with the progress of the enemy's mining operations. This was not enough. The blood of the Highlanders was up. Nothing would satisfy them but a raid, involving the bomb, the bayonet, the bludgeon, in fine, warfare at close grips. They were not disappointed. A raid was carried out at dead of night against the enemy garrison holding the " New Year Crater," the blowing of which had destroyed so many of the Highlanders, and upon the trench system connecting the crater with the German lines. With blackened hands, legs and faces, bomb and bludgeon in hand, and bayonet in support, a company of Highlanders was concentrated for the assault behind the western lip of the crater. To create a diversion in the German lines, a large mine was sprung some 600 yards further south, and five minutes later, "heavies" and field guns, trench mortars and machine guns opened an intense bombardment upon the area surrounding that intended to be raided, forming what was technically known as a " box barrage," isolating, unknown to themselves, the enemy garrison from any possibility of support. Under cover of the deafening roar of the guns, the Highlanders leapt to the assault. Here and there an enemy machine gun opened its stuttering fire, but this was undirected. The garrison was overwhelmed. The "arme blanche" in the hands of proved experts, did its execution quickly and thoroughly. The garrison was annihilated, being either killed or captured to a man. But shortly after the Battalion suffered great loss in the death of Lieutenant-Colonel H. de B. Purvis, M.C., an officer who had served with great distinction since 1914, killed by a stray bullet. He was succeeded in command by Lieutenant-Colonel A. Sprot.

Technically, there were two types of raid: first, the "raid and stay"; secondly, the "raid and away," or the "smack and back." This raid was of the first type, for the Argyll and Sutherland Highlanders now occupied both lips of the crater, having taken the place of the former enemy garrison. Tactically, this little operation was of great importance, for, owing to our proximity to the German front line, it was now necessary for the enemy to reconsider the whole of his mining activity opposite this front, because of the danger to himself of causing an explosion so close to his own lines. This danger rested upon a technicality—soil strata and sub-strata, tamping of charges, and resistance to explosive force.

Not every raid was successful. In the communiqué we never read of failure, but failures there were. Some little thing forgotten; some little piece of preparation not perfected; and the whole operation was inevitably a fiasco. In one raid, perhaps, the artillery observer, owing to ground mist, and after many hours watching with tired eyes thought that the shrapnel had done its work and cut a path for the infantry through the enemy's wire. And it was not so! In another, the boy with "one pip" guiding his platoon on his compass bearing, had not remembered the existence of a "true" and a "magnetic north," and led his men too far to the left; stumbled against the uncut wires; and, memory asserting itself, had made endeavour to correct his bearing and fulfil his task; but had not only thrown himself in desperation and reckless gallantry on the wire, to hang there a corpse for many days, but had at the same time sacrificed his platoon to the murderous chattering fire of enemy machine gun nests. In another raid we have in mind, it was necessary to clear our own front and support lines in order that a monstrous mine might be exploded. The falling debris would have imperilled the lives of our raiders if the latter were concentrated near the front lines, prior to their following in its wake and completing the destruction of the enemy garrison. A part of the garrison in the forward trenches was placed in the strong dug-outs of our front line, whilst the raiders were concentrated in the support line about fifty yards in the rear. The effect of the mine, owing to the fact that unlocated galleries of an enemy shaft had been dug in a stratum above the position of the charge, thereby lessening the pressure, was far greater and more widespread than had been anticipated. The wreckage was complete. Even our communication trenches were so filled that the whole terrain, some seventy yards forward of the position of the raiding party, resembled No-Man's Land. The Captain in charge of the raiding party was deceived. When he reached our front line he thought that he had already crossed No-Man's Land. By the dim light, through mountains of debris, he could detect the yawning mouths of dug-outs, at the bottom of which he could see lights, and hear the murmur of voices. He thought that these were German dug-outs and fit sport for bombs. He organized his party, attacked with bombs, and then himself entered a dug-out, revolver in hand. He saw no enemy, but the torn and bleeding bodies of men of the Battalion which he knew had garrisoned our front line. An error of judgment.

We did not read of this in the communiqués; but in this experimental stage of war when we were testing our New Armies, such incidents have occurred not only in our little sector, but over and over again, along the British front. We were amazed more than once to see the *Daily Intelligence Summary* thrown on one side with only a superficial glance, and labelled " *Comic Cuts.*" There was no doubt that the officer or N.C.O. who conscientiously did his job as a leader, spent his time in restless, remorseless study, not only of the art of war, but of enemy practice and ruse, and of map and plan and photograph. Only such leaders could expect success; even they could not be sure.

An important raid was carried out by the 2nd Royal Welch Fusiliers, two companies of which Battalion had suffered very heavy casualties from the explosion of a gigantic mine beneath their lines, just north of the La Bassée Canal, shortly after the New Year. In revenge for this a very successful raid was carried out by the Battalion, which amply set off their own misfortune.

Further raids were carried out by the 16th Battalion Middlesex Regiment under Lieutenant-Colonel T. H. Hall, and by the 16th Battalion King's Royal Rifle Corps under Lieutenant-Colonel C. E. Wyld, but these were not so successful. In the former Second-Lieutenant Samuel was killed and in the latter Second-Lieutenant Cork went unassisted after the raid in an effort to discover the commander of the raid who was missing, and was awarded the Military Cross for his gallantry.

A most notable raid was carried out by the Glasgow Highlanders opposite Cambrin on the 27th June, 1916. It was a raid on a grand scale. It was "smack and back." Sir Douglas Haig reported upon it in his communiqué as the finest raid which up to that date had taken place. Nothing was overlooked. No eventuality not anticipated. It was carried out by Captain A. C. Frame, who was awarded the D.S.O. for his exploit. Under cover of a creeping barrage which during the raid was formed into a box barrage, the Highlanders entered into a section of the German front line and communication trenches. This section included two mine-shaft heads. Not only did they "make hay" of the defence works themselves, and bomb the dug-outs, but assisted by a small party of Royal Engineers, they entered the enemy's mine galleries, destroying them by camouflets, and captured sixty-one prisoners and two machine guns, whilst they themselves only suffered three casualties, all of which were light. So delighted were the Jocks

9

with their success that in several instances it was a case of "smack and back" and "back and smack" again! One Highlander, at least, made three journeys backwards and forwards across No-Man's Land, securing prisoners and booty.

Many individual acts of gallantry were performed during this period, but perhaps none greater than that of Captain R. McCowan Hill, Royal Army Medical Corps, attached to the Argyll and Sutherland Highlanders. Subsequent to a mine explosion under the Brick-stacks his aid was called to a wounded man imprisoned by the pressure of many tons of masonry on his leg. The Brick-stacks were at the time being shaken to their foundations by a hail of shells and mortars. Captain Hill, although in very great personal peril from falling masonry, undertook the successful amputation of the leg of the wounded Highlander, thus saving his life. During part of the time it was necessary for Captain Hill to bear the weight of much of the overhead masonry on his shoulders before Engineer assistance arrived. For this splendid act of devotion in the cause of his humane calling Captain Hill was awarded the D.S.O. Later for a similar act, during the Menin Road operations in September, 1917, whilst still serving as M.O. to this Battalion, he was awarded a clasp to his D.S.O. Captain Hill completed a very remarkable career as an officer in the Royal Army Medical Corps, serving always with the same Battalion, when he was wounded in November, 1918, just before the Armistice.

Trench mortar batteries, both light and heavy, performed most excellent services during these raids, whilst day by day and night after night carrying out well planned schemes with which to harass the enemy.

The artillery was perfecting their art. The barrage was new. Mysteries of zone and cone had to be talked over. Experiments with "common" as against "high explosive" shrapnel, as a protective or creeping barrage had to be conducted. Liaison with infantry and machine guns had to be perfected.

The proof of the pudding is in the eating thereof. At the end of the Big Push we were to find that we were yet only in the experimental stage. We suffered appalling and unnecessary casualties. The machine was by no means perfect.

But our consultations with our seconds had done us good, for even if we took heavy punishment, we certainly succeeded in winning the round on points.

Within the Division various changes in command took place :—Brigadier-General C. R. G. Mayne, D.S.O., relieved Brigadier-General P. R. Robertson, C.M.G., D.S.O., promoted Major-General; Brigadier-General A. W. F. Baird, C.M.G., D.S.O., relieved Brigadier-General H. Twigg, C.B.; whilst Brigadier-General E. P. Strickland, C.M.G., D.S.O., on promotion to Major-General to command the 1st Division, was relieved by Brigadier-General E. P. Carleton, D.S.O., until the appointment of Brigadier-General J. D. Heriot Maitland, C.M.G., D.S.O., in August. All three Brigadiers maintained their commands until the Armistice, a very notable fact and record.

CAMBRIN AND CUINCHY.

A most successful Horse Show was held in Bethune by the Division in April, 1915. This was one of the first, if not the first held by any Division in France. To this and subsequent similar Shows was certainly attributable the high standard maintained by the Transport, a most hard-working and worked, service, both in and out of the line. Of the regimental transport officers several were subsequently decorated for gallantry under fire, in charge of ammunition and supply wagons, including Captains Harrison of the Queen's and L. R. Hutchison of the Machine Gun Battalion. The former, together with Captain Lipscomb, of the 16th King's Royal Rifle Corps, a familiar figure at Horse Shows in the Jumping ring with his "farmer's seat," served throughout the campaign with their Units, most notable achievements.

CHAPTER II.

THE BATTLE OF THE SOMME.

FIRST PHASE : 1ST JULY TO 1ST AUGUST, 1916.

Leadership and the Personal Equation—High Wood, Gallantry of the 100th Brigade—Heavy fighting by 19th and 98th Brigades.

ORDER OF BATTLE.

HEADQUARTERS, 33RD DIVISION.

Commander	Major-General H. J. S. Landon, C.B.
Aide-de-Camp to Commander	Captain C. Bushell, The Queen's (Royal West Surrey Regiment).
Aide-de-Camp to Commander	Lieutenant F. A. Wilson, Scottish Rifles.

GENERAL STAFF BRANCH—

General Staff Officer, 1st Grade	Lieutenant-Colonel A. Symons, C.M.G., 13th Hussars.
General Staff Officer, 2nd Grade	Major G. de la P. B. Pakenham, D.S.O., Border Regiment.
General Staff Officer, 3rd Grade	Captain H. W. M. Paul, Middlesex Regiment.

ADJUTANT AND QUARTERMASTER-GENERAL'S BRANCH—

Assistant Adjutant and Quartermaster-General	Lieutenant-Colonel P. R. C. Commings, D.S.O., South Staffordshire Regiment.
Deputy-Assistant Adjutant and Quartermaster General -	Captain J. W. Oldfield, General List.
Deputy-Assistant Quartermaster-General ..	Major C. L. Taylor, South Wales Borderers.

ADMINISTRATIVE SERVICES AND DEPARTMENTS—

Assistant Director of Medical Services ..	Colonel T. Daly.
Deputy-Assistant Director of Medical Services	Major G. W. G. Hughes, D.S.O., Royal Army Medical Corps.
Assistant Director of Veterinary Services..	Major R. A. Plunkett, Army Veterinary Corps.
Deputy-Assistant Director of Ordnance Services	Lieutenant C. S. Mulkern, Army Ordnance Department.

SPECIAL APPOINTMENT—

Assistant Provost-Marshal	Major J. D. S. Lloyd, Welsh Horse Yeomanry.

THE BATTLE OF THE SOMME.

HEADQUARTERS, DIVISIONAL ARTILLERY—
Commander .. .. Brigadier-General C. F. Blane, C.M.G.
Aide-de-Camp to Commander .. .. Second-Lieutenant M. Howell, Royal Artillery.
Brigade-Major .. .. Major H. K. Sadler, Royal Artillery.
Staff Captain .. .. Captain T. C. Usher, Royal Artillery.

HEADQUARTERS, DIVISIONAL ENGINEERS—
Commander .. .. Lieutenant-Colonel F. M. Westropp, Royal Engineers.
Adjutant .. .. Lieutenant J. S. Baines, Royal Engineers.

HEADQUARTERS, 19TH INFANTRY BRIGADE—
Commander .. .. Brigadier-General C. R. G. Mayne, D.S.O., Highland Light Infantry.
Brigade-Major .. .. Captain E. K. Twiss, 10th Jats.
Staff Captain .. .. Captain A. H. W. Landon, Royal Canadian Regiment.

HEADQUARTERS, 98TH INFANTRY BRIGADE—
Commander .. .. Brigadier-General F. M. Carleton, D.S.O., Royal Lancaster Regiment.
Brigade-Major .. .. Captain R. M. Watson, D.S.O., Royal Dublin Fusiliers.
Staff Captain .. .. Captain J. D. Hill, Scottish Rifles.

HEADQUARTERS, 100TH INFANTRY BRIGADE—
Commander .. .. Brigadier-General A. W. F. Baird, C.M.G., D.S.O., Gordon Highlanders.
Brigade-Major .. .. Captain O. C. Downes, D.S.O., Rifle Brigade.
Staff Captain .. .. Captain V. Ward Brown, General List.

19TH INFANTRY BRIGADE—
Headquarters.
20th Royal Fusiliers.
2nd Royal Welch Fusiliers.
1st Scottish Rifles (Cameronians).
5/6th Scottish Rifles.

———

19th Brigade Machine Gun Company.

———

19th Trench Mortar Battery.

98TH INFANTRY BRIGADE—
Headquarters.
4th The King's (Liverpool) Regiment
1/4th Suffolk Regiment.
1st Middlesex Regiment.
2nd Argyll and Sutherland Highlanders.

———

98th Brigade Machine Gun Company.

———

98th Trench Mortar Battery.

100TH INFANTRY BRIGADE—
Headquarters.
1st The Queen's (Royal West Surrey Regiment).
2nd Worcestershire Regiment.
16th King's Royal Rifle Corps.
1/9th Highland Light Infantry (Glasgow Highlanders).

———

100th Brigade Machine Gun Company.

———

100th Trench Mortar Battery.

THE THIRTY-THIRD DIVISION.

DIVISIONAL TROOPS—

Headquarters, 33rd Division.

156th Brigade, Royal Field Artillery (" A," " B," " C," " D," Batteries), 12 18-pounders and 4 4·5 in. howitzers.

162nd Brigade, Royal Field Artillery (" A," " B," " C," " D," Batteries), 12 18-pounders and 4 4·5 in. howitzers.

166th Brigade, Royal Field Artillery (" A," " B," " C," " D," Batteries), 12 18-pounders and 4 4·5 in. howitzers.

167th Brigade, Royal Field Artillery (" A," " B," " C," Batteries), 12 18-pounders.

X 33 Trench Mortar Battery, Royal Artillery.

Y 33 Trench Mortar Battery, Royal Artillery.

Z 33 Trench Mortar Battery, Royal Artillery.

33rd Divisional Ammunition Column.

11th, 212th and 222nd Field Companies, Royal Engineers.
33rd Divisional Signal Company.
Pioneer Battalion, 18th Middlesex Regiment.
33rd Divisional Train (170-173 Companies, Army Service Corps).
19th, 99th and 101st Field Ambulances.
No. 73 Sanitary Section.
43rd Mobile Veterinary Section.

At the beginning of July, 1916, the Division moved down to the Somme area to take part in the great offensive battle.

Having detrained near Amiens it proceeded by march route to Fricourt in intense heat and dust, and bivouacked there on the night of the 13th July. The offensive had just commenced. Probably none of us had any conception of the enormous preparations for the " Big Push." We had certainly witnessed the massing of guns and concentration of all the paraphernalia of war for the little efforts of Neuve Chappelle and Loos. But the activity on the roads, the long columns of infantry, ambulances, ammunition lorries, the deep ranks of guns of all calibres, almost locked wheel to wheel ; the huge dressing stations, and the ever growing cemeteries impressed all immediately with the magnitude of the task before us.

Previously, as part of a Division, Brigade, or Battalion, or even as an individual, one had felt oneself a definite unit of the army. One now seemed to be engulfed in the colossal panoply of war. A man seemed to lose his identity as an individual. Divisions were swallowed up in terms of Corps and Armies. Probably, for this reason, from this point in the war one seemed no longer to regard death as individual. Death claimed so many friends and men one had never seen before. Reinforcements would arrive ; one never knew their names, they disappeared so quickly through the Dressing Stations, or to swell the number of the little wooden crosses. The individual man was gone. His soul survived despite the orders which moved him from point to point in the battlefield, not as a man but as a molecule in a body of 120,000 troops. This remarkable fact must be appreciated. For it was a factor which from this point began to influence the whole of our national life until it laid such a grip upon us that in the later days of the war we

14

were in peril of coming entirely under the spell of the Military system. Conscription, Bureaucracy, Officialdom, must all have started from this point when our Government began to think in terms of Armies and not in terms of Platoons.

The personal equation is a definite force in an army. A high moral is its strongest quality. Individual moral is the germ of its success. It was left for the regimental officer who understood this to see that so great a quality did not perish whilst the Staff of necessity became absorbed in questions of Grand Tactics and Strategy. In our national life, also, it was left for the Little Man to preserve this quality in the national heart, whilst the bureaucrat and official chivied him from pillar to post in a mad endeavour to turn a free people into a militarised and a bureaucratic state. We do not blame the bureaucrat. In his neglect of the idea of a National Ideal, he was only attempting to perform a task of which he had had no previous experience. He boasted of framing his policy and modelling his schemes upon those of organized Germany. Probably few other than the humble recruiting officer at home, before the days of conscription, and the Regimental Officer in the field, fully realized that an appeal to the soul of our Ideal, of which there was the germ in every Briton's heart, could make men do what rules and orders and laws could never accomplish.

We had lost sight of the greatest factor of success in leadership—leadership in war, no less than leadership in industry. The personal equation was lost, where, with a great civilian army, it should have been paramount. In the armies of France—the civilian force of a Republic—the personal equation was the keystone of their training, efficiency, and *esprit de corps*. In our army, such expressions as " on vous aura ! " and " ils ne passeront pas ! " were seldom heard. Marshals Foch and Joffre referred to their troops in the inspiring and personally affectionate term, " Mes enfants ! " Such terms of affection were mostly deprecated in our army. Those officers who knew the value of perfect cameraderie and were daring enough to practise it, did so in the teeth of active opposition. Yet there must have been many who felt it strongly. We are not the cold, unbending race we are so often supposed to be. Even the American can now appreciate this. But we are invariably fearful of exposing our hearts. Common danger forced this. The Higher Command, who rightly were not called upon to sit freezing in a bitter wind in the hell of a bombardment could seldom feel how this new Freemasonry bared the soul of spoiling conventionalism, and left the heart of peer and peasant stripped naked before its God. It could think in no terms less than those of divisions ; and so it forgot man and his throbbing heart, his soul ; his weakness and his love—a love passing the love of woman.

Man's soul never died. It was triumphant. Its very vitality formed the new Freemasonry—that of common danger. The Freemasonry of the Trenches had its various degrees. The Grand Master was no more necessarily General or Commanding Officer than private soldier. This was a question of degree—

the first degree of Mons, the second of the Marne, the third of Ypres, the fourth of La Bassée, the fifth of Loos, and so on. The cynic may think the point is laboured. We of that Masonry know it is not so, and never in this generation will it be so. Its secret sign, if there is a secret, is that of the straight-set eye and the square shoulder. It lives in our very midst to-day.

Through dust and heat and a myriad flies the sweating Division moved up through Fricourt across the captured German trench system on the 14th July, with the 100th Brigade leading, followed by the 98th Brigade, and with the 19th Brigade in reserve, up the road through Montauban, where the enemy still grinned in his ghastly sleep, and eastwards to Caterpillar Valley, through the Valley of Death, just west of Bazentin le Grand.

On the evening of the 14th, orders were received for a further general attack upon a wide front, the 100th Brigade being allotted the task of capturing Martinpuich, and High Wood on the Flers Ridge, this being part of the German Switch Line, and of extending the attack eastwards. Patrols were immediately pushed into High Wood from the 9th Highland Light Infantry, under Lieutenant-Colonel Stormonth Darling, and the 1st Queen's Regiment, under Major Palmer, accompanied by one section of the 100th Machine Gun Company. Very little time was possible for reconnaissance. At dawn on the 15th July a thick ground mist covered the whole of the valley lying east of the Village of Bazentin, and completely obscured High Wood and Martinpuich.

The Glasgow Highlanders reported the wood to be strongly held by machine guns. It was necessary to concentrate and deploy the 100th Brigade in the open valley, under enemy observation at a mile range, without any covered approaches or other cover. General Baird repeatedly asked for a hurricane bombardment of the wood. In reply he was told, " Nothing can live there, my dear fellow, nothing can live there." We were to prove the truth of these words. So a bombardment was found to be impracticable ; but the success of the attack, as General Baird reported, depended on the complete possession of the Wood. The Brigade was therefore concentrated in the valley about 800 yards west of High Wood. The Queen's were ordered to attack on the left, and the 9th Highland Light Infantry on the right, the attack being supported by the 16th King's Royal Rifle Corps, under Lieutenant-Colonel C. E. Wyld, with the 2nd Worcestershires, under Lieutenant-Colonel T. K. Pardoe, in reserve.

Each battalion in the forward wave was supported by one Machine Gun Section. Under cover of the mist the transport was able to get right forward to the area of concentration. Meanwhile the 98th Brigade with its Machine Gun Company was concentrated in position in the eastern outskirts of Bazentin le Petit. At 9 a.m. the mist rose. The attack was ordered at 9.30 a.m. Under cover of a weak bombardment the attack swept forward, to be met on both flanks by murderous machine gun fire from the wood itself and from Martinpuich.

BRIGADIER-GENERAL A. W. F. BAIRD, C.B., C.M.G., D.S.O. (GORDON HIGHLANDERS),

WHO COMMANDED THE HUNDREDTH INFANTRY BRIGADE FROM MARCH, 1916, TO APRIL, 1919, WITH HIS BRIGADE-MAJOR, CAPTAIN O. L. DOWNES, D.S.O. (RIFLE BRIGADE), AND ARTILLERY OBSERVATION OFFICER, IN MAMETZ WOOD, BATTLE OF THE SOMME, JULY, 1916.

HIGH WOOD.

On the left the Queens, personally led by Major Palmer, revolver in hand, swarmed forward up the slopes towards the village of Martinpuich. These slopes were covered with long grass. In this grass during the night the enemy had ingeniously laid out two lines of thin wire. This the Queens reached, but never passed. In a few minutes the ground was a shambles. It was impossible to advance; equally impossible to retire. Not a particle of cover other than the grass which was raked with machine gun fire existed anywhere. The attack on the left was a failure, Major Palmer being killed at the head of his men.

On the right, the 9th Highland Light Infantry, who were established in the wood deployed from its north-western edge to join up with the Queens. Cunningly laid machine gun nests prevented their advance. At the same time a battery lying to the west of Martinpuich, which, owing to the advance of the Queens, had temporarily been out of action, now opened fire into the backs of the 9th Highland Light Infantry. The trees of High Wood itself hid many a German sharp-shooter. Not one inch of the ground in this ghastly valley between the wood and the Bazentin Village was safe. The Highlanders clung to their position; their casualties were very severe. In support the 16th King's Royal Rifle Corps lost nearly all their officers before they had reached the position held by the 9th Highland Light Infantry.

By 10 a.m. the attack was held up. Captain Hutchison then moved forward the remaining two sections of his Machine Gun Company to the edge of High Wood and rushed forward two companies of the 16th King's Royal Rifle Corps in support of his guns. The Machine Gunners, in a few moments, had lost seventy per cent. of their personnel, killed.

The Rifles and the Machine Gunners, with the small remainder of the 9th Highland Light Infantry, fearlessly commanded by Lieutenant-Colonel Stormonth-Darling, had taken up such positions as they could in the newly created shell holes. Riflemen and machine gunners opened a vigorous fire upon High Wood and Martinpuich.

It may be said that in this gruesome position in which were so many dead, dying, and badly wounded, it was amusing to observe the German marksmen falling from the trees, with a heavy thump, to the ground. The moral effect of this touch of humour, which instantly struck all, was amazing. The wounded became cheery; the exhausted gained new life, and, as the 2nd Worcestershires, under Lieutenant-Colonel Pardoe, from reserve, swept forward to the attack and passed into the Wood, we forgot the heavy sacrifices which had already been made, and proceeded with rifles and machine guns in our turn to mow down the columns of the enemy.

The 100th Brigade was now thrown forward like a wedge into the enemy's front. By 12 noon the Worcestershires had obtained a definite footing in the Wood, and the 98th Brigade began to come up on the left and filled the gap in which the 1st Queens had been annihilated.

The safety of the 100th Brigade lay in the maintenance of its right flank. The Brigade on the right was showing signs of weakness and began to dribble back,—mixed bodies of men of various regiments. The wounded and the exhausted began to retire.

An attempt was then made, by a body of Indian Cavalry, to break through and drive the enemy from the High Wood ridge. No troops could have presented a more inspiring sight than these natives of India, with lance and sword, dashing in mad cavalcade, up the sunken road on to the sky-line. Some disappeared over it; they never came back. The remainder became the target of every gun and rifle. They were useless—impotent! Turning their horses' heads, with shrill cries, these masters of horsemastership galloped back to safety through a hell of fire, lifting their mounts lightly over yawning shell-holes; turning and twisting through the barrage of great shells, the bursting point of which they seemed to anticipate. It was a mad ride. It was magnificent.

It was apparent at 5 p.m. that the whole attack had been a most costly failure. General Baird wrote of his Brigade that it had behaved with the greatest gallantry. The slopes lying to the West of Martinpuich and High Wood were a grim slaughter house. Dead, dying, and wounded lay thickly upon the blood-stained turf.

During the night the remains of the Brigade occupied a small trench just West of the Wood. The enemy bombardment became so severe that it was decided to retire still further. Had this decision not been made there is no doubt that the Brigade would have perished to a man, but, miraculously, elements of the 2nd Worcestershires and 9th Highland Light Infantry held their position, which itself was surrounded by dead and wounded. On the morning of the 16th, the 19th Brigade relieved the 100th Brigade, and the remains of the Brigade returned to defensive positions on the North side of Mametz Wood.

Fighting of the bitterest nature followed, in which both the 19th and 98th Brigades were involved. The 19th Brigade, with the 2nd Worcestershires covering their left flank, again attacked at dawn on July 20th, and after severe fighting lasting all the day, occupied the whole of the Wood shortly before dusk. At 2.5 a.m. the 1st and 5th Scottish Rifles had been drawn up in the open ground just outside our wire; and preceded by a line of scouts attacked the Wood supported by the 20th Royal Fusiliers, three sections of the 11th Field Company, Royal Engineers, two Companies of the 18th Middlesex Regiment (Pioneers). The attack began satisfactorily, prisoners being taken, but enemy machine gun nests inflicted very severe casualties, particularly in officers. Bearing in mind a message received that the Commander-in-Chief attached the greatest importance to the capture of High Wood, the Brigadier commanding the 19th Brigade flung the 20th Royal Fusiliers into the battle; and later the 2nd Royal Welch Fusiliers, under Major Crawshay, who, despite heavy casualties from the enemy's barrage, which was particularly severe, advanced with great steadiness and courage.

18

HIGH WOOD.

Aided by Stokes mortars, the 19th Brigade displaying fine fighting qualities and spirit, gallantry and tenacity, stuck to their task until the whole of the Wood was in our hands. The line handed over, although frequent attempts were made to do so, was not advanced until September 27th, when the Switch Line was finally captured with the aid of Tanks. It was apparent that the attack was held up, and retention of the ground gained became more and more costly owing to very heavy shell fire. Trenches and communications were dug by night by the 18th (Pioneer) Battalion Middlesex Regiment, under Lieutenant-Colonel Storr, only to be obliterated in daylight. It was possible to sit on the Western edge of High Wood, and actually to see the heavy shells in the air, for about the last forty feet of their descent, before the deafening roar of their explosion and the upheaval of earth and roots and clouds of brown dust.

Early in August, the Division was relieved for a short rest and was bivouacked in the battle area round Mametz Wood. The 100th Machine Gun Company was ordered to place guns in the 1st Division area at Contalmaison to reduce the fire from Martinpuich flanking our High Wood position. Finally, we were withdrawn for an all too brief rest beside the River Ancre at Albert.

Message from Major-General H. J. S. Landon, C.B. :—

" The behaviour of the whole Division throughout the operations " they have recently been engaged in has been worthy of their " reputation.

" In the face of a series of most severe bombardments, and in " spite of heavy losses, the Division most gallantly carried and held the " objective of their second attack, the seizure of which will have a great " effect on the success of further operations.

" My admiration and pride at the splendid spirit shown under most " trying and difficult circumstances is unbounded.

" I feel confident in the ability and readiness, after a period of " reorganization, to continue active operations.

" (Signed) H. J. S. LANDON,
" *Major-General,*
" Commanding 33rd Division.

" *July 23rd, 1916.*"

CASUALTIES : 15TH TO 22ND JULY.

	OFFICERS—			OTHER RANKS—		
	Killed.	Wounded.	Missing.	Killed.	Wounded.	Missing.
19th Infantry Brigade ..	17	61	8	202	1,016	649
98th Infantry Brigade ..	15	48	—	142	857	128
100th Infantry Brigade ..	18	58	4	247	1,023	347

THE THIRTY-THIRD DIVISION.

BATTLE OF THE SOMME.

Fighting by the 19th and 98th Brigades—Attacks on Delville Wood and High Wood—The First Machine Gun Barrage—Capture of Delville Wood.

The 33rd Division, having been reinforced, resumed the offensive upon High Wood and the high ground between High Wood and Delville Wood on the 18th August. During the interval which had elapsed between the 15th July and this date, the Germans had considerably strengthened their positions ; and it was necessary by minor operations to seize certain important trenches before a general attack could be made. This done, an attack on a wide front was planned for the 24th August. It is believed for the first time in the history of machine guns, a machine gun barrage was planned to cover this attack, the guns employed being those of the 19th and 100th Machine Gun Companies and of the 14th and 23rd Divisions.

Both the 19th and 98th Brigades had already obtained tactical advantages previous to this date at High Wood, a portion of which during the absence of the Division had again lapsed into enemy hands, where Captain R. J. Mackay, M.C., of the Argyll and Sutherland Highlanders, showed great gallantry with Major G. E. H. Sim, M.C., of the Royal Engineers, both being severely wounded and receiving the D.S.O., their attack being frustrated by the use of liquid fire ; also in the capture of Orchard Trench by the 1st Queen's under Lieutenant-Colonel L. M. Crofts ; and of Black Watch Trench and a snipers' post east of it, in a further attack through High Wood by the Glasgow Highlanders. The 4th King's and 1/4th Suffolk Regiments also had made clever and determined advances but lost heavily. In the latter regiment Second-Lieutenant Bedwell, the only officer to get forward was killed immediately after the successful capture of Wood Lane, an important tactical point. A further seven hundred and ninety-nine officers and men were lost during these operations.

The 100th Brigade was ordered to carry out the big attack on the 33rd Divisional front. For this attack six machine guns were grouped in Savoy Trench, from which a magnificent view was obtained of the German line at a range of about 2,000 yards. These guns were disposed for barrage. On August 23rd and the night of the 23rd-24th the whole Machine Gun Company was, in addition to the two companies of the 9th Highland Light Infantry lent for the purpose, employed in carrying water and ammunition to this point. Many factors in barrage work which are now common knowledge had not then been learned or considered. It is amusing to-day to note that in the orders for the 100th Machine Gun Company's barrage of ten guns the Officer commanding ordered that rapid fire should be maintained continuously for twelve hours, to cover the attack and consolidation. It is to the credit of the gunners and of the Vickers gun itself that this was done ! During the attack on the 24th, 250 rounds short of one million were fired by ten guns ; at least four petrol tins of water per gun besides all the water bottles of the Company and the urine tins from the neighbourhood were emptied into the guns for cooling purposes ; and a continuous party was employed carrying ammunition. A belt-filling machine in action, without stopping for a single moment, was maintained by one man for twelve hours. At the end of this time many of the N.C.O.'s and gunners were found asleep from exhaustion at their posts. A prize of five francs to the members of each gun team firing the greatest number of rounds was offered, and was secured by a gun team with a record of just over 120,000 rounds.

The attack on the 24th August was a brilliant success, the operation being difficult and all objectives taken within a very short time. This was carried out by the 2nd Worcestershires, the 9th Highland Light Infantry, and 16th King's Royal Rifle Corps, with the 1st Queens in close support. Particular gallantry upon this occasion was shown by Captain W. Henderson, of the 2nd Worcestershires, a man of fifty years of age, who mounted the parapet at zero, and calling out, " Come on the Worcestershires ! " headed the attack straight through to the final objective, himself taking many prisoners. He was awarded the Military Cross.

Prisoners examined at Divisional and Corps Headquarters reported that the effect of the machine gun barrage was annihilating, and the counter-attacks which had attempted to retake the ground lost were broken up whilst being concentrated east of the Flers Ridge and of High Wood.

The work of the transport during these operations was particularly arduous. No driver in charge of ammunition and rations will ever forget the perils and horrors of the " Valley of Death " and the " Green Dump," the valley itself being continuously soaked in gas, and an unceasing bombardment being maintained along its whole length.

The operations ended in the capture of Delville Wood, but the north-east corner of High Wood still remained in the hands of the enemy.

EXTRACT FROM " FOURTH ARMY TELEGRAM," DATED 25TH AUGUST, 1916.

" Please convey to the 33rd Division and especially to General " Baird the Army Commander's congratulations on their performance " yesterday, which he thinks was especially creditable to all concerned " at the end of such a long period in the front line as the 33rd Division " have now had."

At the end of September the Division was withdrawn from the forward area and proceeded by train to Longpre to the Longpre-Airaines area, where it was billeted. This will always be remembered as one of the few pleasant and long rests that the Division had spent in France.

For a very short period the Division took over the line opposite Gomme-court Park, where attacks of the London troops on the 1st July had broken down. This sector which had previously been occupied by the French was a much enjoyed rest and a period of reorganization. For the young officers of the Glasgow Highlanders it was a time of great activity. Whenever shells fell in the little village of Foncvillers they invariably did so in synchronisation with the stentorian voice of Sergeant-Major Lewis, D.C.M., of that Battalion. There is little doubt therefore that his voice could be as easily heard in the German lines as it could be at Divisional Headquarters.

At this period Major-General R. J. Pinney, from the 35th (Bantam) Division, was appointed to command the Division, replacing Major-General H. J. S. Landon, C.B. This command, with a brief interval late in 1917, he held throughout the following strenuous months until March, 1919.

THIRD PHASE : 1ST NOVEMBER, 1916, TO 1ST MARCH, 1917.

BATTLE OF THE SOMME.

Les Bœufs—British and French Attacks opposite Le Transloy— Fine Exploit by 2nd Battalion Worcestershire Regiment— Rancourt and Bouchavesnes—Trench Feet—Clery.

ORDER OF BATTLE.

Commander .. .. Major-General R. J. Pinney.
    Aide-de-Camp to Commander .. .. Major H. C. C. Batten, Dorsetshire Regiment.
    Aide-de-Camp to Commander .. .. Second-Lieutenant A. S. G. Kennard, Hampshire Yeomanry.

GENERAL STAFF BRANCH—
    General Staff Officer, 1st Grade .. .. Lieutenant-Colonel A. Symons, C.M.G., 13th Hussars.
    General Staff Officer, 2nd Grade .. .. Major G. W. S. Sherlock, 6th Gurkha Rifles.
    General Staff Officer, 3rd Grade .. .. Captain H. W. M. Paul, M.C., Middlesex Regiment.

ADJUTANT AND QUARTERMASTER-GENERAL'S BRANCH—
    Assistant Adjutant and Quartermaster-General .. .. Lieutenant-Colonel P. R. C. Commings, D.S.O., South Staffordshire Regiment.
    Deputy-Assistant Adjutant and Quarter-master-General .. .. Captain J. W. Oldfield, M.C., General List.
    Deputy-Assistant Quartermaster-General .. Major F. G. Lawrence, D.S.O., South Wales Borderers.

THE BATTLE OF THE SOMME.

ADMINISTRATIVE SERVICES AND DEPARTMENTS—

Assistant Director of Medical Services .. Colonel T. Daly, Royal Army Medical Corps.

Deputy-Assistant Director of Medical Services .. .. Major G. W. G. Hughes, D.S.O., Royal Army Medical Corps.

Assistant Director of Veterinary Services.. Major R. A. Plunkett, Army Veterinary Corps.

Deputy-Assistant Director of Ordnance Services .. .. Lieutenant A. M. E. Beavan, Army Ordnance Department.

SPECIAL APPOINTMENT—

Assistant Provost-Marshal .. .. .. Major J. D. S. Lloyd, Welsh Horse Yeomanry.

DIVISIONAL ARTILLERY—

Commander .. .. Brigadier-General C. F. Blane, C.M.G.
    Aide-de-Camp to Commander .. .. Second-Lieutenant M. Howell, Royal Artillery.
Brigade-Major .. .. Major H. K. Sadler, Royal Artillery.
Staff Captain .. .. Captain T. C. Usher, Royal Artillery.

ROYAL ARTILLERY—

156th Brigade, Royal Field Artillery .. Lieutenant-Colonel H. C. Rochfort Boyd, D.S.O.
162nd Brigade, Royal Field Artillery .. Lieutenant-Colonel O. M. Harris, D.S.O.
166th Brigade, Royal Field Artillery .. Lieutenant-Colonel C. G. Stewart, C.M.G., D.S.O.
33rd Divisional Ammunition Column .. Lieutenant-Colonel A. G. Johnson.
Divisional Trench Mortar Officer .. .. Captain C. C. W. Havell.
X 33 Trench Mortar Battery .. .. Lieutenant H. C. Powell.
Y 33 Trench Mortar Battery .. .. Lieutenant A. V. Nicholson.
Z 33 Trench Mortar Battery .. .. Lieutenant C. C. Fitzgerald.

DIVISIONAL ENGINEERS—

Commander .. .. Lieutenant-Colonel F. M. Westrop, Royal Engineers.

Adjutant .. .. Lieutenant J. S. Baines, Royal Engineers.

ROYAL ENGINEERS—

33rd Divisional Signal Company .. .. Captain G. W. Williams.
11th Field Company, Royal Engineers .. Captain H. A. S. Pressey.
212th Field Company, Royal Engineers .. Captain H. T. Morshead.
222nd Field Company, Royal Engineers .. Captain C. le T. Turner Jones.

19TH INFANTRY BRIGADE—

Commander .. .. Brigadier-General C. R. G. Mayne, D.S.O., Highland Light Infantry.

Brigade-Major .. .. Captain E. K. Twiss, 10th Jats.
Staff Captain .. .. Captain A. H. W. Landon, Royal Canadian Regiment.

1/5th Scottish Rifles .. .. .. Lieutenant-Colonel E. R. Clayton.
2nd Royal Welch Fusiliers .. .. .. Major C. H. R. Crawshay.
20th Royal Fusiliers .. .. Lieutenant-Colonel W. B. Garnett.
19th Machine Gun Company .. .. Captain W. H. C. Pery-Knox-Gore.
19th Trench Mortar Battery .. .. Lieutenant H. D. D. C. Tiley.

THE THIRTY-THIRD DIVISION.

98TH INFANTRY BRIGADE—

Commander	Brigadier-General J. D. Heriot-Maitland, C.M.G., Rifle Brigade.
Brigade-Major	Captain R. M. Watson, D.S.O., Royal Dublin Fusiliers.
Staff Captain	Major E. P. Clarke, Suffolk Regiment.
1st Middlesex Regiment	Lieutenant-Colonel J. W. L. Elgee.
2nd Argyll and Sutherland Highlanders ..	Lieutenant-Colonel P. W. Brown, D.S.O.
4th King's (Liverpool) Regiment	Lieutenant-Colonel E. M. Beall, D.S.O.
1/4th Suffolk Regiment	Lieutenant-Colonel H. C. Copeman, D.S.O.
98th Machine Gun Company	Captain C. D. Jay.
98th Trench Mortar Battery	Captain C. E. Paternoster.

100TH INFANTRY BRIGADE—

Commander	Brigadier-General A. W. F. Baird, C.M.G., D.S.O., Gordon Highlanders.
Brigade-Major	Captain O. C. Downes, D.S.O., Rifle Brigade.
Staff Captain	Captain C. Bushell, The Queen's (Royal West Surrey Regiment).
1st Queens (Royal West Surrey) Regiment	Major H. A. Hunter.
2nd Worcestershires	Lieutenant-Colonel T. K. Pardoe.
16th King's Royal Rifle Corps	Lieutenant-Colonel C. L. Porter.
1/9th Highland Light Infantry	Lieutenant-Colonel J. C. Stormonth Darling, D.S.O.
100th Machine Gun Company	Captain G. S. Hutchison, M.C.
100th Trench Mortar Battery	Captain A. H. Popert.

DIVISIONAL TROOPS—

18th Middlesex Regiment (Pioneers) ..	Lieutenant-Colonel H. Storr, Middlesex Regiment.
33rd Divisional Train	Lieutenant-Colonel P. J. P. Lea, D.S.O., Army Service Corps.
19th Field Ambulance	Major W. B. Purdon, Royal Army Medical Corps.
99th Field Ambulance	Major C. R. Morris, Royal Army Medical Corps.
101st Field Ambulance	Lieutenant-Colonel A. S. Arthur, Royal Army Medical Corps.
43rd Mobile Veterinary Section	Captain A. G. L. Lalor, Army Veterinary Corps.
73rd Sanitary Section	Captain J. E. Wilson, Royal Army Medical Corps.

The Division moved again to the forward area, and bivouacked on the 2nd November, beside Trones Wood, in the open. During the Division's absence from the forward area and on the Gommecourt Front, High Wood and the Flers Ridge had eventually been captured by the employment of more than ten Divisions.

The weather had entirely broken. The roads were a morass of treacly mud through which stuck out tree stumps and branches at all angles, which were supposed to form their foundation. Cover of every description had been swept aside by shell fire, and every yard of ground was pitted by deep shell holes. The artillery on both sides had continually increased as the fighting became more and more local.

LES BŒUFS.

On the 22nd of October the Division moved forward to the Gillemont-Guinchy Ridge in order to participate in a further general attack, in which the French were to co-operate with ourselves. The French appeared to be anxious to accelerate the attacks. On the Les Bœufs front, however, " Dew Drop " Trench had already been attacked four times without success. The policy of General Headquarters in continuing this onslaught has been subjected to severe criticism. It must be remembered, however, that the Roumanian situation at this time was very uncertain ; and it was necessary to hold the German attack to our front wherever possible. On October 25th, Marshal Foch had an all day conference. Our troops were already in line on the immediate left of the French. The French on this date decided to attack with their 152nd Division, under General Andrieu, in order to anticipate a German counter-attack. Information had been received by the Intelligence Staff of Lord Cavan's Corps, that the Kaiser had been round " straffing " Von Arnim and other generals for not counter-attacking this Corps.

Attacks were continued between 26th and 30th October in conjunction with the French. Owing to there being no unity of command, however, there was little or no co-operation between the French and ourselves, despite the hard work of the liaison officers. The wings on the left of the French and the right of the British were, in consequence, almost invariably in the air,—a source of extreme danger to both armies.

But the 98th Brigade, on 28th October, captured Dewdrop Trench, which had already been assaulted four times, in a very gallant attack by the 4th Suffolk Regiment and the 2nd Worcestershire Regiment of the 100th Brigade, incurring very heavy casualties and taking 136 prisoners. The Corps Commander, Lord Cavan, sent the following message :—

To MAJOR-GENERAL PINNEY, 33rd Division,

" Hearty congratulations on capture of Dewdrop and 100 prisoners " after so many unsuccessful efforts by other Divisions. Please thank " Brigadier and Worcesters and Suffolks."

Following this the 19th Brigade assaulted " Hazy " Trench and captured the " Gun Pits." Owing to the uncertainty of the exact position of the Boche, equally with that of our troops, it was impossible for the heavy artillery to be used. In addition, water, food, and ammunition had to be man handled for 5,000 yards of thick mud. It is little wonder, therefore, that the 19th Brigade had to evacuate their position. The 100th Brigade lost two very able and gallant officers in Captain W. Henderson, M.C., of the Worcestershires, and Lieutenant-Colonel J. C. Stormonth Darling, D.S.O., of the Glasgow Highlanders, both killed by snipers while reconnoitring.

THE THIRTY-THIRD DIVISION.

EXTRACT FROM "THE TIMES," DATED 30th OCTOBER.

"BRITISH RIGHT ADVANCED.

"A welcome series of successes in the Transylvanian passes are
"reported from Bukarest. On the Moldavian side, where for some time
"the Roumanians, with the help of Russia, have had the upper hand,
"over 900 of the enemy have been taken prisoners in the Uzal valley.
"Falkenhayn's troops have also been heavily defeated in the Torzburg
"Pass and South of the Vulcan Pass, where thay had made a deep
"incursion into Roumania.

"At the Predeal, the principal pass between Brasso and Bukarest
"through the Prahova valley, a counter-attack against the invaders
"failed. Telegraphing from Bukarest on Friday, our Correspondent says
"that the Roumanians have taken 20,000 prisoners since the outbreak
"of war. The German prisoners, for the most part youths or men over
"50, badly clothed and hungry, are said to be extremely dejected.

"North-east of Les Bœufs, on the right of the British line North
"of the Somme, our troops on Saturday captured several important
"enemy trenches. We took prisoners two officers and 138 other ranks.
"Our gain in this region was extended yesterday morning when the
"British troops captured another enemy trench.

"The French on the Somme have also made slight progress in the
"Somme region, at Sailly-Saillisel, North of the river, and Biaches,
"South of the river."

EXTRACT FROM THE "DAILY MAIL," DATED 30th OCTOBER.

"The 'grit' of our soldiers, their persistence against every sort of
"enemy, was never more highly tested than in the succession of fights
"renewed to-day in front of Les Bœufs. If they did not 'fight upon
"their stumps' as at Chevy Chase, on occasion they waded in mud
"much beyond their knees, and not a few were only salved from
"foundering by their companions tugging them to firmer berths.

"A certain number of the wounded have bayonet wounds—a form
"of injury much rarer among our soldiers than among the German.
"And the butt of the rifle was used as well as the point of the bayonet.

"The weather to-day was less repellant, and yet rather worse for
"fighting than ever. The wind was stiff,—excellent, doubtless, for drying
"the ground, but a trouble both to the artillery and the observers.
"Nevertheless, the airmen faced the bumps as gaily as the infantry in
"the mud. The artillery fire was properly observed, and in spite of
"all, the men charged once more the crazy system of shell holes,
"emplacements, and trenches to which some humorist has appended
"a list of meteorological terms—'hazy,' 'misty,' 'rainbow' and the

26

LES BŒUFS.

" rest. The hundred or so prisoners who waded back this afternoon
" were armoured with mud, and every man who returned after the walk,
" whether wounded or not, fell into deep sleep the instant opportunity
" offered, so weary were they all.

   " It had been a winter fight ; and winter troubles, such as trench
" feet, have to be faced and prevented. Every ounce of weight—of
" food, water, bombs, wire, special guns, boots, and all the ponderous
" paraphernalia necessary in trench warfare—counts doubly. Yet, at the
" very worst, the men have attacked and won local struggles. In one
" of these, carried through during the very foulest of the foul days, the
" storming party found at their goal as welcome a reward as the hot
" tea that greets the walking wounded at the clearing hospital. They
" arrived at the German trench a few minutes after the enemy's parcel
" post, which was a full one. Nearly all the parcels contained food and
" many of them rum. Never was an alfresco meal more thoroughly
" seasoned with the ' Spartan sauce ' or better enjoyed. It is, after all,
" no bad thing that as a means towards the maintenance of moral the
" Germans have spent extra trouble in perfecting their postal
" arrangements to the front."

On the 3rd November, the 19th and 98th Brigades, with the French
on the immediate right of the Division, took over the line East of Les
Bœufs and Ginchy, with their supports lying in the old German trench known
as the Flers Line. From the Flers Line itself could be seen the towers of
Bapaume ; and it was obvious that the intention was to capture Le Transloy
and Rocquigny and then to outflank Bapaume itself, which lay about three
miles distant. It was equally obvious, however, to those who took over
the line, that owing to the state of the ground in the valley between Les
Bœufs and Le Transloy, the thick ground mists which prevented accurate
artillery observation, and the large amount of wire which the enemy had
already put out, that an attack at this time of the year across a quagmire
completely intersected with shell holes would be an almost impossible task.
The repeated attacks carried out on the 3rd and 4th November, by the
Division upon Hazy Trench, which was indeed " hazy," since it could not
be found on the ground but only on the map, Antelope Trench, German
Trench, Brimstone Trench and trenches with other evil sounding names ;
the very heavy casualties incurred ; the extreme difficulty of getting back
wounded across the ground on which it was almost impossible for an armed
man to move himself, let alone carry a wounded comrade ; the lowering,
sunless skies and the torrents of rain, will never be forgotten by those who
were forced to take part in these hideous operations. The horror of the
day spent in shallow, waterlogged trenches under unceasing fire was even
surpassed at night when the full fury of the German guns was let loose.
Men disappeared into the night ; one knows not to this date their fate,

27

whether destroyed by shell fire, or swallowed up in the yawning shell holes, stifled with mud and water, gripped and paralysed with cold and wounds. The scream of shells, the dull boom of the burst, the chatter of machine guns and the "spat, spat" of heavy rain drops lashing the surface of the quagmire were incessant. The sole duckboard track was torn up or sunken beneath the oozing surface of the ground. Boots were torn from the feet of the men held fast in the octopus grip of the mud. Men were seen working without any clothing except their shirts and · jackets. Exhaustion became a plague. Horses and mules remained to die stuck fast in their tracks. Wagons were abandoned and became the sport of shells. The little wooden crosses daily increased. Every man was buried where he fell, it being impossible to bear him away.

On the 5th November it was decided to have a gala Guy Fawkes day, and the remains of the Division which had repeatedly attempted the feat, only to be "bogged" a few yards from our line, and easily shot to pieces like bottles in a fair, were hurled across to take the German trenches surrounding Le Transloy. Success was obtained by the 2nd Worcestershires, who had been concentrated in the French area, and who, under Lieutenant E. Bennett—who won the V.C. for his exploit—struggled forward some hundreds of yards to the objective and squatted like ducks in the mud, known as "Bennett Trench," opposite Le Transloy. In view of the conditions this attack, although little was gained of tactical advantage, must be regarded as one of the most brilliant exploits recorded.

Extract from "The Times," 6th November.

"Most of Saillisel Captured.

"The French and British troops on the Somme pushed forward "again yesterday. The French took most of the Saillisel, and to the "south-east attacked the wood of St. Pierre-Vaast on three sides.

"On the northern side they took three trenches, and on the south-"western fringe captured the whole of the enemy position. Fighting "was very violent, and German counter-attacks were brilliantly repulsed. "More than 500 prisoners were taken.

"The British in their centre made progress on a front of about "1,000 yards, and took the high ground near the Bätte de Warlencourt. "They attacked too, on their extreme right towards Le Transloy, and "cleared a pocket of Germans. At Verdun the French have now taken "all the village of Vaux. On their right they have occupied Damloup, so "that all the former main defences of Verdun have been recaptured."

Machine gunners, who fared badly during this period, commenced their first experience of carrying intolerably heavy loads across several miles of country, which in peace time they would have said it would be impossible

28

to cross unsupported by drag ropes or without salmon waders. The difficulties of keeping guns cleaned and in action in this area was seldom appreciated, and certainly not understood. Only Heaven knows how the Royal Artillery fared during these operations ; few live to tell the tale. But their guns were never silent.

From this area the Division, which had lost heavily, was withdrawn for a short period into the wasted areas behind the Somme battlefields, and was moved south on the 3rd December, and took over from the 30th French Division in the Rancourt-Bouchavesnes Sector, opposite St. Pierre Vaast Wood, with its rear echelons and transport lines in the Maurepas Ravine about three miles behind. The conditions in this area were even worse than those of the previous month in the Les Bœufs Sector. Roads did not exist ; not a stick of vegetation was living, nothing but stunted trees and tangled scrub remained of the vast boar forests and pleasant parks of this district in pre-war days. Only one communication trench, three kilometres long, existed ; and this was subjected from morning till night to a heavy bombardment ; and, in any case, the water-logged condition of the ground made it almost impassable.

The commencement of this trench was known as " Angostura." Had its end been termed " Bitters," it would have not been a misnomer. Over and over again men were stuck in the mud, often up to their shoulders for many hours. Some lived for two days in this bitter cold, buried round the neck in mud, under continuous shell fire, it only being possible to render them assistance, or give them hot stimulants under cover of darkness, until they were dragged out with ropes almost insane, and hideously frost-bitten.

A new plague, which in a minor form in 1914-15 had revealed itself, now descended upon the Division, to be known as " Trench Feet." The whole energy of the Administrative Services of the Division was required to grapple with this problem, which caused us heavy casualties.

The number of cases during the first two eight days tours, where each company performed forty-eight hours duty in the wet, were as under :—

98TH BRIGADE—		100TH BRIGADE—	
1st Middlesex	25	1st Queen's	209
2nd Argyll & Sutherland Highlanders	11	2nd Worcestershires	104
4th King's	81	9th Highland Light Infantry	259
1/4th Suffolks	5	16th King's Royal Rifle Corps	82

From these figures it can be realized how serious was this malady, which in many cases caused death and in many others necessitated amputation. It was undoubtedly due to the energy and foresight of the A.A. and Q.M.G., Lieutenant-Colonel P. R. C. Commings, that these casualties were speedily reduced, whilst within a short time the Division, even in the line was replete with every comfort which the resources of the Army could provide. He carried out the organization of tea kitchens, canteens, and other comforts which until the end were not only a great safeguard of the health of the troops, but a great moral factor in fighting efficiency.

Christmas was spent in this area, probably the worst Christmas in the history of any man who experienced it.

It is amusing to note that on Christmas Day two Russian prisoners came in, naturally thought to be Boche. They met other Russians amongst our prisoners who told them we were English. They all kissed each other. When the Provost-Sergeant came in he was immediately kissed by five Russians.

In January the Division side-shuffled still further southwards, and took over the line from Bouchavesnes, inclusive, to the bend of the Somme at Clery, including the Island of Ommiecourt, in the river itself.

The Clery front was taken over from General Lancrenon of the 17th French Division, who left behind him not only good maps and plans, but much advice chiefly as to " Lying doggo," also " a warning concerning a mysterious dog which went and visited a cellar in Clery, full of dead Huns, and a complete telephone exchange " used by the dog or the Boches (—?—) We never discovered which.

Fortunately, a heavy frost, followed by snow and followed again by hard frost set in at this period and lasted well into February. Conditions became considerably more agreeable ; and, as the Somme and its canals froze over, it was possible to take much more interest in life ; besides which the French had constructed admirable tunnelled dug-outs, whilst an excellent supply of " Tommy's Cookers," cocoa and comforts was obtained from the Division.

The Division, too, established and maintained an excellent tea kitchen at Clery, which was generously patronised, particularly by ration parties.

At this period the weather was not only cold and windy, but we experienced 15 to 20 degrees of frost. In consequence, as many as possible, except sentries on duty, kept underground for the sake of warmth.

The operations in the Sector were confined mostly to raids ; keeping oneself warm ; and to experiments, both by our own and the Boche gunners, in trying the effect upon ice of high explosive shells. Of the raids, a particularly fine one was carried out on the 23rd February by a Company of the 2nd Battalion Worcestershire Regiment, under Captain E. A. O. Durlacher and Lieutenant E. L. Hopkins, under the personal direction of Brigadier-General Baird, in which two officers and forty-one other ranks of the Alexandra Guard Grenadier Regiment were taken prisoners, and the whole of the trench system destroyed, at a cost to ourselves of only three casualties. Another raid in which a machine gun and several prisoners were taken was carried out by the Glasgow Highlanders, under Lieutenants W. Mc. C. F. Coulter and A. Wilson, the latter being killed whilst gallantly searching for a missing man after the raid. Both these raids were supported by machine gun barrage fire. This was particularly effective from Ommiecourt, which was apparently unsuspected, and from which enfilade fire could be brought to bear and outflank the whole of the German line.

The first machine gun barrage in action on modern lines was carried out on 18th February, covering an attack by the 4th Division opposite Bouchavesnes, when forty-eight guns of the 4th and 33rd Divisions were grouped in batteries in one area. This was organized by Lieutenant-Colonel R. G. Clarke, then 15th Corps Machine Gun Officer. It was curious that, although the batteries were under the direct observation of Mount St. Quentin, and were observed in action, the shells fired at the batteries, although pitched amongst the guns, ricochetted off the hard, battered and frozen ground and burst in the bank about fifty yards to the rear. Not a single casualty was sustained amongst the gunners on this occasion.

The Eastern situation was, at this time, most obscure. There was great fear that Russia and Austria would drop out " paired." There were also grave rumours that if the Asquith-Grey Cabal remained longer in office they would drift into Peace, a Peace which could have been nothing but ignoble. It is on record that Lord Cavan was lunching with Lord Derby when Sir Douglas Haig and Mr. Lloyd George came in late,—both very pale. After lunch, Sir Douglas Haig tapped Mr. Lloyd George on the shoulder and said " Thank you." They had just come from the supreme War Council, and Mr. Lloyd George had taken the soldiers' part against the policy of " Wait and See," drift, or an ignoble peace.

Major-General Pinney was awarded the C.B. in the New Year's Honours Gazette of 1917, and on the 17th February he was decorated as Commander of the French Order of the Legion of Honour by General Nivelle,—a small man with a dull eye, evidently of strong character, but only noticeable if one looked at him carefully. A Colonel on the Staff tied the ribbon behind the General's neck as he stood facing the French Commander-in-Chief. The latter, under his breath, scolded the Staff Officer, who fumbled over the operation, muttering in French " I ought to have brought a *jeune fille* instead of a slow man like you." When the decoration was at last secure a stage kiss was given to General Pinney on both cheeks, followed by a word of congratulation whilst shaking hands.

A pleasant and entertaining diversion in this area was found in the defences of Ommiecourt Island, which was uninhabited, except by one platoon of Infantry and by two Sections of Machine Gunners.

A tale which will illustrate the inventive genius, broad humour and resource of our men may be aptly told.

A French pontoon was " obtained " by the Transport of the 100th Machine Gun Company and towed up the canal from Suzanne into the Somme opposite the island. The boat was converted into an armoured gun-boat. In order to give her the necessary armoured plating, " scrounged " steel helmets were tacked round her sides down to the " Plimsoll mark " and

Machine Guns were installed fore and aft. By the time the boat was ready the thaw had already commenced ; and it was hoped to manœuvre the boat through the thin ice up to the German line, and co-operate with a Machine Gun landing party in a raid which was planned for the Glasgow Highlanders. A preliminary reconnaissance was carried out by the Officer Commanding and an orderly across the ice. In order to ensure them both against mishap they were secured with telephone wire. The orderly, unfortunately for himself decided to fall through a small hole in the ice, and was salved half drowned. The Commanding Officer proceeded as far as the Island, about 100 yards from the German Line, when he floundered through the ice. Twelve " good men " at the end of his telephone cable immediately jerked it taut and proceeded pulling. By a series of these jerks the Major was retrieved about half the distance across the ice when, owing to a slackening of the wire, he was able to get on to his feet and proceed homewards on his own. But no sooner was he once more started than another jerk came upon the hawser and he was jerked off his feet and toboganned across the ice. This experiment was repeated several times until he reached home, and was immediately carried to hospital, from whence, having been curiously diagnosed as a case of spotted fever, he escaped and returned to his Company.

No use was finally made of the gun-boat, for, early in March the Division was withdrawn from the line and concentrated for a few days in so-called camps, most of them below water-level near Suzanne ; and then proceeded by march route to Corbie, to undergo intensive training for the Spring Offensive. Intensive training consisted chiefly of football matches, field manœuvres and a well-earned rest, in which military tattoos and entertainments by " The Shrapnels," the Divisional Concert Party, and Cinema were frequent and at their highest standard.

The casualties sustained by the Division from October, 1916, until February, 1917, inclusive, amounted to 299 officers and 7,812 other ranks from all causes.

CHAPTER III.

THE BATTLE OF ARRAS, 1st March to 1st July, 1917.

The Hindenburg Line, 19th Brigade engaged—Fontaine les Croisilles—April, Attacks by 98th and 100th Brigades—Especial gallantry of 2nd Battalion Argyll and Sutherland Highlanders, 1st Battalion Middlesex Regiment, 4th Battalion The King's Liverpool Regiment, 1st Battalion The Queen's Regiment and 16th Battalion King's Royal Rifle Corps—Heavy Counter Attacks—May, Further Attacks upon the Hindenburg Line—Brilliant Exploit by the 100th Brigade—Final Capture of the Line—Heavy Counter Attacks withstood by Glasgow Highlanders and 2nd Battalion Worcestershire Regiment—Officers' Casualties—"The Arras Spring Meeting"—Horse Show at Cavillon.

ORDER OF BATTLE.

HEADQUARTERS, 33RD DIVISION.

Commander	Major-General R. J. Pinney, C.B.
Aide-de-Camp to Commander	Major H. C. C. Batten, Dorsetshire Regiment.
Aide-de-Camp to Commander	Second-Lieutenant A. S. G. Kennard, Hampshire Yeomanry.

GENERAL STAFF BRANCH—

General Staff Officer, 1st Grade	Lieutenant-Colonel D. Forster, D.S.O., Royal Engineers.
General Staff Officer, 2nd Grade	Captain B. L. Montgomery, D.S.O., Royal Warwickshire Regiment.
General Staff Officer, 3rd Grade	Captain J. F. L. Fison, M.C., Suffolk Regiment.

ADJUTANT AND QUARTERMASTER-GENERAL'S BRANCH—

Assistant Adjutant and Quartermaster-General	Lieutenant-Colonel P. R. C. Commings, D.S.O., South Staffordshire Regiment.
Deputy-Assistant Adjutant and Quartermaster-General	Captain J. W. Oldfield, M.C., General List.
Deputy-Assistant Quartermaster-General	Major O. B. Foster, M.C., Northumberland Fusiliers.

ADMINISTRATIVE SERVICES AND DEPARTMENTS—

Assistant Director of Medical Services	Colonel S. de C. O'Grady, Royal Army Medical Corps.
Deputy-Assistant Director of Medical Services	Captain L. G. Brown, Royal Army Medical Corps.
Assistant Director of Veterinary Services	Major R. A. Plunkett, Army Veterinary Corps.
Deputy-Assistant Director of Ordnance Services	Lieutenant A. M. E. Beavan, Army Ordnance Department.

THE THIRTY-THIRD DIVISION.

SPECIAL APPOINTMENT—
    Assistant Provost-Marshal ..   ..   .. Captain J. D. S. Lloyd, Welsh Horse Yeomanry.

HEADQUARTERS, DIVISIONAL ARTILLERY—
    Commander ..   .. Brigadier-General C. F. Blane, C.M.G.
    Brigade-Major ..   .. Major H. K. Sadler, Royal Artillery.
    Staff Captain ..   .. Captain W. E. Bownass, Royal Field Artillery.
    Staff Officer for Reconnaissance .. Lieutenant T. R. Jackson, Royal Field Artillery.

HEADQUARTERS, DIVISIONAL ENGINEERS—
    Commander ..   .. Lieutenant-Colonel G. F. Evans, D.S.O., Royal Engineers.
    Adjutant   ..   .. Lieutenant J. S. Baines, Royal Engineers.

HEADQUARTERS, 19TH INFANTRY BRIGADE—
    Commander ..   .. Brigadier-General C. R. G. Mayne, D.S.O., Highland Light Infantry.
    Brigade-Major ..   .. Major E. K. Twiss, D.S.O., 10th Jats.
    Staff Captain ..   .. Captain A. H. W. Landon, Royal Canadian Regiment.

HEADQUARTERS, 98TH INFANTRY BRIGADE—
    Commander ..   .. Brigadier-General J. D. Heriot-Maitland, C.M.G., Rifle Brigade.
    Brigade-Major ..   .. Brevet Major R. M. Watson, D.S.O., Royal Dublin Fusiliers.
    Staff Captain ..   .. Major E. P. Clarke, D.S.O., Suffolk Regiment.

HEADQUARTERS, 100TH INFANTRY BRIGADE—
    Commander ..   .. Brigadier-General A. W. F. Baird, C.M.G., D.S.O., Gordon Highlanders.
    Brigade-Major ..   .. Captain H. W. M. Paul, M.C., Middlesex Regiment.
    Staff Captain ..   .. Captain W. J. J. Coats, Highland Light Infantry.

It had been rumoured for some time that the Division was to take part in the second big British Offensive in the neighbourhood of Arras. It was moved from Corbie in the last week of March. Concurrent with its arrival in the concentration area west of Arras, the offensive had already started brilliantly with the capture of the Vimy Ridge, and villages further south, and a footing had been obtained in the Hindenburg Line.

From North to South the battle had gone well for us. On April 9th the Canadian Corps had obtained all objectives on the Vimy Ridge ; the 17th Corps had also taken all its objectives and formed a defensive flank to the North ; the 6th Corps had had equal success, securing all objectives South of the Scarpe ; but the 7th Corps had only succeeded in reaching the Hindenburg Line, and had incurred heavy casualties.

As on the Somme, it was again the misfortune of the Division not to be employed in the first successes. By the time the Division arrived at Hamelincourt preparatory to taking over the line, and to resuming the offensive, the

BRIGADIER-GENERAL J. D. HERIOT-MAITLAND, C.M.G., D.S.O., (RIFLE BRIGADE),

WHO COMMANDED THE NINETY-EIGHTH BRIGADE
FROM AUGUST, 1916, TO NOVEMBER, 1918.

enemy, having recovered from his first surprise, had already greatly strengthened his defence, particularly with artillery. On the 14th April the Division was moved into line, relieving the 21st Division. The same day General Allenby, commanding the 3rd Army, published an order stating, "We are in pursuit of a beaten enemy," whilst General Sir Thomas Snow, commanding the 7th Corps, stated that "attacks by Corps formations against machine guns in position are 'rot'." The latter proposed, therefore, that the attack should be carried out in the form of strong patrols and raids.

The 19th Brigade had been detached from the 33rd Division on the 12th, and, on the 13th, headed the 21st Division in an attempt to capture further trenches, part of the Hindenburg Line defence system, North-west of Fontaine les Croisilles. These attacks were unsuccessful, and at the same time the Boche commenced a heavy counter-attack against our left at Monchy le Preux. During the night of the 15th/16th the 20th Royal Fusiliers and 1st Cameronians, of the 19th Brigade, attempted a further attack upon the Hindenburg Line. The former Battalion was unsuccessful; and the latter Regiment got well forward, but ran out of bombs. When the Division took over, the 19th Brigade was established in the Hindenburg Line, and, to the South, the 100th Brigade occupied posts east of Croisilles, with patrols gradually moving across the Sensée Valley by night, and pushing forward posts towards the Hindenburg Line, as far south as "The Hump" near Bullecourt. To cover these operations the machine gunners were very fully occupied with harassing fire; whilst the 33rd Divisional Artillery was heavily engaged supporting the infantry attacks before Monchy le Preux with enfilade fire, and in stemming off the enemy counter-attacks. By this time the Army had succeeded in capturing 100 guns and 100,000 prisoners.

In the area in which we were now operating the Boche had carried out a deliberate plan of devastation. Not only were farmhouses and villages destroyed by explosives, but even the orchards, trees and village crucifixes had been cut down at their roots. This system had been carried out over a very wide area, and left not a vestige of cover for our troops; whilst most of the damage done, from a military point of view, was quite unnecessary.

An attack on a very large scale was planned for the 23rd April. In this attack the 98th Brigade to the North was ordered to force its way southwards down the Hindenburg Line, chiefly with bombs, and make a junction with the 100th Brigade in the Sensée Valley; the 100th Brigade, itself delivering a frontal attack upon the Hindenburg Line. The attack was particularly difficult to carry out. The Hindenburg Line consisted of a highly fortified front and second line with concrete machine gun emplacements, some of them with two storeys, about every fifty yards along it. Both lines were defended in front by strands of the thickest wire to a depth of about twenty yards, and were connected by the most complete system of tunnels and dug-outs that has ever been seen in the history of warfare.

The initial assault of the 98th Brigade attack was carried out by the

35

2nd Argyll and Sutherland Highlanders, under Lieutenant-Colonel P. W. Browne, and the 1st Middlesex Regiment, under Lieutenant-Colonel J. W. L. Elgee. The first objective for the 98th Brigade was Fontaine les Croisilles. The Argyll and Sutherland Highlanders attacked across the open on the left, whilst the Middlesex bore right down the trench system. At zero, 4.45 a.m., the big barriers across both front and support lines were destroyed by mines. The attack early met with opposition. Even before the troops had got down the slope to the Sensée River, one company each of the Argyll and Sutherland Highlanders and Middlesex Regiment found themselves cut off by the enemy between them and our own lines. Several local attempts were made to rescue them, but without success. The position in which this party found themselves was such that it enabled them to bring enfilade fire to bear upon that part of the Hindenburg Line to the south of the Sensée River, which had been captured by the 1st Queen's Regiment. Although under extreme difficulties and suffering heavy casualties from fire, both in their front and in their backs, this party, under Captain Henderson and Company-Sergeant-Major Todd, of the Argyll and Sutherland Highlanders, succeeded in holding the position, and destroyed large numbers of the enemy, until it perished almost to a man. Captain Henderson, who was awarded a posthumous V.C., himself with three men, led a bayonet charge on a large body of the enemy. By 5.45 a.m. the 98th Brigade had captured 240 prisoners of the 61st German Division, whilst the 4th Suffolk Regiment, assisted by two tanks, had obtained a junction with the 100th Brigade astride the Sensée River. During these operations Second-Lieutenant T. M. B. Lock, the Signalling Officer of the 1st Middlesex Regiment, also greatly distinguished himself. By this time a great deal more was expected of the machine guns than heretofore, and the Infantry had learned to have considerable faith in the overhead barrage. The idea of grouping guns together and of central control had already made itself felt in the Division ; and General Pinney ordered that the guns of the 19th and 100th Brigade should be grouped to cover the attack of the 100th Brigade. During the night of the 22nd April a very remarkable exploit was carried out by the 100th Machine Gun Company. The whole transport drove down the Sensée Valley into " No Man's Land," protected only by a small patrol of the Worcestershire Regiment, and deposited twelve guns in their battery positions and many thousands of rounds of ammunition. The transport returned without any mishap, although it had driven within 300 yards of the German Line, and possibly closer to the German patrols across " No Man's Land."

A battery of twelve guns was established within 200 yards of the Hindenburg Line on the high ground east of the Sensée River, so that direct fire could be brought to bear on the enemy in Fontaine les Croisilles, and upon those who should be manning the Hindenburg system. In addition, an enfilade barrage was arranged to flank the front of the 98th Brigade attack. Three other batteries of four guns each were established east of Croisilles.

A forward observation post was placed in the bed of the Sensée River within 100 yards of Fontaine Village, every battery being connected to it by signal communication.

At dawn on the 23rd the 100th Infantry Brigade also advanced to the attack, and during the first half-hour it was thought that success would be achieved. The 98th Brigade had already taken about 300 prisoners, whilst the Queens, under Captain Godfrey, penetrated the wire and established themselves well in the Hindenburg Line, with very light casualties. As daylight came, however, it was seen that the Sensée Valley was completely commanded by machine gun nests and pill-boxes both north and south of the River. The attack had not yet succeeded in capturing these nests. Very heavy bomb fighting was being carried on, and the air could be seen filled with German stick bombs. The bombardment became exceptionally fierce, particularly in the area of the Quarry, and up the Sensée Valley. All communication was destroyed. Light mists hung in the Valley, which prevented visual communication. It was during this period that a groom was the only connection between the forward Battalion and Brigade Headquarters. He rode repeatedly up and down the Sensée Valley with despatches through a hail of shrapnel, high explosives, and machine gun fire. It was apparent that the Queen's, for the time being at any rate, were cut off from the rest of the Brigade, it being impossible to move up to the Hindenburg Line owing to the very heavy shell and machine gun fire, without incurring the heaviest possible casualties. Moreover, both tanks with the 100th Brigade had failed to leave their starting point. By 10 a.m. the situation of the Queen's was desperate. Their bombs were exhausted, and it seemed an impossible task to supply them. Nevertheless, the 16th King's Royal Rifle Corps who were in support, under Lieutenant-Colonel A. V. Johnson, with the greatest gallantry, and despite the heaviest losses, repeatedly made their way up and down the valley, under Captains Scott and Gonner, who was killed, carrying bombs to the Queen's. Owing to the tunnel system it was, on the other hand, an easy matter for the Germans to feed their own troops with bombs and grenades. About 11 o'clock a determined counter-attack by the enemy, who seem thoroughly to have appreciated the awful plight of the Queen's, drove them and elements of the 16th King's Royal Rifle Corps from the Hindenburg Line. The 98th Brigade, then losing touch, were themselves driven back from their objective. As the men came back, the well posted enemy machine guns, picked them off like rabbits, and scarcely a man returned unwounded, whilst many were shot down in their tracks. The Queen's, after the attack, mustered only forty-three men. Meanwhile the machine guns, particularly the forward battery, had rendered very valuable services, and were again and again thanked by the Queen's during the operation for their help, where no one else could render assistance. It is a remarkable fact that the battery of twelve guns, although, as previously noted, within 200 yards of the German line under direct observation, incurred not a single casualty, the bombardment, which was so hideously destructive, falling the whole time about twenty yards behind it.

By twelve noon it was ascertained that the attack of the whole Army had been held up, the 6th Corps just east of Guemappe, and, on our front, except for a small party of Suffolks in the front trench of the Hindenburg Line, the situation was as it had been at zero. At 3 p.m., a new attack was made. It was by now positively plain that it was impossible to attack south of the Sensée Valley until the high ground to its north had been captured, so that in this new attack the 98th Brigade only was employed. The second attack was carried out at 7 p.m., by the 4th King's Liverpool Regiment, under command of Lieutenant-Colonel E. M. Beall, who, in his shirt sleeves, personally conducted his leading bombing party. At the same time the 30th Division on our left threw a Battalion forward as a flank protection. During the night the Boche repeatedly attacked the 98th Brigade, especially the Hindenburg support line, and at one time succeeded in closing in upon General Maitland's Headquarters. The fact, however, that elements of one company of the Middlesex and one of the Argyll and Sutherland Highlanders were still in their rear, forced the Boche to retire at dawn.

The partial success of this battle was a very great disappointment to all. It was only by the 98th Brigade being held up that it was prevented from being a great victory.

Some idea of the artillery preparation and bombardment to cover these operations may be gathered from the following figures :—

ARTILLERY AMMUNITION EXPENDITURE.

ON DIVISIONAL FRONT.

	April 21st-22nd.	22nd-23rd.	23rd-24th.
18-pr. Shrapnel	4,176	11,174	10,440
18-pr. H.E.	3,628	8,197	9,750
4.5 in. H.E.	1,845	6,023	6,161
18-pr. Smoke	—	506	—
4·5 in. Howitzer	—	15	—
4·5 in. Smoke	—	173	—

ON CORPS FRONT.

60-pr. Shrapnel	1,570	3,003	4,082
60-pr. H.E.	2,092	3,183	4,074
6 in. Howitzer	5,253	9,773	6,992
6 in. Shrapnel	100	187	283
6 in. H.E.	343	336	234
8 in. Howitzer	1,307	2,284	2,341
9·2 in. Howitzer	1,155	1,239	1,282

The following wire was received by the Division from the Commander-in-Chief :—" The fierce fighting yesterday has carried us another step forward. I congratulate you and all under you on the result of it and in the severe punishment you have inflicted on the enemy."

The following letter also was received from General Snow, Corps Commander, on the 26th April, when General David Campbell, with the 21st Division, relieved us from the line :—

> "On the occasion of the Division leaving the line for a well-earned
> "rest, the Corps Commander wishes to record his appreciation of the
> "high fighting qualities of your Division. The fighting of the last few
> "days has been severe, and in open fight your Division, in a difficult
> "situation, outfought and inflicted severe losses on the enemy. The
> "incident of the two companies (one of the 1st Middlesex and one of
> "the Argyll and Sutherland Highlanders) being isolated for nearly
> "twenty-four hours, but holding out until relieved, will no doubt live
> "in the history of those distinguished Regiments."

The Division was transferred to the Bienvillers-Pomera area to refit and receive drafts for further operations.

During the period of rest an important Conference was held. At this it was decided that "the pace of the artillery barrage should be 100 yards for two minutes on dry ground and three minutes on wet ground, over the open ; heavy guns to do little or no counter battery work. 'Mopping up' most necessary. Objectives must be limited when the Boche has concentrated."

Meanwhile, fighting had continued with great violence. General Braithwaite's 62nd Division had attacked and failed on the 3rd of May, whilst the 7th Division was heavily engaged in fighting in Bullecourt. At the same time a German Officer, captured on the 15th May, stated that a general retirement would be made on that date. He also stated that the Boche had breakfast about 8 o'clock, having stood to since 3 a.m.

On the 16th it was reported that the Boche was withdrawing, whilst General Shoubridge's 7th Division had succeeded in taking Bullecourt and had been relieved by the 58th Division. On the 16th May the 33rd Division again relieved the 21st, but it was found that the enemy on our front had not retired. Not much ground had been made during the absence of the 33rd Division. An attack was ordered for the 20th May by the 3rd Army, under General Allenby, and by the 5th Army, under General Gough, on a wide front. The 98th Brigade, under the command of Brigadier-General Heriot-Maitland, was ordered to carry out its attack on identical lines with the attack on the 23rd April. The 100th Brigade was given the most ambitious scheme of a frontal attack on the Hindenburg Line between the Sensée River and the "Hump," just North of Bullecourt, inclusive.

The plan, in the minutest detail, for this latter part of the attack was most ingeniously carried out by Brigadier-General Baird. Instead of at dawn, the attack was to be made during the Boche breakfast hour, shortly before 9 a.m., when the German sentries would be unsuspecting. In order to make them still more unalert, it was arranged that a squadron of aeroplanes should perform a " stunt " flight low over their lines between the hours of 8.30 and 9 a.m.

There was to be no previous bombardment, but, for four minutes covering the initial assault, a hurricane bombardment followed by a protective bombardment for two hours covering consolidation. The machine guns of the 100th and 19th Companies were again grouped for this operation, whilst those of the 98th remained independent. The night preceding the attack a camouflaged trench was dug again within 300 yards of the Hindenburg Line under full observation of the enemy position. Twelve guns were placed in this, and the teams were all ready before dawn. A battery of dummy guns and gunners was placed about 100 yards in front, and to a flank, of the battery position in order to deceive the enemy. As a special enterprise two Lewis guns, in the hands of the Machine Gun Corps, were given a free hand to work themselves forward by the Sensée Valley into the Hindenburg Line under cover of darkness, and to bring fire to bear on any Machine Guns which opened on the attacking troops at zero. So successful was this enterprise that one man succeeded in working his way right into the line before dawn, and in capturing several prisoners before zero hour.

At zero, with three battalions in line, the 2nd Worcestershires, under Major G. J. L. Stoney ; 16th King's Royal Rifle Corps, under Major E. Wenham ; and the Glasgow Highlanders, under Lieutenant-Colonel J. Menzies ; the attack upon the Hindenburg Line began, and, owing to General Baird's skilful handling, it succeeded in capturing the whole of the front system with a loss of only one man wounded, and with the capture of a large number of prisoners. Very soon, however, the enemy opened up his usual fierce bombardment ; and the further attack upon the Hindenburg Support Line, afterwards known as " Tunnel Trench," was unsuccessful, although the infantry succeeded in establishing themselves between the two lines.

During the afternoon determined counter-attacks were made by the enemy to retake the Hindenburg Line, particularly against the 2nd Battalion Worcestershire Regiment, on our right flank in " The Hump," where a strong point had been established. Some excellent direct fire sniping was obtained by the 19th and 100th Machine Gun Battery. It had been our experience on the 23rd April that the Germans had consistently and deliberately shot down our stretcher bearers. We were able to return the compliment by the annihilation of nineteen stretcher bearers who were not carrying wounded, but ammunition. This was later confirmed by prisoners.

Late in the afternoon and during the evening the enemy bombardment increased to extreme violence, and was followed by counter-attacks of the most determined nature. These thrusts were directed chiefly against the front held by the Glasgow Highlanders. In a short time all the Company Commanders had become casualties, including Captain A. E. Murray, Captain W. Coulter, killed ; Captain R. C. Reid, wounded ; and Lieutenant Anderson, captured. It was at this time that Second-Lieutenant D. Mac K. Greenshields, showing complete disregard to danger and splendid soldierly qualities, not only consolidated our line, moving from point to point, organizing defence, but maintained command of this battalion for a period of twenty-four hours under extreme difficulty. For his work he was awarded the D.S.O. Second-Lieutenant Mather, of the same battalion, also did extremely fine work, but as was so often the case, was not lucky enough to obtain a concrete reward for his gallant services. After the loss of the Commander of " A " Company of the 9th Highland Light Infantry, Company-Sergeant-Major McElveney took command of this Company, and conducted its operations with splendid heroism. Every Battalion engaged lost valuable and experienced Officers, killed or wounded.

It would be an impossible task for us to relate of all those who at moments of crises, in the absence of their Commanders, have taken command of situations and merited high reward.

In recording this history, we can only draw upon our own memory, or upon the scant records and memories of those few who are still left to tell the tale. Doubtless, not only during these operations, but in all others we have described, we have omitted mention of a hundred acts and more names which should, undoubtedly, be chronicled in this memoir.

During the height of the bombardment, and at a time of extreme peril, when our troops in the line were short of both bombs and ammunition, Captain Harrison of the Queen's, acting as Brigade Transport Officer, galloped the whole of the Brigade ammunition limbers up the Sensée Valley along the Fontaine Road, and succeeded in replenishing with bombs and ammunition the whole line, with the loss of only one limber. This feat was not only very spectacular, but needed the highest qualities of resource, initiative, and daring. Undoubtedly, Captain Harrison's act saved the 100th Brigade from again being driven out of the Hindenburg Line as on the 23rd of April.

EXTRACT FROM " THE TIMES," MAY 21ST, 1917.

" 9.12 p.m.—As the result of an attack carried out by us early this " morning, our troops have established themselves in a further section of " the Hindenburg Line, on a front of over a mile, between Fontaine-les- " Croisilles* and Bullecourt. The enemy has made several unsuccessful " attempts to shake our hold on this position, and fierce fighting has " taken place in this neighbourhood throughout the day. Heavy

---

* Fontaine-les-Croisilles is north-north-west of Bullecourt from which it is distant about two miles.

" casualties have been inflicted on the enemy, and a number of
" prisoners have been taken by us. Fighting continues in our favour.
" Hostile raiding parties were driven off last night in the neighbourhood
" of Oppy and south-west of Wytschaete. We carried out a successful
" raid south of Armentières. Three German aeroplanes were brought
" down yesterday in air fighting, one of which landed in our lines. Five
" other hostile machines were driven down out of control, and one
" German observation balloon was destroyed. Four of our aeroplanes
" are missing."

BERLIN STORY OF BRITISH REPULSES.

" *Saturday.*—Front of Crown Prince Rupprecht. Between the coast
" and St. Quentin the artillery activity has increased in several sectors.
" It attained great intensity during the night between Acheville (east of
" Vimy) and Gavrelle (south of Acheville). An attack launched by the
" English—under the protection of this fire—on both sides of the Arras-
" Douai road broke down under our defensive fire. Enemy attacks east
" of Monchy were also unsuccessful.

" *Sunday.*—Near Arras the fighting activity has again increased.
" On both sides of Monchy, after short artillery preparation the English
" attacked during the evening with strong forces. They were completely
" repulsed. During the night the artillery activity between Acheville
" and Queent (south-west of Bullecourt), was extraordinarily lively. At
" daybreak the strongest drumfires commenced on the line, and south of
" the Scarpe this was followed by English attacks.

" *Evening.*—The English attacks announced this morning south of the
" Scarpe have been repulsed with heavy losses to the enemy."

EXTRACT FROM " THE TIMES," MAY 22ND, 1917.

" ENEMY VERSION OF THE FIGHTING.

" Only a demolished trench lost.—German report May 21st.

" *Front of Crown Prince Rupprecht.*—Yesterday's attacks by the
" English were delivered on both sides of the Arras-Cambrai Road on a
" front of twelve kilometres (about $7\frac{1}{2}$ miles). Wherever the enemy
" thrusting troops between the Scarpe and the Sensée brook succeeded
" in advancing out of their trenches they were shot to pieces by our
" destructive fire. Enemy troops which penetrated into our lines to the
" east of Croisilles were driven back again by a strongly delivered
" counter thrust. Many times repeated attacks between Fontaine and
" Bullecourt during the afternoon, evening, and night met with the same
" fate. We maintained our positions, with the exception of one completely

" demolished trench, which we left in possession of the enemy in
" accordance with our plan.

" *Evening.*—In the morning English attacks at Bullecourt (Artois),
" and French local attacks to the south-west of Nauroy (Champagne)
" failed. Throughout the day there were artillery duels of varying
" intensity in several sectors of the Arras, Aisne and Champagne fronts,
" as well as on the eastern bank of the Meuse."

HINDENBURG LINE CONQUESTS.

Bullecourt Gains Secured—Severe German Losses.

" 12.25 p.m. Our operations in the Hindenburg Line between
" Bullecourt and Fontaine-les-Croisilles were continued with success
" during the night. Our troops, who had carried the front trench of the
" Hindenburg Line yesterday morning and had repulsed several counter
" attacks, renewed the attack in the evening, and after fierce hand-to-
" hand fighting captured the support trench also. Hostile counter attacks
" were again beaten off with heavy loss to the enemy, whose troops were
" engaged in the open by our massed artillery. A large number of the
" enemy's dead were found in the captured positions. About 150
" prisoners have so far been taken by us in these operations. Two
" German divisions have been engaged in the fighting in this neighbour-
" hood since yesterday morning. We carried out a successful raid last
" night near Loos. Early this morning a party of the enemy endeavoured
" to enter our trenches south-west of Messines, but was driven off.

" 9.12 p.m. Our new positions in the Hindenburg Line north-west
" of Bullecourt have been secured during the day with little interference
" from the enemy. All information received confirms the severity of the
" German losses in the recent fighting in this area. With the exception
" of a sector about 2,000 yards in length immediately west of Bullecourt,
" we now hold the whole of the Hindenburg Line from a point one mile
" east of Bullecourt, to Arras. Hostile artillery has again shown
" considerable activity on the north bank of the Scarpe. There was
" great activity in the air yesterday. A number of successful bombing
" raids were carried out, and our aeroplanes co-operated actively with our
" Infantry in their attacks, engaging German troops in the enemy's front
" line trenches with machine gun fire. In air fighting seven German
" aeroplanes were brought down, one of which fell in our lines, and eight
" others were driven down out of control. Another hostile machine was
" shot down out of control by our anti-aircraft guns. Four of our
" aeroplanes are missing."

At 4 o'clock in the afternoon, the 19th Brigade was ordered to continue
the attack through the 100th Brigade. This was carried out by the 5th

Scottish Rifles and 1st Cameronians, and their orders were to capture Tunnel Trench. The attack by these Battalions were unsuccessful and were held up with very heavy losses, whilst it was found increasingly difficult, owing to the uncertain positions of the 98th Brigade, to give an effective artillery barrage. The attack of the 98th Brigade had gone well forward, some troops having reached the village of Cherisy, but owing to the fact that neither the 19th nor the 100th Brigade were able to capture Tunnel Trench, which connected the Sensée Valley through Fontaine, it was impossible for them to hold their ground ; and the attack upon Fontaine Village was again a failure, although the whole of the Hindenburg front line was now entirely in our hands.

On the 26th and 27th, further attacks were ordered. These were carried out by the 2nd Royal Welch Fusiliers, under Lieutenant-Colonel Williams, and by the 5th/6th Scottish Rifles, supported by the guns of the 19th Machine Gun Company.

For the first time the fire of eight machine guns was organized as a creeping barrage in front of the advancing troops. At 2 p.m. the infantry attacked in three waves, the men advancing shoulder to shoulder. But the enemy was fully prepared. His artillery opened simultaneously with our own. His machine guns had been taken from their emplacements and placed on the parapet in order to increase their field of fire. When our infantry reached the enemy front line—a distance of about 200 yards—there were many guns in the line. Devastating fire from the machine guns had accounted for many hundreds of men. As they fell in the leading wave, men from the second were rushed forward to take their comrades' places. Thus the second and third waves gradually merged into the first wave. The enemy fought stoutly and climbed out of their trench, lining the parapet to meet our attack. Officers, N.C.O.s and most of the men were in shirtsleeves. For more than an hour the bitterest hand-to-hand fighting took place and many an individual contest was decided without weapons in " Catch-as-catch-can " style, the combatants locked together frequently rolling off the parapet and falling into the trench to be seen no more. When the fighting had reached its height, and with the result still doubtful, the enemy rushed up reinforcements from his reserve trenches and forced back all that were left of our exhausted men. Our two forward machine guns remained intact, covering the withdrawal of the infantry by placing an impenetrable curtain of fire across the front.

The barbarous methods of the enemy were much in evidence after the attack. Until nightfall enemy snipers kept up a continuous fire on our wounded, many of whom were writhing in agony near his line. After dark, enemy patrols came into " No Man's Land," collected our killed and wounded, heaved them into a big pile, and lighted an enormous human bonfire.

"THE HINDENBURG LINE"—CROISILLES.

" British troops are pushing towards Fontaine-les-Croisilles from the
" West and North-west. This German fortress on the Sensée River has
" been made more open to attack by the penetration of the Hindenburg
" Line West of Bullecourt. On Saturday night British troops made
" a very successful raid near St. Quentin."

" Between Ypres and Armentières, near Hulloch, and on both sides
" of the Scarpe, good fighting conditions prevailed and artillery
" engagements developed.

" About midnight several English companies were repelled by
" a counter-attack West of Wytschaete. Between Cherisy and Bullecourt
" stubborn engagements took place throughout the night on both banks
" of the Sensée River. Repeated English attacks made in this Sector
" failed with heavy losses before the resistance offered by our troops."

Between May 28th and June 19th, further attacks were carried out by
the 33rd Division, by the 21st and by Fanshawe's 58th London Division.
A great attack was ordered for June 25th, but, after the troops of the 100th
Brigade were in the line, the attack was, at the last moment, cancelled.

On 1st July, the Division was relieved by the 50th Division, and proceeded
to the Hamelincourt Area to refit and for a rest.

The Division sustained heavy casualties during these operations, the
totals being 240 officers and 5,431 other ranks ; but those of the enemy
must have been far heavier. Amongst officers, we lost :—

ROYAL ARTILLERY.

Killed.	*Wounded.*
2nd Lieut. N. S. Bastock.	2nd Lieut. G. G. Barlow.
2nd Lieut. N. Grant.	2nd Lieut. S. N. Beall.
Capt. B. R. Heape.	Major Bennell-Stanford.
	Capt. M. M. I. Body.
	2nd Lieut. W. E. Harrison.
	2nd Lieut. R. J. Marjores.
	2nd Lieut. A. B. Neate.
	2nd Lieut. R. E. Oldham.
	Lieut. W. G. Sheares.
	2nd Lieut. A. R. Tucker.

ROYAL ENGINEERS.

Killed.	*Wounded.*	*Missing.*
2nd Lieut. F. M. McCutchan.	2nd Lieut. P. Melhuish.	2nd Lieut. R. N. Montgomery.
	2nd Lieut. H. C. Williams.	

19TH BRIGADE.

20TH ROYAL FUSILIERS.

Killed.

2nd Lieut. U. P. Davis.
Lieut. E. L. Powell.
Lieut. R. Q. Scott.
2nd Lieut. W. Soro.

Wounded.

2nd Lieut. C. Aberdeen.
2nd Lieut. C. H. Bryant.
Capt. E. F. Chapman.
2nd Lieut. S. R. Davies.
2nd Lieut. A. Garrity.
2nd Lieut. A. C. Graham.
Capt. D. S. Hodgson-Tines.
Lieut.-Col. L. F. Leader.
Lieut. T. Millard.
2nd Lieut. J. Morrison.
2nd Lieut. A. Murgatroyd.

2ND ROYAL WELCH FUSILIERS.

Killed.

2nd Lieut. S. L. Blaxley.
2nd Lieut. E. V. Brooks.
2nd Lieut. J. Jackson.
2nd Lieut. W. O. Lewis.
Capt. J. M. Owen.
2nd Lieut. A. Phillips.

Wounded.

2nd Lieut. J. Farraud.
Lieut. R. C. J. Greaves.
2nd Lieut. R. H. Hanmer.
2nd Lieut. R. Jones.
2nd Lieut. W. G. Lloyd.
2nd Lieut. G. W. Lowe.
Capt. L. M. Omerod.
Capt. H. G. Picton-Davies.
2nd Lieut. S. L. Sassoon.
2nd Lieut. R. C. Shelley.
2nd Lieut. R. N. Siddall.
2nd Lieut. E. S. Storey-Cooper.
2nd Lieut. J. Tackington.

Missing.

Lieut. J. R. Conning.
2nd Lieut. F. E. G. Davies.
Lieut. E. L. Orme.
2nd Lieut. J. D. M. Richards.
2nd Lieut. J. B. Williams.

1ST CAMERONIANS.

Killed.

2nd Lieut J. D. Clark.
2nd Lieut. L. A. Forbes.
Capt. D. C. Foster.
Capt. J. W. Kennedy.
Lieut. K. D. L. Macfarlane.
2nd Lieut. S. L. L. Newlands.
2nd Lieut. J. A. Oppe.
2nd Lieut. J. Scott.

Wounded.

2nd Lieut. A. C. Alston.
Capt. A. C. Brown.
2nd Lieut. W. J. Craig.
Lieut. J. B. Hamilton.
2nd Lieut. G. Kerr.
2nd Lieut. J. P. Macgregor.
Lieut. J. McMurray.
2nd Lieut. R. Mirrie.
Capt. D. Moncreiff-Wright.
2nd Lieut. A. E. Phillips.
2nd Lieut. J. R. Taylor.

THE BATTLE OF ARRAS.

5TH SCOTTISH RIFLES.

Killed.

Capt. K. A. Brown.
Capt. C. M. A. Gunn.
2nd Lieut. R. W. McEwan.
2nd Lieut. D. Murchison.

Wounded.

Lieut. & Q.-Mr. J. Brown.
2nd Lieut. N. Clark.
2nd Lieut. A. S. Collins.
2nd Lieut. R. Downie.
2nd Lieut. R. S. Hamilton.
2nd Lieut. M. G. McCulloch.
2nd Lieut. J. Mc. G. Maguire.
2nd Lieut. J. Meikle.
2nd Lieut. J. Owen.
2nd Lieut. D. A. Rigby.
2nd Lieut. J. I. Scott.
Lieut. A. F. Struthers.
2nd Lieut. D. Wood.
Lieut. J. T. Wylie.
2nd Lieut. R. M. Young.

98TH BRIGADE.

4TH KING'S (LIVERPOOL) REGIMENT.

Killed.

2nd Lieut. H. S. Aslachsen.
2nd Lieut. W. A. Back.
2nd Lieut. A. Corbridge.
2nd Lieut. H. B. Hubble.
2nd Lieut. F. James.
Capt. R. T. Patey.
2nd Lieut. J. Robinson.

Wounded.

2nd Lieut. F. C. Ager.
2nd Lieut. C. Burton.
2nd Lieut. A. R. B. Littlar.
2nd Lieut. R. Moore.
2nd Lieut. R. Reid.

4TH SUFFOLK REGIMENT.

Killed.

2nd Lieut. H. W. Woods.

Wounded.

2nd Lieut. F. Dallimer.
2nd Lieut. B. S. Evans.
2nd Lieut. D. Glen.
2nd Lieut. A. W. Hare.
Capt. J. C. Rash.
2nd Lieut. B. C. Rigby.
2nd Lieut. W. R. Walton.
2nd Lieut. S. C. Williams.

THE THIRTY-THIRD DIVISION.

1ST MIDDLESEX REGIMENT.

Killed.
2nd Lieut. G. L. J. Baker.
2nd Lieut. E. G. Clark.
2nd Lieut. A. R. Henry.
2nd Lieut. W. Murray.
2nd Lieut. F. M. Packhouse.
2nd Lieut. H. T. Parker.

Wounded.
2nd Lieut. P. H. Barber.
Capt. A. L. Cooper Key.
2nd Lieut. R. B. Halley.
2nd Lieut. R. B. Holman.
2nd Lieut. H. Lawson.
2nd Lieut. F. E. Molz.
2nd Lieut. H. E. Pechell.
2nd Lieut. F. E. D. Rutter.
2nd Lieut. D. L. Skippon.

2ND ARGYLL AND SUTHERLAND HIGHLANDERS.

Killed.
Lieut. H. D. Allan.
2nd Lieut. A. Fulton.
Capt. A. Henderson.
Lieut. A. B. Murray.
2nd Lieut. R. P. Spiers.
Capt. A. B. Tyson.
2nd Lieut. A. A. Wilson.

Wounded.
2nd Lieut. R. C. Allan.
Lieut. R. C. B. Anderson.
2nd Lieut. F. Blest.
2nd Lieut. G. O. Hallifax.
2nd Lieut. J. M. H. Maitland.
2nd Lieut. H. Murray-Campbell.
Lieut.-Col. C. B. J. Riccard.
2nd Lieut. F. Whitaker.

Missing.
2nd Lieut. W. Clark.

100TH BRIGADE.

1ST QUEEN'S (ROYAL WEST SURREY) REGIMENT.

Killed.
2nd Lieut. G. H. V. Burghope.
2nd Lieut. N. J. Fowler.
2nd Lieut. D. E. H. Millard.

Wounded.
2nd Lieut. J. N. F. Barnard.
Capt. H. Battiscombe.
2nd Lieut. F. J. Bower.
2nd Lieut. H. J. Carpenter.
2nd Lieut. K. A. Frazer.
2nd Lieut. S. M. Howcroft.
2nd Lieut. C. G. Kemp.

Missing.
Capt. F. S. Ball.
2nd Lieut. O. V. Botton.
Capt. R. Brodhurst-Hill.
Capt. F. Godfrey.
2nd Lieut. J. Holliday.
2nd Lieut. G. P. S. Jacob.
2nd Lieut. H. M. Thompson.
2nd Lieut. R. G. Walker.

2ND WORCESTERSHIRES.

Killed.
Capt. E. A. O. Durlacher.
2nd Lieut. P. W. Potter.

Wounded.
2nd Lieut. W. A. Cross.
Capt. H. C. Downes.
2nd Lieut. J. L. Gillespie.
2nd Lieut. F. J. D. Gunston.
Lieut. R. Harrison.
2nd Lieut. E. L. Hopkins.
2nd Lieut. H. B. Ludlow-Smith.
2nd Lieut. G. Mason.

48

THE BATTLE OF ARRAS.

16TH KING'S ROYAL RIFLE CORPS.

Killed.	*Wounded.*	*Missing.*
2nd Lieut. R. H. Garrad.	Lieut. N. K. Balshaw.	2nd Lieut. R. Allan.
Capt. E. M. Gonner.	Capt. G. T. Edwards.	Capt. A. B. Bernard.
Capt. J. R. Smith.	Lieut. F. C. Giddens.	2nd Lieut. L. B. Forrest.
Lieut. H. B. Smith.	2nd Lieut. W. Howat.	2nd Lieut. E. F. Peacocke.
	2nd Lieut. C. E. Howard.	2nd Lieut. G. L. Spreckley.
	2nd Lieut. C. W. Miller.	
	2nd Lieut. V. S. Northan.	
	2nd Lieut. F. J. Page.	
	2nd Lieut. G. M. Welsford.	

1/9TH HIGHLAND LIGHT INFANTRY.

Killed.	*Wounded.*	*Missing.*
2nd Lieut. D. W. Binnie.	2nd Lieut. G. W. Brown.	2nd Lieut. W. M. Andrew.
2nd Lieut. R. P. Cole.	2nd Lieut. S. Coulter.	2nd Lieut. A. Maitland.
Capt. W. Mc F. Coulter.	Capt. W. F. M. Donald.	
2nd Lieut. T. McGregor.	2nd Lieut. A. Glendinning.	
Capt. A. C. Murray.	Capt. R. C. Reid.	
2nd Lieut. W. Morrison.		
2nd Lieut. D. O. Muir.		
2nd Lieut. H. O. Munro.		

MACHINE GUN CORPS.

Wounded.

Lt. A. D. D. Bonner.
2nd Lieut. H. E. Hales.
2nd Lieut. A. W. P. Wouldham.

As an illustration of the constant changes from desperate fighting and casualties to leisure and amusements, we continue with the account of the Arras Spring Meeting, which we undertook directly after the Battle of Arras.

THE THIRTY-THIRD DIVISION.

THE ARRAS SPRING MEETING.

(Reproduced by the Courtesy of the Proprietors, from the "Illustrated Sporting and Dramatic News," June 20th, 1917.)

COSTERS.

THE 1917 Flat Racing Season in the B.E.F. was opened by a Divisional Spring Meeting, last month. The course, situated on a rolling down in a recent "No Man's Land," stretching between three piles of debris and brickdust—lately Epsom, Banstead and Tadworth!—sprang up in a night. It is a short one of five furlongs, and practically straight. Fine weather gave a very enjoyable meeting, and the turf was in splendid condition.

The arrangements made by the Stewards were amazing. The Enclosure and Grand Stand, "For County Gentlemen and Officers Only," with the added legend beneath, "Beware of Pickpockets"; Tattersall's Ring; Paddock and Weighing-in Rooms; Clerk of the Scales; Judge's Box; the white railed course—nothing had been forgotten. "Charlie's Bar" was transferred by special request from Newmarket, with a welcome alteration in prices, which were calculated not to injure the pockets of even heavy drinkers. Had more of the racegoers been aware of this fact earlier, the strain on the barmen might have been severe. A tea room on the same lines was also in evidence and proved almost as popular as its neighbour. The Divisional Staff was most generously "At Home." Tattersall's Enclosure on the other side of the course also provided tea for the asking, provided that the request was accompanied by a mess tin. A crowd representing many English County Regiments, Highland, Lowland, Rifles, and every arm of the Service, besieged the marquee with a babel of noise the whole day.

The tracks leading to the course were a scene of busy movement early in the afternoon.

The runners, not forgetting a large number of mules, totalled several hundred, and these with the crowd who travelled by wagon, by bicycle, by motor, or on foot, resembled big columns, those of some other Divisions, on the march. We had not looked for the "Coach Club" on the battlefield. But Brig.-General Baird with that initiative which has made him so distinguished both on the battlefield and in

"DROPPING THE PILOT."

50

the sporting world turned out two light draught horses with his own two chargers as leads, in a four-in-hand, which coach, carrying his own Headquarters as "party," bore a suspicious resemblance to the wagon which brings our rations. A long whip and equally long cigar completed a picture of the late Mr. Vanderbilt at Richmond. The roads leading to the course did not perhaps present such a kaleidoscopic appearance as those to Epsom Downs on Derby Day, due to the lack of variety

A NON-STARTER.

of the vehicles officially issued to the Army; but the banter, pleasant or otherwise, between the racegoers, was, if anything, even more pronounced. That there is latent eloquence of a high order in every Army driver was demonstrated wherever there was a collision.

The familiar figures with little black bags and large blackboards were absent, doubtless making munitions elsewhere. Nevertheless, Tattersall's Silver Ring was the scene of considerable financial activity among those who had been paid out the same morning, whilst a surreptitious traffic, carried on by orderlies and batmen from the Officers' Enclosure, filed across the course to "Black and White," "Old Joe," and the fraternity, before every race. The odds uncontrolled by any of the aforesaid little gentlemen in broad bowlers, changed with alarming rapidity. The solitary tipster who ventured into the enclosure was unceremoniously dealt with by the only member of the police force in evidence during the day, who showed characteristic promptness on his reappearance in Tattersall's.

H.M.S. LANDHORSE.

In the paddock could be seen little knots of owners criticising the horseflesh paraded there, some of them, moreover, very temporary owners, who imagine that every animal lent them by a benevolent Government can go "some"—and they can! To stand and listen to the names of the runners being bellowed by relays of heated and thirsty Stewards—hence the relays—was more than amusing. Three mules of vicious tendency—"Faith, Hope and Charity," the most vicious, the greatest of these, "Love," of the Worcestershire Regiment. The

Highland Regiments, Argylls and H.L.I. produced such classics as " Flying Fox," " White Heather," " Persimmon " and " Lemberg," amongst animals as nobby and tufted as only the after effects of a winter campaign can make light draught horses. The Middlesex, Queen's and Royal Fusiliers were local and homely, as behoves Cockney humour, " Napoo," " Umteen," " Farrier's Friend "—the unshoeable " U-Boat," and the Bing Boys " George " and " Alfred." The Staff, enjoying the privilege of frequent leave in London and Paris, favoured the stage, thus " Gaby," " Delysia," " Zena " and " Phyllis."

Colour was lent to the scene by members of the chorus of " The Shrapnels Revue Company," who are touring the district. Miss Sadie Sthaies, Miss Clarice Corcette, and Miss Nida Nytie appeared in ravishing toilettes. Two mules were observed to bolt on their approach—presumably to bring their friends. The ladies, to the chagrin of the A.S.C. Sergeant-Majors and other magnates, were escorted by their friends of the Company.

The first race on the programme was the Adinfer Stakes for N.C.O.'s and men, for which there were no fewer than eighty entries, representing all arms of the Service, with the exception of the " Tanks," though an element of the parade gave one an impression that they had entered. This proved one of the most popular events, won by Private Reece's " Billy " by a neck from the Queen's " Black Bess." At the moment the race was ended a diversion was caused by a coster and his wife driving their cart at a gallop the whole length of the course. The man then handed the strings to his wife, leapt out, and with lightning rapidity fooled numerous county gentlemen of the Enclosure with the three card trick. He disappeared with his spoils as rapidly as he had come.

AT CHARLIE'S BAR.

Meanwhile the runners for the 3.30 p.m. race, the Ayette Maiden Plate, for Officer riders, catchweights, were parading. It was won in the last half-furlong by Lieutenant Kennard's (A.D.C.) " Netta," owner up, from Lieutenant Edward's (Worcestershire Regiment) " Frugal," Captain Paul up, after a race which he kept well in hand. The field numbered forty-two.

The " Domino Stakes," flat race, open to horses belonging to and ridden by members of the Military Mounted Police, followed. It was won by Sergeant Fletcher's " Paddy," from the A.P.M.'s " Black Jester."

The " Boiry Maiden Plate," for Infantry Officers' chargers, catchweights, a very keenly contested race, was won by the Worcestershire Regiment's " Cuthbert," from H.L.I.'s " Ruby," Major Stoney on the former riding a great race from Captain Paul on the latter. Field of thirty-seven.

The " St. Ledger Stakes," named not after the famous classic race, but after a captured village in the vicinity, was the event of the day. Open flat race, 12 st., previous winners 14 lb. extra. The R.W.F.'s " Girlie," ridden by Lieutenant Yates at 13 st. 13 lb., won from A.S.C.'s " Francois," Captain Jackson up, with Captain Gordon's (A.V.C.) " Jack Straw," third. It is interesting to recall that " Girlie " was captured from the enemy on the retreat from Mons, and has served with this Battalion throughout the

LT. YATES WINS THE "ST. LEDGER" STAKES ON GIRLIE.

campaign, as has her jockey. She started a hot and popular favourite, being well known for her speed throughout the B.E.F.

The final race at 5.30 p.m. the Prix d'Alphonso, Open Flat Race for Mules, was run in two spasms, owing to the enormous number of entries. It was ridden bareback, and proved most quixotic. The parade to the starting point before the race was almost as interesting as the race itself. Several of the mules, as a protest against delayed feeds, left their riders at the starting point to complete the course on foot. Some remarkable feats of horsemanship, all over the mule, were performed by many riders. In the middle of the first spasm two mules made for home in front of the whole field, scattering the crowd right and left, whilst the coster's wife, still voteless, in spite of Mr. Asquith's recently expressed adherence to her cause, flung her masculine proportions across the course. To those who witnessed this and the episode at Tattenham Corner, the former was the more heroic.

Throughout the afternoon, owing to the proximity of the battle, a squadron of the Royal Flying Corps patrolled overhead, and effectively kept at a distance the scouts of the enemy. This arduous duty did not prevent some of the pilots exhibiting their skill by looping the loop amid the plaudits of the crowd beneath. The only other guard considered necessary was mounted behind the Enclosure, conceivably behind Charlie's Bar !

GENERAL BAIRD'S " COACH."

The Divisional Commander, who rode on to the course with his A.D.C.s early in the afternoon, was the conspicuous figure in the Judge's box, and carried out his duties with that good humour and joviality which has endeared him to all ranks of his Division. Of the jockeys Captain Paul, M.C. who rode in three races, finishing second in two, was outstanding.

The brilliant success of the meeting was entirely due to Major-General R. J. Pinney, C.B., Commanding the Division, who not only fostered the original idea, but personally supervised every detail of the arrangements. These were most ably carried out by Lieut.-Colonel P. G. Lea, D.S.O., A.S.C.,

Captain B. L. Montgomery, D.S.O., and the indefatigable Hon. Secretary and Treasurer, Major H. C. C. Batten, together with other Stewards.

A silver trumpet presented by Captain B. L. Montgomery, D.S.O., for the Unit gaining the highest number of points in the meeting was won by the 2nd Battalion of the Worcestershire Regiment. It is a trophy which, as a souvenir alone, will always have an honoured place in the mess of that Battalion in years hereafter.

The meeting was a triumphant success, and as such is ample proof of the wonderful moral and spirit of our troops lately engaged in very heavy fighting.

* * * * * *

On the 2nd June the Division was reviewed by Lieut.-General Sir Thomas Snow, the Corps Commander, who presented Medal Ribbons, and the Division again returned to the line in this area on the 3rd June for offensive operations. These, however, were at the last moment indefinitely postponed, and nothing but a minor attack by the 1st Queen's was carried out. After one other short relief and tour in the line the Division was finally withdrawn to Bienvillers-Pommera Area.

A REPETITION OF THE TATTENHAM CORNER INCIDENT.

Unquestionably, as the result of the successful example set by the 33rd Division and a few other Divisions in the grouping of their machine guns, now for over a year, the Machine Gun Corps decided to take its first step towards the formation of Machine Gun Battalions; and as a thin end of the wedge a Divisional Machine Gun Officer was appointed.

From Bienvillers-Pommera Area the Division marched into the rest area between Cavillon-Picquigny and Hangest for four weeks. Undoubtedly this was the best period that the Division ever spent in France.

The weather during this period was perfect sunshine every day. The fullest use was made of the Somme River and its Canals, fishing, swimming, and diving competitions being held, daily bathing parades and voluntary bathing being carried out not only once each day, but all day. A regatta went off with great success. Daily leave was given to Amiens and, as the "largest plum in the pudding," a Horse Show was organized by the Division.

55

THE THIRTY-THIRD DIVISION.

The Horse Show was conducted on the same generous lines as the Race Meeting at Ayette; and was held in brilliant weather at Cavillon on the 17th and 18th of July.

Our Show, in the opinion of good judges was quite equal to a big County Show. Many distinguished French Officers, including Lieut.-Colonel du Tiel, organizer of the French Olympia, put in an appearance, besides large numbers of local inhabitants, headed by the Comtesse de la Hauteclocque, whose eldest daughter gave away the prizes.

A GENERAL VIEW OF THE COURSE. (NOTE PROTECTING AIRCRAFT.)

The results of the Horse Show are here recorded:—

CLASS I. SINGLE HORSE TURNOUT.

1st	.. .. ..	No. 1 Company, Divisional Train.
2nd	.. .. ..	19th Field Ambulance.
3rd	.. .. ..	18th Middlesex Regiment (Pioneers).
Commended	.. ..	19th Field Ambulance.

CLASS IIA. PACK ANIMALS (PONIES).

1st	.. .. ..	9th Highland Light Infantry.
2nd	.. .. ..	4th King's (Liverpool) Regiment.
3rd	.. .. ..	19th Machine Gun Company.
Commended	.. ..	Divisional Headquarters.

THE HORSE SHOW AT CAVILLON.

CLASS IIB. PACK ANIMALS (MULES).

1st	18th Middlesex Regiment (Pioneers).
2nd	18th Middlesex Regiment (Pioneers).
3rd	1st Cameronians.
Commended	16th King's Royal Rifle Corps.
Commended	16th King's Royal Rifle Corps.

CLASS IIIA. PAIRS L.D. HORSES (RIDE AND DRIVE).

1st	101st Field Ambulance.
2nd	1st Queen's (Royal West Surrey) Regiment.
3rd	No. 2 Company, Divisional Train.
4th	2nd Royal Welch Fusiliers.
Commended	No. 3 Company, Divisional Train.
Commended	19th Field Ambulance.

CLASS IIIB. PAIRS L.D. MULES (RIDE AND DRIVE).

1st	2nd Worcestershire Regiment.
2nd	16th King's Royal Rifle Corps.
3rd	16th King's Royal Rifle Corps.
Commended	9th Highland Light Infantry.
Commended	20th Royal Fusiliers.

CLASS IVA. PAIRS H.D. HORSES (LONG REIN).

1st, 2nd and 3rd ..	No. 1 Company, Divisional Train.
Commended	19th Field Ambulance.

CLASS IVB. PAIRS H.D. HORSES (RIDE AND DRIVE).

1st	No. 1 Company, Divisional Train.
2nd	101st Field Ambulance.
3rd	19th Field Ambulance.

CLASS IVC. (COMPLETE COOKER TURNOUT).

1st	20th Royal Fusiliers.
2nd	10th King's Royal Rifle Corps.
3rd	2nd Royal Welch Fusiliers.
Commended	2nd Royal Welch Fusiliers.

CLASS VA. (TEAMS OF SIX MULES).

1st	33rd Divisional Signal Company.
Commended	222nd Field Company, Royal Engineers.

THE THIRTY-THIRD DIVISION.

CLASS VB. (TEAMS OF FOUR MULES).

1st	100th Machine Gun Company.
2nd	18th Middlesex Regiment (Pioneers).
3rd	222nd Field Company, Royal Engineers.

CLASS VIA. H.D. HORSES (Stripped).

1st, 2nd, 3rd and 4th. No. 1 Company, Divisional Train.

CLASS VIB. L.D. HORSES (Stripped).

1st	No. 1 Company, Divisional Train.
2nd	101st Field Ambulance.
3rd	No. 2 Company, Divisional Train.
4th	33rd Divisional Signal Company.

CLASS VIC. MULES (Stripped).

1st	16th King's Royal Rifle Corps.
2nd	212th Field Company, Royal Engineers.
3rd	2nd Worcestershire Regiment.
Commended ..	16th King's Royal Rifle Corps.

CLASS VIIA. OFFICERS' CHARGERS (Over 15 hands).

1st	"Satan"	Major Batten, Divisional Headquarters.
2nd	"Ginger"	Captain McCosh, 9th Highland Light Infantry.
3rd	"Cygnet"	Lieutenant Kennard, Divisional Headquarters.
Commended ..	"Caesar's Wife" ..	Lieutenant Pinney, Divisional Headquarters.

CLASS VIIB. OFFICERS' CHARGERS (15 hands and under).

1st	"Daisy"	Major Batten, Divisional Headquarters.
2nd	"Billy"	Lieutenant-Colonel Garnet, 2nd Royal Welch Fusiliers.
3rd	"Polly"	Major Pretty, 2nd Royal Welch Fusiliers.
Commended ..	"Mugwamp" ..	2nd Lieutenant Harries, 2nd Royal Welch Fusiliers.

CLASS VIIC. INFANTRY OFFICERS' CHARGERS (15.2 and under).

1st	"Billy"	Lieutenant-Colonel Garnet, 2nd Royal Welch Fusiliers.
2nd	"Mugwamp" ..	2nd Lieutenant Harries, 2nd Royal Welch Fusiliers.
3rd	"Polly"	Major Pretty, 2nd Royal Welch Fusiliers.

CLASS VIID. RIDERS—W.O.s, N.C.O.s AND MEN.

1st	"Putney" ..	Staff-Sergeant Filler.
2nd	"Bunkey" ..	Company Sergeant-Major Eastwood.
3rd	"Zebra" ..	Lance-Corporal Crump.
Commended ..	"Sybil".. ..	Company Sergeant-Major Ferguson.
Commended ..	"Pedlar" ..	Sergeant Robertson.

THE HORSE SHOW AT CAVILLON.

CLASS VIIIA. JUMPING (Officers' Chargers over 15 hands).

1st	" Francois "	Captain Jackson, Army Service Corps.
2nd	" Ginger "	Lieutenant Fox, 2nd Worcestershire Regiment.
3rd	" Yola "	Captain Petre, Army Service Corps.

CLASS VIIIB. JUMPING (Chargers 15 hands and under).

1st	" Tim "	Captain Boumphrey, 2nd Royal Welch Fusiliers.
2nd	" Ginger "	Lieutenant-Colonel Chaplin, 1st Cameronians.
3rd	" Betty "	Lieutenant Lipscomb, 16th King's Royal Rifle Corps

CLASS VIIIC. JUMPING (W.O.s, N.C.O.s AND MEN).

1st	" Zebra " ..	Lance-Corporal Crump.
2nd	" Tino "	Sergeant Turner.
3rd	" Beauty " ..	Sergeant Sankey.

CLASS VIIID. JUMPING DIVISIONAL CHAMPIONSHIP.

Winner—" Francois," Captain Jackson, Army Service Corps.

The Major-General's Cup for the highest aggregate in Classes I.–VI. was won by No. 1 Company, Divisional Train, Army Service Corps.

CHAPTER IV.

NIEUPORT, AUGUST, 1917.

YPRES, SEPTEMBER, 1917, TO MARCH, 1918.

Night Bombing and Mustard Gas—Fine Raid by 1st Battalion The Cameronians —The Third Battle of Ypres, Machine Gun Batteries—Fierce Fight at Polygon Wood—Great Gallantry of the whole Division—Special Mention of the Royal Field Artillery, 1st Battalion Middlesex Regiment, 2nd Argyll and Sutherland Highlanders, 2nd Worcestershire Regiment, 9th Highland Light Infantry, and 4th King's Liverpool Regiment—German Charges of Contravention of International Law—Neuve Eglise—In the Passchendaele Salient.

ORDER OF BATTLE.

HEADQUARTERS, 33RD DIVISION.

Commander .. .. Major-General R. J. Pinney, C.B.
    Aide-de-Camp to Commander .. .. Lieutenant B. F. S. Pinney, General List.
    Aide-de-Camp to Commander .. .. Second-Lieutenant A. S. G. Kennard, Hampshire Yeomanry.

GENERAL STAFF BRANCH—
    General Staff Officer, 1st Grade .. .. Brevet Lieutenant-Colonel D. Forster, D.S.O., R.E.
    General Staff Officer, 2nd Grade .. .. Brevet Major H. D. Denison-Pender, M.C., 2nd Dragoons.
    General Staff Officer, 3rd Grade .. .. Captain A. M. Bankier, M.C., Argyll and Sutherland Highlanders.

ADJUTANT AND QUARTERMASTER-GENERAL'S BRANCH—
    Assistant Adjutant and Quartermaster-General .. .. Brevet Lieutenant-Colonel P. R. C. Commings, D.S.O., South Staffordshire Regiment.
    Deputy-Assistant Adjutant-General .. Major H. C. C. Batten, Dorsetshire Regiment.
    Deputy-Assistant Quartermaster-General .. Major O. B. Foster, M.C., Northumberland Fusiliers.

ADMINISTRATIVE SERVICES AND DEPARTMENTS—
    Assistant Director of Medical Services .. Colonel S. de C. O'Grady, D.S.O., Royal Army Medical Corps.
    Deputy-Assistant Director of Medical Services .. .. Captain J. H. Fletcher, M.C., Royal Army Medical Corps.
    Deputy-Assistant Director of Veterinary Services .. .. Major R. A. Plunkett, Army Veterinary Corps.
    Deputy-Assistant Director of Ordnance Services .. .. Captain A. M. E. Beavan, Army Ordnance Department.

NIEUPORT.

ADMINISTRATIVE SERVICES AND DEPARTMENTS—
continued.

Assistant Provost-Marshal	Major Hon. E. G. French, General List.
Senior Chaplain to the Forces, Church of England	Reverend W. G. Mayne.
Senior Chaplain to the Forces, Nonconformist	Reverend Hugh Brown.

DIVISIONAL ARTILLERY—

Commander	Brigadier-General C. G. Stewart, C.M.G., D.S.O., R.A.
Brigade-Major	Major T. E. Durie, M.C., Royal Field Artillery.
Staff Captain	Captain W. E. Bownass, Royal Field Artillery.
Staff Officer for Reconnaissance ..	Lieutenant T. R. Jackson, Royal Field Artillery.
Divisional Trench Mortar Officer ..	Captain C. C. W. Havell, M.C.
156th Brigade, Royal Field Artillery	Lieutenant-Colonel B. A. B. Butler.
162nd Brigade, Royal Field Artillery	Lieutenant-Colonel E. J. Skinner, D.S.O.
Divisional Ammunition Column ..	Colonel L. Forde, C.M.G.

HEADQUARTERS, DIVISIONAL ENGINEERS—

Commander	Lieutenant-Colonel G. F. Evans, D.S.O., Royal Engineers.
Adjutant	Captain E. L. Gale, M.C.
11th Field Company	Major C. P. L. Balcombe.
212th Field Company	Major J. E. Anderson, M.C.
222nd Field Company	Captain C. D. A. Fenwick.

19TH INFANTRY BRIGADE—

Commander	Brigadier-General C. R. G. Mayne, D.S.O., Highland Light Infantry.
Brigade-Major	{ Captain A. F. G. Walker, General List. { Major C. la T. Turner-Jones, M.C., R.E.
Staff Captain	Captain A. H. W. Landon, Royal Canadian Regiment.
1st Battalion The Cameronians ..	Major C. C. Scott, (Temporary).
5th Scottish Rifles	Lieutenant-Colonel H. B. Spens.
2nd Royal Welch Fusiliers	Lieutenant-Colonel W. B. Garnett, D.S.O.
20th Royal Fusiliers	Lieutenant-Colonel Modera, M.C.
19th Machine Gun Company ..	Captain W. Lewthwaite.
19th Trench Mortar Battery ..	Lieutenant Borthwick.

HEADQUARTERS, 98TH INFANTRY BRIGADE—

Commander	Brigadier-General J. D. Heriot-Maitland, C.M.G., Rifle Brigade.
Brigade-Major	Captain H. F. Wailes, East Yorkshire Regiment.
Staff Captain	Major E. P. Clarke, D.S.O., Suffolk Regiment.
1st Middlesex Regiment	Lieutenant-Colonel J. W. L. Elgee.
2nd Argyll and Sutherland Highlanders ..	Lieutenant-Colonel L. L. Wheatley, D.S.O.
4th King's (Liverpool) Regiment ..	Lieutenant-Colonel E. M. Beall, D.S.O.
1/4th Suffolk Regiment	Lieutenant-Colonel H. C. Copeman, D.S.O.
98th Machine Gun Company ..	Captain A. Lomax.
98th Trench Mortar Battery ..	Captain C. E. Paternoster.

THE THIRTY-THIRD DIVISION.

HEADQUARTERS, 100TH INFANTRY BRIGADE—

Commander	Brigadier-General A. W. F. Baird, C.M.G., D.S.O., Gordon Highlanders.
Brigade-Major	Captain J. I. Muirhead, M.C., Yorkshire Light Infantry.
Staff Captain	Captain W. J. J. Coats, M.C., Highland Light Infantry.
1st Queen's (Royal West Surrey) Regiment	Lieutenant-Colonel L. M. Crofts, D.S.O.
2nd Worcestershire Regiment	Major L. C. Dorman, D.S.O.
16th King's Royal Rifle Corp	Lieutenant-Colonel A. V. Johnson.
1/9th Highland Light Infantry	Lieutenant-Colonel A. H. Menzies, D.S.O.
100th Machine Gun Company	Captain W. C. Andrew.
100th Trench Mortar Battery	Captain C. R. F. Cotgrave.

DIVISIONAL MEDICAL UNITS—

19th Field Ambulance	Lieutenant-Colonel W. B. Purdon, D.S.O., M.C.
99th Field Ambulance	Lieutenant-Colonel C. R. Morris, D.S.O.
101st Field Ambulance	Lieutenant-Colonel G. W. G. Hughes, D.S.O.

DIVISIONAL TRAIN—

Officer Commanding	Lieutenant-Colonel P. G. P. Lea, D.S.O., Army Service Corp.
Senior Supply Officer..	Major D. Dill, Army Service Corp.

DIVISIONAL TROOPS—

18th Middlesex (Pioneers)	Lieutenant-Colonel H. Storr, D.S.O.
Divisional Gas Officer	Captain C. G. Jones, Royal Engineers.
Divisional Claims Officer	Captain D. L. Pigache, Royal Fusiliers.
Divisional Machine Gun Officer	Major G. S. Hutchison, M.C., Argyll and Sutherland Highlanders.
248th Machine Gun Company	Captain F. Wheeler.
43rd Mobile Veterinary Section	Captain A. G. E. Lalor.
Divisional Signal Company	Major R. W. Cardew, M.C., Royal Engineers.
230th Employment Company	} Captain M. B. Hoare, Essex Regiment.
Divisional Salvage Officer	

The Division was then hurried up to the coast, where the Hun had attacked and practically annihilated a Brigade of the 1st Division, and took over the line, Nieuport inclusive to Lombardtsyde, with the Belgians on its right. The period spent in this sector was about three weeks. It was at this time that two fresh nuisances became part of everyday warfare in a marked degree—aeroplane bombing by night and the use of mustard gas.

To those who have only experienced the mild sensation of scurrying into cellars and tubes in London during the night wanderings of the Zeppelin in its palmy days, it is impossible to describe what the civilians immediately behind the battle area, and the troops either billeted or bivouacked, had to put up with at night whilst resting. If one can suppose that all the Zeppelins carried out a combined raid in one night accurately letting loose their bombs upon a given area, some idea of the intensive bombing of the

War Zone can be imagined. Belgium, in particular, is no very difficult problem for the night-flying airman, owing to its network of well defined Canals, its huge forests and its otherwise flat country. All of these landmarks are very plain. England, on the other hand, is so thickly populated, with few prominent landmarks, and was very largely protected with anti-aircraft guns, a luxury with which we were not favoured, that it presented a difficult problem to the " bombster." Scarcely a night passed but a shower of bombs was let loose upon our camps and billets, often with serious results in loss of life.

The horse lines, which had to be regular in form suffered seriously, but it was our good fortune that despite the number of bombs dropped, which gave one chills down the spine when sleeping in the top of a three-storey house, or lying blanketed in a sand dune or Nisson Hut, the majority certainly expended their force in blowing a few more harmless swedes and turnips sky-high. Nevertheless the anxiety undergone by officers commanding troops for their safety, when huddled together in a narrow area preparatory to battle, cannot be exaggerated ; whilst the swish and boom of falling bombs, often only a few yards from the sleepers, was enough to disturb the rest of the most heavy of them.

Mustard gas came as a new form of frightfulness upon us. At first it was difficult to know how to cope with it, owing to the fact that in addition to choking the lungs it also inflicted severe burns upon the flesh. In our Division the first to be submitted to this form of " Frightfulness " was the 2nd Battalion Argyll and Sutherland Highlanders and the 9th Battalion Highland Light Infantry, both kilted Regiments. Those who were unfortunate enough to be smitten suffered most dreadful agonies. A conference was immediately called at Divisional Headquarters to decide as to the best method of dealing with this new gas, and for providing effective measures against it. It was decided that the Highlanders must immediately be equipped with long cotton drawers. Highland Officers were therefore asked to submit proposals as to what form these drawers should take ; and the argument waxed exceedingly high concerning the colour, number of buttons, etc. Eventually these two Highland Regiments were seen in the line rather more resembling standard lamps, their kilts acting as shades, than anything else. We feel sure that Major O. B. Foster, who was responsible for designing these " undies," will do well, should he ever become unemployed, with a smart " frou frou " shop in Bond Street. He certainly put all his latent genius into producing pants made from Ordnance linen, which were both serviceable and becoming.

The sector itself was unpleasant and uninteresting, except for excellent sea bathing when out of the line.

The 248th Machine Gun Company (called the Divisional Company) had joined the Division towards the end of July, and was now put into the line for the first time with the 19th and 98th Machine Gun Companies.

THE THIRTY-THIRD DIVISION.

On August 24th, the 1st Battalion Cameronians raided the German posts on the Geleide Brook taking one Officer and eight men prisoners, and killing many of the enemy. Our casualties in this operation were only one killed and sixteen wounded.

On the 25th, the enemy counter-attacked and succeeded in retaking the most easterly post, and on the 26th very heavily assaulted the 19th Brigade, succeeding with a 17 inch shell in obtaining a direct hit upon Brigade Headquarters, completely demolishing the top of it and breaking the concrete of the cellar. No less than fifteen of those gigantic shells fell into Nieuport, with the net result that the sole casualty was the complete wreckage of the Brigadier's breakfast.

We were able at this time to see a good deal more of our Belgian Allies than we had done in the past, for a Belgian Division was on our immediate right, beside Lombartsyde. They had held this line continuously since October, 1914, and had made themselves most comfortable in a network of islands in which they had constructed splendid shelters, with even field bakeries in the front line.

Major-General Pinney, C.B., to the regret of all in the Division, was obliged to relinquish his command temporarily, owing to an injured leg, and was relieved by General P. Wood, C.B., D.S.O., from the 43rd Infantry Brigade.

The Division was withdrawn from the Nieuport Sector to the Eperlecques Training Area early in September.

Meanwhile a new offensive was being hatched at General Headquarters. It was intended that whilst a frontal attack was carried out on the Nieuport front, a landing force under cover of the Naval guns should proceed on rafts from Dunkirk, and land and assault at Ostend, thus throwing back the right wing of the German Army and hurling it into confusion ; whilst the German troops were, at the same time to be blotted out of the Belgian Hills on the Dixmude-Ypres Front. In their recent assault the Germans had crossed the Yser Canal, however, and the heavy casualties which our troops incurred on the Ypres-Menin Road made this plan, for the time being, an impossible enterprise to carry out.

Lack of men was now very much felt. Orders were issued in August to comb out one hundred thousand Infantry from the Transportation Services. These orders were issued in order to enable the fight on the Ypres Front to be continued until November. As will be shown, very heavy fighting was continued with large forces until well into December. Mr. Lloyd George was of the opinion, firstly, that the Belgian Hills could not be carried without a far greater expenditure in men than Sir Douglas Haig anticipated ; secondly, that we should require every available man to meet the great German offensive of March, 1918, which he, in common with all intelligent statesmen, had anticipated must come. His deduction, therefore, was that the offensive before Ypres should not be continued. The results of the further fighting were shown later when raw recruits, old men and boys, together with nearly the whole of the home Army were hurled into the line as a haphazard combination to stem the tide of the offensive.

By now it had been fully realized both by the unfortunate Officer who held the appointment, and by the four Machine Gun Companies, that the position of a Divisional Machine Gun Officer was ludicrous. In the Army, one gives or receives orders; one neither gives nor receives advice. The giver, at any rate, is likely to be told to mind his own business. A further step in the formation of the Machine Gun Battalion was therefore seriously considered.

The third great battle of Ypres had already begun. So obsessed by now was the higher command with the machine gun barrage, that the Machine Gun Companies of every available Division were crowded into the line to support the new offensive. Accordingly, half the 19th and 248th Machine Gun Companies were despatched by train from Watou to Dickebusch, where they camped, to construct barrage positions and carry up ammunition to the neighbourhood of Stirling Castle, a fortnight before the operation was undertaken. A week later, the remaining half of these two Companies joined the advanced party, and these two Companies were "brigaded" for operations under the 23rd Division. The whole scheme consisted of many hundreds of guns co-ordinated by Lieutenant-Colonel Bidder, the 10th Corps Machine Gun Officer. The Division with the 98th and 100th Machine Gun Companies followed into the Dickebusch Area on the 18th September, and by this time the 19th and 248th Companies with the Divisional Machine Gun Officer, co-operating with the 23rd Division, had moved forward to their barrage positions to take part in the first big assault on the line of the Belgian Hills, which runs through Inverness Copse, Polygon Wood, and thence to Passchendaele and Westroosbeke. On the morning of the 29th the assault was made on our front by the 23rd Division.

The struggle for the possession of Inverness Copse had continued with great violence. General Wood who now commanded the Division had, whilst commanding the 43rd Brigade, himself captured the wood and then held it, personally conducting the operation for a whole week, despite very heavy counter attacks. The enemy, however, succeeded in retaking the wood, and threw back our line on to the Stirling Castle Ridge. The attack for the 20th had been admirably planned, the troops for the assault lying in readiness well in front of the Ridge in what had been the enemy's line. At zero hour troops of the Northumberlands and Durhams swept forward with great violence and courage; and, suffering very few casualties, overwhelmed the machine gun posts in Inverness Copse, bayoneting the German gunners at their posts, and drove through the wood which was their first objective. They consolidated the line to the East of it, on the edge of the boggy morasses, over which, owing to the treacherous nature of the inviting-looking soil it was extremely difficult to pass. Moreover, the wide area of the Lakes was quite impassable. Before, then, the assault could be continued, it was necessary to accomplish a wide turning movement and mass the troops for assault to the North-east of Inverness Copse ; so that they could sweep down to the South, past the Northern extremity of the Lakes ; and from this position assault the Tower Hamlets Ridge. Under cover of a smoke barrage this was done in little under an hour. This movement completed the first and second phases of the attack. It was unfortunate that the position of our Machine Gun Batteries supporting the 23rd Division lay in the middle of the German barrage line. This had never happened to us previously, nor did it happen again, and on this occasion the position was none of our selection. During the first and second phases of the attack, the Machine Gun Barrage Batteries suffered very heavy casualties, losing, in addition to many valuable N.C.O.s and men, the Officers commanding all the Companies. The capture of Inverness Copse and Dumbarton Lakes was a complete success. For the next phase it was necessary to move the barrage positions forward to the edge of Inverness Copse. This was an exceedingly arduous operation, but was most ably carried out to time under very heavy fire, by Captain E. Faulkner. The machine guns were thus able to cover the third phase of the attack, which included the capture of the Tower Hamlets Ridge.

Already orders had been issued for a second attack upon the Ridge to include the capture of Polygon Wood, the Reutelbeeke and Polderhoek Chateau on the 33rd Divisional Front. Even by this date the casualties of the British Army had exceeded those which it is understood that the Prime Minister had agreed could be the maximum to be expended on this adventure. Regardless, however, apparently, of its preconceived ideas, of the available manhood of Great Britain, General Headquarters committed itself to the task of continuing the onslaught, when it must have been known only too well that such a task could only be extremely costly. General von Clausewitz, probably the greatest military writer and critic, has written that no military operation can be termed a success, unless the strategical or tactical advantages obtained are commensurate with the losses incurred. It was obvious to all who took part in these operations, which led to the boggy morasses of Passchendaele, that such could never be the case. Had this been realized at the time, the agonies which our troops suffered in March and April, 1918, might probably have been largely prevented.

This criticism is made from the limited information available for a man in the fighting line. There probably were weighty reasons which reciprocated this up hill fighting which were not apparent to those in the actual battle.

Very little time was available for reconnaissance and for the dumping of ammunition in the forward area. It seemed inconceivable at the time that those who were directing these operations could so blindly continue to issue orders to troops whose fatigue was so great and whose casualties were so heavy in their execution that nothing but almost superhuman grit could urge them to be carried into effect. Probably, in the history of our nation, its manhood has never been called upon to carry out so many futile tasks as those to which it was committed between September and December, 1917.

66

THE BATTLE OF THE YPRES-MENIN ROAD.

By 12 midnight, 24th–25th September, both the 98th and 100th Brigades were concentrated for the attack. In the 98th Brigade, the 2nd Argyll and Sutherland Highlanders, under Lieutenant-Colonel L. L. Wheatley, the 1st Middlesex, under Lieutenant-Colonel J. W. L. Elgee, and 4th King's, under Lieutenant-Colonel E. M. Beall; and in the 100th Brigade the 9th Highland Light Infantry, under Lieutenant-Colonel A. H. Menzies, and 1st Queen's, under Lieutenant-Colonel L. M. Crofts, were the leading Battalions, concentrated on a line running from the South across the Tower Hamlets Ridge, thence across the Reutelbeeke, and to the East of Cameron Copse. These Battalions were strongly supported by the Machine Gun Groups of their Brigade Companies, together with the 207th (Independent) Machine Gun Company.

The attack of the Second Army, including the 33rd Division, was ordered for dawn on the 26th instant. At 3.30 on the morning of the 25th the enemy opened a bombardment of hitherto unparalleled intensity. So vicious was this bombardment, and in such great depth upon our rear communications, that it was impossible to move transport or troops upon the roads. The S.O.S. signal was seen at every point along our lines. Our guns of all calibres and machine guns immediately opened fire. So great was the roar of guns that not only could they be heard in Boulogne, but it was possible in that place to feel the vibration of the ground. Following up their bombardment, the enemy counter attacked in massed formation upon our lines, no less than six Divisions being used in this attack upon our Divisional front. On the right, the posts of the 1st Queen's were overwhelmed, the enemy debouching from the village of Gheluvelt armed with flame throwers. The stream of burning oil thrown from these devilish weapons reached a length and height of 100 yards, and set fire to the trees, which being as dry as tinder, immediately took fire. In Inverness Copse was concentrated the 2nd Battalion Worcestershire Regiment, under Lieutenant-Colonel T. K. Pardoe. Two Companies of this Regiment had already been destroyed by the bombardment. The Glasgow Highlanders moved forward and with great dash covered up the exposed flank of the 1st Queen's; whilst the 2nd Worcestershire Regiment, although it had already suffered heavy losses, particularly that of Lieutenant H. V. Fox, the Adjutant, consolidated its position. At the same time the 4th Battalion The King's threw out their right flank, gaining touch with the Worcestershires who had moved Southwards to keep connection with the 9th Highland Light Infantry, who were by now covering the Queen's, and with deliberate rifle and Lewis gun fire thinned out the enemy attacks. The 1st Battalion Middlesex and the 93rd, however, held their ground, one Company of each Regiment being completely cut off from the rest of their Battalion, with the enemy in between them and their friends. This was the second occasion on which the Ninety-third, living up to its ancient tradition of the " Thin Red Line " held its ground; for, as at Fontaine, so now did the Highlanders refuse to give way. Very valuable service was also rendered by Lieutenant-Colonel Pardoe and his Adjutant Lieutenant Fox, who, as has been noted, was killed, both of whom with the Chaplain, The Reverend Tanner, held out at a Pill Box, itself almost submerged in water.

The 207th Machine Gun Company, which was close behind our front line grouped in batteries, opened fire with sixteen guns at almost point blank range into the massed hordes of the enemy. Captain M. Gelsthorpe so skilfully directed the fire of his Company that, by holding it until the German officers, at the head of their troops, had topped the ridge and advanced down the forward slope, he could see the massed formation behind, coming over the ridge, as low down as the knee. As each mass advanced in this manner, he opened fire upon their ranks. The enemy was thus so far committed to the assault that he could not retire, but must advance. Low flying aeroplanes, however, soon detected him and both by machine gunning and directing artillery fire upon the gunners the enemy inflicted very severe casualties amongst them. So heavily did this Company suffer that Captain Gelsthorpe, who withdrew his whole Company in perfect order to a new position, was assisted only by his one surviving Officer, who was badly wounded, and one N.C.O. During the action, so heavy was the German counter battery bombardment, that despite the fact that we had undoubtedly a preponderance of artillery, guns of all calibres being locked almost wheel to wheel along the whole front, and in many lines, our artillery could appreciably be felt to grow weaker and weaker. Every form of communication had disappeared early in the day. The only possible means left was that of runners ; but as it took a runner nearly three hours to reach the imagined front line from the Brigade Headquarters at " Tortops," the direction of the battle became almost an impossibility. Lance-Corporal Hamilton acting as a runner of the 9th Highland Light Infantry was awarded the Victoria Cross for his services in this battle. It is not too much to say that the Runners of all Battalions and formations were worthy of a similar award. It is indeed marvellous that any survived. Only supreme scout and shell craft and complete disregard of personal safety made this in any way possible. It is improbable that any General knew what became of the troops he committed to battle five minutes after he had seen them disappear into the cloud of gun smoke and dust. Many of the platoons who were ordered forward in support of the shaken lines disappeared for ever.

During the whole period of this battle most gallant services had been rendered by the 33rd Divisional Artillery. These services are best described in detail :—

" A " Battery, 156th Brigade, R.F.A.

Commanded by Lieutenant (Acting Major) H. McA. Richards, R.F.A.

From 18th to 21st September, 1917, this Battery was in action South of Zillebeke in support of the Infantry during the Big attack on the 20th.

THE BATTLE OF THE YPRES-MENIN ROAD.

During this period the Battery got shelled nearly all day chiefly with 21 cm. Howitzer shells, but also with shells of a lighter nature. They lost in four days, thirteen guns knocked out, and twenty-one all ranks including nine Nos. 1 killed and wounded. Two complete detachments were killed serving the guns and all pits were completely destroyed by the 22nd. Reference this period the following message was received by Officer Commanding, 156th Brigade, R.F.A.—the comments of the Officer Commanding Brigade are also given :—

"The Officer Commanding, 156th Brigade, R.F.A., is more than "proud to have received the following letter. He knows how magni-"ficently all the Officers, N.C.O.'s and men have behaved at the guns "in all the Batteries. Their gallantry is emulated by the Drivers and "N.C.O.'s in charge of horses. The Colonel thinks it a great honour "to work for them."

The letter then read as follows :—

"I would like to draw your attention to the extremely gallant "behaviour of the Officers and men of "A" Battery of the Brigade "under your Command. On the afternoon of 19th September they were "heavily shelled for an hour and half by 5.9 inch and 8 inch howitzers, "when firing a Barrage. In spite of the fact that one or more guns "were knocked out, and several ammunition pits ignited, they continued "firing all the time, and succeeded in putting out the fires. On this "occasion the N.C.O.'s and men were set a splendid example by "Second-Lieutenants Gallie and Beadle, who continued the whole time "to walk up and down behind the guns encouraging the men assisting "to put out the fires. The second occasion was on the evening of the "21st during an S.O.S. call for assistance from the Infantry. On this "occasion the fire was even more intense, but the Battery, or what "guns remained, continued to fire the entire time. I saw at least one "gun blown up and three ammunition dumps ignited. On this occasion "Second-Lieutenant Gallie again behaved very gallantly, and was ably "assisted by Second-Lieutenant Bloor. I cannot mention the names of "individual N.C.O.'s or men, but the behaviour of the battery was "wonderful ; they showed other batteries in the neighbourhood a splendid "example of what a Battery can do to assist Infantry while under the "heaviest fire.

"(Signed) JAMES ABBEY,
"*Major, R.F.A.,*
"Commanding A/103rd Brigade, R.F.A."

During the period under review the Battery has lost over seventy all ranks and over twenty guns, but still continue to do their work in a highly efficient, and admirable manner.

Second-Lieutenant Gallie was subsequently promoted Captain, awarded the D.S.O. and M.C., and ended a career of exceptional gallantry, killed in action during the last stages of the campaign.

"C" BATTERY, 156TH BRIGADE, R.F.A.

Commanded by Temporary Captain (Acting Major) A. BARKER, M.C., R.F.A.

During the attack on Veldhoek on the 20th September, 1917, the Battery was in action South of Zillebeke. During the whole of the time that the Battery was firing in support of the Infantry, shells from 10.5 cm. howitzers were falling all about the Battery. One shell wounded two Officers, and another completely knocked out a gun and detachment. The Battery continued firing throughout in spite of this heavy shelling. The casualties during the attack were, two Officers and ten other ranks killed and wounded.

Later, after sustaining twenty casualties the Battery moved forward two miles into action near Sanctuary Wood. Directly the trails were dropped, the position was shelled with 8 inch and 5.9 inch. After a most exhausting day, a fresh position five hundred yards away was chosen and by dawn next morning guns and ammunition were manhandled into it, and the construction completed, the Battery being again ready to support the Infantry.

The Battery received a congratulatory message from the Colonel of the Army Brigade Commanding the Group as follows :—

" May I thank you for the excellent way in which you have all " carried out, what has been I fear, an arduous few days.

" (Signed)   L. COCKRAFT,
" *Lieutenant-Colonel,*
" Commanding Left Group."

"C" BATTERY, 162ND BRIGADE, R.F.A.

Commanded by Temporary Captain (Acting Major) L. C. HILL, M.C., R.F.A.
1st September, 1917, to date.

This Battery was in action South of Zillebeke from 13th September, 1917, to date. During this period the Battery underwent severe shelling, losing five Officers and ninety-one other ranks, and having over eighteen guns destroyed or put out of action. At all times the Battery behaved *most* gallantly, always firing their S.O.S., etc., whatever the conditions. On about the 21st September the Battery position had to be cleared owing to heavy shelling with 8 inch, more than one gun being destroyed—the S.O.S. was received—and led by their Officers the men manned their guns and fired till the order " Stop " was received—all the time being heavily shelled. During this episode one Officer was killed and ten other ranks killed and wounded.

On the 4th October the Battery repeated this performance, manning the guns on S.O.S. being given after the position had had to be cleared—they

BRIGADIER-GENERAL C. G. STEWART, C.M.G., D.S.O., R.A.,

WHO, HAVING PREVIOUSLY COMMANDED THE 166TH BRIGADE, ROYAL FIELD
ARTILLERY, WITH THE 33RD DIVISION, COMMANDED THE THIRTY-THIRD
DIVISIONAL ARTILLERY, AUGUST, 1917, TO OCTOBER, 1918.

were again heavily shelled all the time they were firing—one gun was knocked out and twelve other ranks were killed or wounded while manning the guns. This gallant action by the Battery was seen by the Officer Cammanding of another Battery in the neighbourhood belonging to another Division, who was so struck by the gallantry displayed by the Battery that he sent in a written report which was forwarded to Corps. The Battery has not got a copy of this report.

Between September 13th and October 17th, the Battery sustained the following casualties :—

	Killed.	Wounded.	
Officers	4	2	(1 remained at duty).
Other Ranks ..	10	80	(18 remained at duty).

During all this period the conduct of the Battery was invariably exemplary, and the two instances given above are only typical of the general conduct of the Battery, which was the subject of unstinted praise on the part of neighbouring Batteries who themselves were witnesses of the Battery's gallantry. It was not until they had insufficient men to maintain their guns in action, that the Battery reported that it could not carry on efficiently, and it was in consequence withdrawn from action and returned to its wagon lines with four N.C.O.'s and six Gunners left.

No mention has been made of individuals by name, as from the Commanding Officer to the Gunners, the Battery worked as one unit, and no distinction can be made on the work of this splendid Battery.

The Commanding Officer is Major L. C. Hill, M.C., R.F.A. (Wounded and remained at duty 16–10–17).

"D" BATTERY, 162ND BRIGADE, R.F.A.

From 2nd September to 15th October, 1917, this Battery was in action at Maple Copse, East of Zillebeke. This was the period of the successful attacks on enemy's positions on the Ypres-Menin Road, and to the North. The enemy had made a large concentration of artillery and continually shelled the area around Maple Copse with guns of all calibres from 7.7 cm. to 8 inch howitzers. The Battery was in a camouflaged position, the guns being in the open, and the shelter for the detachments being only splinter proof. The Battery was shelled almost daily, there were casualties frequently and the demand made on the men's endurance was very great. Throughout the period the Battery never failed and the devotion of all ranks to their duty was exemplary. This was especially marked on September 19th, while the Battery was firing a preliminary barrage. The position was heavily shelled by the enemy with 5.9 inch and 4.2 howitzers. Very serious casualties were caused, two guns were put out of action and a large dump of ammunition exploded. Regardless of the heavy hostile fire, the Battery continued to fire, the detachments of the guns which were untouched, calmly performing their duties while the Officers walked up and down the Battery cheering their men and directing the removal of the wounded to a place of safety.

This is given as a typical example of the conduct of the Battery and the high spirit which animated all ranks.

The casualties sustained by the Battery between September 13th and October 13th, were :—

	Killed.	Wounded.	
Officers	1	6	
Other Ranks ..	14	55	(20 remained at duty).

The Battery is still in action in the same position.

The Commanding Officer of the Battery is—

Major F. L. Lee.

His predecessors in command were—

Major W. P. Colfox, wounded 19th September.
Major C. E. Beerbohm, killed 26th September.

Except for a lull of about twenty minutes the intensity of the bombardment continued during the whole of the 25th and the night of the 25th/26th. At 9 p.m. orders were received from the Higher Command that the original attack would be carried out according to plan on the morning of the 26th. The Division by this time had suffered five thousand casualties. During the night of the 25th/26th the whole position was reorganized. It seems incredible now that this can have been done. The Divisional Ammunition Column sent up no less than 700,000 rounds on pack-mules to the machine guns, a feat of organization, patience and heroism seldom equalled. At dawn on the 26th the attack, which had been reinforced by the 19th Brigade, swept forward along the whole 33rd Divisional front with extreme bitterness. Very few prisoners were taken. Enormous numbers of the enemy were found dead, and the 93rd and 1st Middlesex Regiment, who had been cut off were found to have maintained their original position of the 25th intact, having endured not only the enemy attack but our own bombardment. The triumph of the 33rd Division in thus capturing the whole of its objective after having endured so severe a bombardment and counter-attack on the day preceding is best described in telegrams sent by Field-Marshal Sir Douglas Haig and General Sir H. Plumer hereunder :—

" *From* the Field-Marshal Commanding-in-Chief, British Armies in France.

" *To* General Sir H. C. O. Plumer, Commanding 2nd Army, General Head-
" quarters, 27th September, 1917.

" The ground gained by the 2nd Army yesterday, under your
" command, and the heavy losses inflicted on the enemy in the
" course of the day, constitute a complete defeat of the German

"forces opposed to you. Please convey to all Corps and Divisions
"engaged my heartiest congratulations, and especially to the 33rd
"Division, whose successful attack, following a day of hard fighting,
"is deserving of all praise."

"*From* Xth Corps.

"*To* 33rd Division.   G.G. 131.   26th September, 1917.

"Following received from General Plumer: Please accept my
"congratulations on success of to-day's operations, and convey them
"to the troops engaged. The 33rd Division have done fine work
"under extraordinarily difficult circumstances, and the 39th Division
"have carried out their task most successfully. The Corps Commander
"adds his own congratulations."

"In circulating the above messages I wish to congratulate all Officers,
"Non-commissioned Officers and men of the Division on having gained by
"their fine fighting qualities, such marks of appreciation from the
"Commander-in-Chief, and from the Army and Corps Commanders.
"Captured enemy documents show what efforts the enemy made on
"the 25th September, 1917, against the front held by the Division
"between the Ypres-Menin Road and the Southern edge of the Polygon
"Wood.
"I wish this Order to be read on parade to all ranks of the
"Division, as a mark of my appreciation of their gallant conduct in
"the past, and as a proof of my confidence in their being able to
"maintain their high reputation in the future.

"(Signed) P. Wood,
"*Major-General,*

"*September 29th, 1917.*   "Commanding 33rd Division.

An aeroplane photograph of the battlefield alone gives some idea of
the difficulties experienced by our troops, no less than of the enormous
number of shells used in the attack. Not a square yard of ground exists
which is not pock-marked with craters—a photograph, resembling rather
some hideous disease than a once beautiful wooded country side.

In this, the Battle of Polygon Wood, Officers, N.C.O.'s and certainly one
man, Private O'Conor, of the King's Liverpool Regiment, had led platoons
and groups in the attack and in protecting exposed flanks. Mules had been
led up through the hottest shell-fire with ammunition, food and water.
Machine and Lewis Gunners had shot Germans for hours. Signallers and
Runners had kept communication regardless of personal danger. Medical
Officers and Stretcher-bearers had performed their gallant and humane duty

in looking after wounded and injured in spite of enormous pressure of work and heavy casualties in their own ranks.

It was after this Battle that some interesting correspondence took place between Great Britain and Germany concerning an allegation that orders had been given to the 1st Battalion Middlesex Regiment, to shoot any armed stretcher-bearer falling into British hands. This allegation was absolutely denied.

Translation.
(215118/318/T.)
III a 20043.
156817.

" NOTE VERBALE.

" According to information from British prisoners of war the order " has been given to the British 1st *Middlesex Regiment, 19th Brigade,* " 33rd *Division,* to shoot any armed German stretcher-bearer falling into " British hands. Even a revolver carried by the stretcher-bearer is " considered as armament.

" This order is at variance with the provisions of Article 6 of the " Geneva Convention of July 6th, 1906, according to which medical units " are to be respected and protected by the belligerents, and with " Article 8 (1) of the Convention, according to which the protection " guaranteed by Article 6 is not to be forfeited by the personnel of the " unit being armed and using its arms for its own defence or for that " of the sick and wounded under its charge.

" The German Government therefore enters the most energetic protest " against this order given in contravention of International law by responsible " British Commanders, and expects the British Government as soon as " it learns the foregoing to cause the order to be repealed at once.

" Should a satisfactory reply not reach the German Government by " the 10th December next it would be obliged to proceed to suitable " retaliatory measures.

" The Foreign Office would be grateful to the Swiss Legation if it " would kindly cause the foregoing to be brought by telegraph, through " the intermediary of the Swiss Legation in London, to the knowledge of " the British Government, and the latter's reply to be communicated to " it by telegraph also.

" Copy of the note verbale is being sent to the Netherland Legation " (British Division) in this City.

" BERLIN.
" *November 6th,* 1917.

" *To* THE SWISS LEGATION,
" (German Interests)."

PASSCHENDAELE.

From Polygon Wood and Inverness Copse the Division was withdrawn
and took over the newly-captured line East of Messines. Owing to the
heavy nature of the ground, for the river Douve had flooded its banks, this
was a place of practical inactivity, except for considerable shelling in the
evening. Divisional Headquarters were camped at the Ravelsberg, with the
reserve and support Brigades at Kortepyp and Neuve Eglise respectively.
As at a later date the Division was engaged in the heaviest fighting in this
locality, it is interesting to note that it had previously had a good
opportunity of studying its topography.

Early in November a further move was ordered and the Division was
again moved North of Ypres, where on the 6th of November it relieved the
3rd Canadian Division in the Passchendaele Salient.

There was no man in the Division who was not more than pleased to
see its old Commander return once more, Major-General R. J. Pinney, C.B.,
relieving Major-General Wood, C.B., D.S.O., in Ypres at the end of this month ;
although we sincerely regretted the loss of General Wood who had led us
to Victory on the Menin Road.

The winter experiences of the 33rd Division, which had gone from
worse to worse, undoubtedly culminated in unpleasantness and horror during
its tours in the Passchendaele Salient.

The Passchendaele Salient extended to a depth of about three thousand
yards and a width of only one thousand yards. The whole area was overlooked
by the enemy from Westroosebeke, and suffered from shell fire and gas of all
descriptions continuously both night and day. The only places in the Salient
when the Division first took it over, which could in any degree be said to

be safe were the remains of the German concrete " mebus," or more commonly called " pill-box." The enemy, unfortunately, however, knew this, and these little Island-refuges were for ever shelled with gas shells and having no protective apparatus against the fumes of gas poison, they were practically uninhabitable. The entry into the Salient was nothing more or less than a plunge into a slough of filthy shell holes, amongst which hundreds of unburied dead grinned and gesticulated from amongst miles of tangled wire and stunted trees.

The Ravibeeke, a little stream, which flowed from the neighbourhood of Passchendaele Church down the ravine to Zonnebeeke, owing to heavy rains, had flooded its banks ; and not only were the shell holes then filled with water, in which lay rotting equipment, ammunition, horse flesh and rations, but the whole terrain was sticky as treacle, yet slippery as ice, whilst the stench from gas-fumes exuding from the ground combined with that of rotting corpses made life almost unbearable. The communications consisted only of a single duck-board track which showed up so plainly upon the enemy's aeroplane photographs that it was heavily shelled at all times. Owing to its peculiar position, and the fact that the Salient was destined to be the concentration point of troops for the capture of Westroosebeke to the North and high ground East of Passchendaele, it was strongly garrisoned to prevent its seizure by the enemy in counter-attack. The roads which ran from Passchendaele to Broodseinde and Zonnebeeke, which apart from the duck-board track furnished the only safe means of reaching the extremity of the Salient without losing one's way and disappearing into the enemy's line, were also well marked by the enemy artillery as a target. These roads were a perfect shambles of unburied dead whose number increased daily. Those who, fearful of the death walk of these roads, essayed the open country, perished in the mud or wandered into the German lines, thereby increasing the number of our missing. The Reliefs carrying complete rations for the " period of relief " were lost to sight in a sea of mud for four days. It was decided therefore to sink two large shafts and galleries. One, " Primus Shaft," situated beside the Passchendaele Road on the Keerslahoek mound, and another at Crest Farm, a considerable eminence which served as a pivot point for the concentration of troops in the event of Hostile counter-attacks from the North or from the East. These galleries had at least a foot of water in the bottom of them, although hand pumps were kept going both day and night. The life lived in these underground passages was very much like that of the water rat, so much so that there were as many of these animals as there were troops. Each of these galleries held two Infantry Companies. Two attacks to capture Westroosebeke and the high ground to the East of Passchendaele were carried out in the early part of December, in which the 1st, 29th, 32nd, 33rd and 49th Divisions took part. The whole of these five Divisions had to be concentrated, prior to the hour of assault, in the Passchendaele Salient. As a result of these attacks,

76

with their very heavy casualties, not one yard further of ground was captured, for the enemy was well posted with machine guns in immensely strong concrete pill-boxes; and it was a physical impossibility for our troops to struggle across the swamps to capture them.

The Engineer and Pioneer services, working under the most difficult and dangerous conditions, succeeded in "doubling" the duck-board track, and extending it to important centres in the Salient within a short period. When the Infantry were relieved from the line they were immediately formed into daily working parties and continued the arduous task of perfecting what came to be known as the "Mule Track," which extended from "Frost House" to "Tyne Cotts," a distance of about three miles. Upon this track it was later possible to bring up ammunition for the guns, rations and material. The journey upon this track, however, was always full of danger; and was regarded by the drivers as a gamble with life. Men and animals were shot down in their tracks by huge explosives which splintered the track and blew their wagons sky high.

The perfecting of these communications was jealously guarded by Lieutenant-General Sir A. Hunter Weston, K.C.B., D.S.O., the Corps Commander, himself an Officer of the Royal Engineers. Under enormous difficulties he succeeded in establishing the "Decouville Track" from Ypres to Crest Farm, upon which ran an almost regular service of trains consisting of six to eight open trucks driven by a miniature motor engine. Undoubtedly this railway not only saved many lives, but owing to the stealth with which it moved, and the "shell-craft," which is indeed a science, of the drivers, the little trains completed their daily journeys almost without mishap. In fact, the relief train became to be known as the "Passchendaele Express." Nevertheless, the casualties from shell fire, from gas and exposure, sustained by the Division were very considerable. Too high a tribute cannot be paid to the services of the Divisional Field Companies, companies of miners, gas experts, railway men of the Corps of Royal Engineers. The former, commanded by Majors C. P. L. Balcombe, T. E. Anderson and G. D. A. Fenwick, under the direction of Lieutenant-Colonel G. F. Evans, must take much of the credit for making the Salient at all inhabitable :—Railway communications, timbered tracks, concrete dug-outs, all had the mark of their arduous and unstinted labours. The miners, being heterogeneous bodies of skilled miners from the pits of Wales, Nottinghamshire, Staffordshire, Derby, Scotland, Canada and Australia, constructed the only homes of real safety; though always faced with the supreme difficulty of keeping pumping operations going, and the lesser difficulty of transporting masses of heavy gear to assist them in their task. Nor would concrete dugouts, pill-boxes or mined galleries have been of any value but for the services of the gas experts who cunningly fitted little gas-proof window blinds. The credit for all these comforts, far more than perhaps was realized at the time, was due to the Corps Commander. And not only as to the Engineering Services but in all matters affecting the tactics, efficiency, sanitation and salvage, Sir Aylmer Hunter-Weston displayed an unabateable energy and versatility, both mentally and physically.

The time spent in the Passchendaele Salient was one very full of the memory of gas. At this period the enemy commenced employing a mixture of phosgene and some non-poisonous effluvia which served only as an irritant to the nose. It was impossible to tell the difference between these two gasses. It was a frequent occurrence, therefore, for men who imagined that they had only suffered slight inconvenience from nose irritation, after the violent exertion of walking from the Passchendaele Salient to Ypres to drop dead suddenly in the Square, at the threshold of the Cloth Hall which served as a canteen. However, it must not be supposed that we were not quite the equals of the Boche in this respect. We remember Captain Thomas of the " Special Royal Engineers," who came cheerily into the line announcing that he could " do in " the Boche with poison gas at 2s. 9d. per head !

Divisional Headquarters at Ypres was exactly like a rabbit warren. The passages and rooms were most cunningly burrowed out under the City Ramparts. The walls and ceilings were supported by rails, and the whole interior was " wondrous neat and clean " and lit by electricity run by the electric light lorries of the Motor Transport Service. The whole interior was absolutely shell and aerial torpedo proof, but the atmosphere was close and stale, and it was no " cushy job " to have to work and sleep in such a place week after week. Outside, the duck-boards led down to the roadside. Against the wall every few yards dug-outs had been made so that the Staff could " dodge the shelling " when Fritz was " Hating " the place. General Pinney was very happy there, for his soul loved, as Esau's did, the smell of savoury meat, the scent of danger, and the sound of battle.

The Division was most energetically supported and assisted by both Lieutenant-Colonel E. C. Gepp, and Major H. Denison Pender, of the Divisional Staff. It was relieved after its first tour in this Sector on the 12th December. During the night of relief, a very serious fire occurred in the Ramparts, Ypres, with serious loss of life and property to the personnel of Divisional Headquarters and a Heavy Artillery group attached to them.

During this tour the front of the 33rd Division was considerably lengthened to embrace not only Passchendaele Church inclusive, but the Broodseinde cross-roads and the whole of the Keerslahoek Ridge. This was the result of the reduction of each Brigade from the strength of four Battalions to that of three. In the 33rd Division the following Battalions disappeared, to the very great regret of the whole Division in losing such fine fighting Battalions :—

> 20th Battalion Royal Fusiliers.
> 4th Battalion Suffolk Regiment.
> 2nd Battalion Royal Welch Fusiliers (which went to the Welch Division).

78

PASSCHENDAELE.

The Division was reconstituted as under :—

19th Brigade—
> 1st Battalion Queen's (Royal West Surrey) Regiment.
> 1st Battalion The Cameronians (Scottish Rifles).
> 5th–6th Battalion Scottish Rifles.

98th Brigade—
> 4th Battalion King's (Liverpool) Regiment.
> 2nd Battalion Argyll and Sutherland Highlanders.
> 1st Battalion Middlesex Regiment.

100th Brigade—
> 2nd Battalion Worcestershire Regiment.
> 9th Battalion Highland Light Infantry (Glasgow Highlanders).
> 16th Battalion King's Royal Rifle Corps.

The Division was relieved by the 50th Division and moved back to the Steenvoorde Area for Christmas. Christmas went with unusual éclat and gaiety in a heavy snowfall, with concerts, dinners and many football matches.

In the first week of January, the Division was moved back into its old Sector at Passchendaele. The Sector was already considerably more pleasant. Communications both for Infantry and Transport had made rapid strides, and many of the old pill-boxes had been made habitable.

On many occasions, the front of the 33rd Division was raided by the Germans, particularly from the "Gasometers," and opposite the railway from the direction of the Passchendaele Station. Notably, there was a raid upon the posts of the 1st Queen's, in which the enemy not only failed to reach the posts, but left at least fifteen dead lying out in front of the wire, in the machine gun barrage line. Another raid upon the Cameronians opposite Passchendaele Church met a like fate. Several successful raids by the 4th King's, 9th Highland Light Infantry and 1st and 5th Scottish Rifles, were carried out. There is no doubt whatever, that by this time the Infantry had the greatest confidence in direct machine gun fire by night, and in the barrage ; and invariably it was asked for.

The 5/6th Scottish Rifles in the 19th Brigade, the 1st Middlesex in the 98th Brigade and the 9th Highland Light Infantry in the 100th, took it upon themselves, in particular, to keep the Boche at a distance ; and so active were their patrols and so successful, that opposite the 100th Brigade front the enemy was seldom to be met within seven hundred to one thousand yards ; whilst in front of the Left Sector, served by the 19th and 98th Brigades, the "Gasometers," a point of considerable tactical importance to the enemy, was finally vacated.

Except for night bombing and violent "shell storms," very little activity was shown by the enemy. Everyone, however, felt that this was only the lull before the storm. On March the 29th the storm broke, not on our front but on that of the 5th Army. No sooner had the storm broken than the 33rd Division was hurriedly withdrawn from the line and relieved by the 49th Division. Before the relief had taken place, the 19th Brigade was moved to the Arras area at Lattre St. Quentin. The rest of the Division was moved by bus and train to this area three days later. Very little news filtered through except that the enemy had made a large number of attacks on a stupendous scale; and rolling up the 4th and 5th Armies had almost broken our line, and that of the French; and was advancing rapidly on the road to Paris; having captured in a few days tens of thousands of prisoners and hundreds of guns, and the whole of the Somme and Arras battle fields; establishing his line in territory which he had not previously occupied since the early days of 1914.

During the last rest period behind the Ypres sector the Infantry Brigades were reduced to three Battalions each; the Division losing the 20th Royal Fusiliers, 2nd Royal Welsh Fusiliers and 4th Suffolk Battalions, the former being disbanded and the last two being transferred to other Divisions.

On the eve of the departure of the 33rd Division for the South, the following message was received from the Corps Commander :—

" *From* Lieutenant-General Sir Aylmer Hunter-Weston, K.C.B., D.S.O., M.P.,
      " Commanding VIII. Army Corps, British Armies in France.

" *To* Major-General R. J. Pinney, C.B., and the Officers, Warrant Officers,
      " Non-Commissioned Officers and Men of the 33rd Division.

                                    " Headquarters, VIII. Corps,
                                          " British Expeditionary Force.
                                                " *April 5th*, 1918.

      " It is with great regret that I part temporarily with the 33rd
" Division. Throughout the time that it has been in the 8th Corps, it
" has done good service to the State, and the conduct, spirit and
" resolution of all ranks has been beyond praise.

      " You are now going to bear your share in the greatest battle of
" all history. You go as the Champions of Right and Justice, and the
" defenders of our homes and liberties and all that makes life worth
" living.

      " The Empire is fortunate in having in you a well disciplined,
" resolute and determined Division, which can be trusted to ' stick it
" out,' to carry on and win through to Victory. I hope it may be
" my good fortune to have the 33rd Division under my command again.

      " Wherever you go I shall follow your doings with the greatest
" interest, and wherever you are my thoughts and best wishes will be
" with you each and all.

                        " (Signed) AYLMER HUNTER-WESTON,
                                          " *Lieutenant-General*,
                                          " Commanding VIII. Corps."

Aylmer Hunter Weston
Lt. General

LIEUTENANT-GENERAL SIR AYLMER HUNTER-WESTON, K.C.B., D.S.O.,

WHO COMMANDED THE EIGHTH CORPS IN WHICH THE THIRTY-THIRD DIVISION
SERVED AT THE BATTLE OF THE YPRES-MENIN ROAD; BEFORE MESSINES,
AND IN THE PASSCHENDAELE SALIENT, SEPTEMBER, 1917, TO MARCH, 1918.

CHAPTER V.

METEREN AND NEUVE EGLISE.

1ST MARCH TO 20TH APRIL, 1918.

Battle of the Lys—Meteren—Brilliant Action of 19th and 98th Brigades and the 33rd Battalion Machine Gun Corps—Neuve Eglise—Stout Defence by 2nd Battalion Worcestershire Regiment and 100th Brigade—Officers' Casualties.

ORDER OF BATTLE.—1ST APRIL, 1918.

33RD DIVISION.

Commander	Major-General R. J. Pinney, C.B.
Aide-de-Camp to Commander	Captain F. C. Hooper, Dorset Regiment.
Aide-de-Camp to Commander	Lieutenant A. S. G. Kennard, Hampshire Yeomanry.

GENERAL STAFF BRANCH—

General Staff Officer, 1st Grade	Lieutenant-Colonel E. C. Gepp, D.S.O., Duke of Cornwall's Light Infantry.
General Staff Officer, 2nd Grade	Lieutenant-Colonel H. C. Sparling, D.S.O., 1st Quebec Regiment.
General Staff Officer, 3rd Grade	Captain A. M. Bankier, M.C., Argyll and Sutherland Highlanders.
Intelligence Officer	Lieutenant W. I. B. Ware, Intelligence Corps.

ADJUTANT AND QUARTERMASTER-GENERAL'S BRANCH—

Assistant Adjutant and Quartermaster-General	Lieutenant-Colonel J. G. Ramsay, D.S.O., Cameron Highlanders.
Deputy-Assistant Adjutant-General ..	Major H. C. C. Batten, Dorset Regiment.
Deputy-Assistant Quartermaster-General ..	Major O. B. Foster, M.C., Northumberland Fusiliers.

ADMINISTRATIVE SERVICES AND DEPARTMENTS—

Assistant Director of Medical Services ..	Colonel S. de C. O'Grady, D.S.O., Royal Army Medical Corps.
Deputy-Assistant Director of Medical Services	Captain J. R. M. Whigham, M.C., Royal Army Medical Corps.
Deputy-Assistant Director of Veterinary Services	Major G. H. Farrell, Army Veterinary Corps.
Deputy-Assistant Director of Ordnance Services	Captain A. M. E. Beavan, Army Ordnance Department.

THE THIRTY-THIRD DIVISION.

SPECIAL APPOINTMENTS—

Army Provost-Marshal   ..   ..   ..   Major Hon. E. G. French, D.S.O., General List.

Senior Chaplain to the Forces, Church of England .. ..   Reverend W. C. Mayne.

Senior Chaplain to the Forces, Nonconformist .. ..   Reverend Hugh Brown.

Officer Commanding French Mission ..   Lieutenant P. F. Girard.

Officer Commanding Belgian Mission ..   Lieutenant Roels.

DIVISIONAL ARTILLERY—

Commander .. ..   Brigadier-General C. G. Stewart, C.M.G., D.S.O., Royal Artillery.

Brigade-Major .. ..   Major T. E. Durie, M.C., Royal Field Artillery.

Staff Captain .. ..   Captain W. E. Bownass, M.C., Royal Field Artillery.

Staff Officer for Reconnaissance ..   Lieutenant T. R. Jackson, Royal Field Artillery.

Divisional Trench Mortar Officer ..   Captain C. C. W. Havell, M.C.

156th Brigade, Royal Field Artillery   Lieutenant-Colonel B. A. B. Butler, D.S.O.

162nd Brigade, Royal Field Artillery   Lieutenant-Colonel F. T. Oldham.

Divisional Ammunition Column ..   Colonel L. Forde, C.M.G.

X/33 Mobile Trench Mortar Battery   Captain T. R. Mayler.

Y/33 Mobile Trench Mortar Battery   Captain T. Wingate, M.C.

HEADQUARTERS, DIVISIONAL ENGINEERS—

Commander .. ..   Lieutenant-Colonel G. F. Evans, D.S.O., Royal Engineers.

Adjutant .. ..   Captain E. L. Gale, M.C., Royal Engineers.

11th Field Company .. ..   Major C. P. L. Balcombe, M.C.

212th Field Company .. .. ..   Major J. E. Anderson, M.C.

222nd Field Company .. .. ..   Major H. T. Morshead, D.S.O.

DIVISIONAL SIGNAL COMPANY, ROYAL ENGINEERS—

Officer Commanding .. ..   Major G. W. Williams, M.C.

19TH INFANTRY BRIGADE—

Commander .. ..   Brigadier-General C. R. G. Mayne, D.S.O., Highland Light Infantry.

Brigade-Major .. ..   Captain C. la T. T. Jones, M.C., Royal Engineers.

Staff Captain .. ..   Captain D. C. Robinson, Royal Lancashire Regiment.

1st Queen's Regiment, Commanding Officer   Lieutenant-Colonel M. Kemp-Welch, D.S.O., M.C.
a/2nd-in-Command ..   Captain N. B. Avery.

1st Cameronians,   Commanding Officer   Lieutenant-Colonel G. Wingate, M.C.
2nd-in-Command ..   Major R. D. Hunter.

5/6th Scottish Rifles,   Commanding Officer   Lieutenant-Colonel H. B. Spens, D.S.O.
2nd-in-Command ..   Major C. C. Scott.

19th Trench Mortar Battery,
Commanding Officer   Captain W. G. Borthwick.

METEREN AND NEUVE EGLISE.

98TH INFANTRY BRIGADE—

Commander	Brigadier-General J. D. Heriot-Maitland, C.M.G., Rifle Brigade.
Brigade-Major	Captain F. C. V. D. Caillard, M.C., Somerset Light Infantry.
Staff Captain	Captain E. J. Whitson, M.C., Highland Light Infantry.

4th King's (Liverpool) Regiment,

Commanding Officer	Lieutenant-Colonel S. E. Norris, D.S.O.
2nd-in-Command ..	Major J. H. L. Browne.

1st Middlesex Regiment, Commanding Officer   Lieutenant-Colonel J. H. Hall, C.M.G., D.S.O.

2nd-in-Command ..	Major G. O. T. Bagley.

2nd Argyll and Sutherland Highlanders,

Commanding Officer	Lieutenant-Colonel Hon. I. M. Campbell, D.S.O.
2nd-in-Command ..	Major A. G. C. Colquhoun.

98th Trench Mortar Battery,

Commanding Officer	Captain C. E. Paternoster.

100TH INFANTRY BRIGADE—

Commander	Brigadier-General A. W. F. Baird, C.M.G., D.S.O., Gordon Highlanders.
Brigade-Major	{ Captain J. I. Muirhead, Yorkshire Light Infantry. { Captain O. C. Downes, D.S.O., Rifle Brigade.
Staff Captain	Captain W. J. J. Coats, M.C., Highland Light Infantry.

2nd Worcester Regiment,

Commanding Officer	Lieutenant-Colonel T. K. Pardoe, D.S.O.
2nd in-Command ..	Major G. J. L. Stoney, M.C.

16th King's Royal Rifle Corps,

Commanding Officer	Lieutenant-Colonel B. J. Curling, D.S.O.
2nd-in-Command ..	Major P. A. W. Laye.

1/9th Highland Light Infantry,

Commanding Officer	Lieutenant-Colonel A. H. Menzies, D.S.O.
2nd-in-Command ..	Major E. McCosh, M.C.

100th Trench Mortar Battery,

Commanding Officer	Captain B. G. T. Hawkes.

18TH BATTALION MIDDLESEX REGIMENT (PIONEERS)—

Commanding Officer	Lieutenant-Colonel H. C. McNeile, M.C., Royal Engineers.
2nd-in-Command	Major W. H. Coles.

33RD BATTALION MACHINE GUN CORPS—

Commanding Officer	Lieutenant-Colonel G. S. Hutchison, M.C., Argyll and Sutherland Highlanders.
2nd-in-Command	Major W. C. Andrew.

230TH DIVISIONAL EMPLOYMENT COMPANY—

Commanding Officer	Captain M. B. Hoare.

THE THIRTY-THIRD DIVISION.

DIVISIONAL TRAIN (ARMY SERVICE CORPS)—

    Commanding Officer .. .. Lieutenant-Colonel P. G. P. Lea, C.M.G., D.S.O.
    Staff Supply Officer .. .. Major A. Clifton-Shelton.

DIVISIONAL MOTOR TRANSPORT COMPANY (ARMY
    SERVICE CORPS)—

    Commanding Officer .. .. Major J. A. H. Waters.
    2nd-in-Command .. .. Captain H. A. G. Denyer.

DIVISIONAL MEDICAL UNITS (ROYAL ARMY
    MEDICAL CORPS)—

    19th Field Ambulance .. .. .. Lieutenant-Colonel W. H. L. McCarthy, M.C.
    99th Field Ambulance .. .. .. Lieutenant-Colonel C. R. M. Morris, D.S.O.
    101st Field Ambulance .. .. .. Lieutenant-Colonel L. F. K. Way.

43RD MOBILE VETERINARY SECTION (ARMY
    VETERINARY CORPS)—

    Commanding Officer .. .. Captain A. G. E Lalor.

    Gas Officer .. .. Captain H. C. Tedd, King's (Liverpool) Regiment
    Salvage Officer .. .. Captain M. B. Hoare, Loyal North Lancashire
        Regiment.
    Claims and Canteen Officer .. .. .. Captain D. L. G. Pigache, Royal Fusiliers.
    Baths Officer .. .. Lieutenant J. H. Currie, Argyll and Sutherland
        Highlanders.
    Acting Salvage and Burial Officer .. .. 2nd-Lieutenant D. McKay, Argyll and Sutherland
        Highlanders.

ARTILLERY (ATTACHED TROOPS)—

    110th Field Artillery Brigade ⎫
    112th Field Artillery Brigade ⎬ 25th Divisional Artillery.
    113th Army Field Artillery Brigade.
    242nd Battery, Royal Garrison Artillery.
    333rd Battery, Royal Garrison Artillery.

ATTACHED TROOPS—

    2nd New Zealand Entrenching Battalion.
    XXII. Corps Reinforcement Battalion.
    33rd Composite Battalion (consisting of Instructors and Students at IX. and XXII. Corps Schools,
        Second Army Sniping School, and stragglers from other units).
    Composite Force, under Brigadier-General L. J. Wyatt, D.S.O., North Staffordshire Regiment
        (consisting of VIII. Corps School Instructors and Students and stragglers from other units).
    5th Tank Battalion.
    4th Tank Battalion.
    IX. Corps Cyclists.
    XXII. Corps Cyclists.
    6th Motor Machine Gun Battery.
    1st Motor Machine Gun Battery.
    Two Groups French Motor Machine Guns and Auto-cannon.

METEREN AND NEUVE EGLISE.

The operations carried out by the Division between the 12th and 20th April, 1918, were without doubt those which called for all the military skill. courage and endurance of which it was capable. The 9th Corps Special Orders have quoted the 2nd Battalion Worcestershire Regiment and the 33rd Battalion Machine Gun Corps as the two Battalions which particularly distinguished themselves between these dates at the Battle of the Lys ; but the whole Division fought with all the courage, energy, self-denial and knowledge with which it was endowed.

The Division was concentrated in the Arras Area on the 8th of April, 1918.

Whilst in its concentration area behind Arras, two days of most valuable training were obtained in the use of ground ; concealment of approach ; use of Transport for ammunition supply ; use of mounted orderlies ; fire direction and control ; mobility ; avoidance of large dumps, except in limbers or on the backs of pack animals.

The great success of this Division in action between the 12th and 18th April could not have been achieved without this training. Undoubtedly casualties would have been far heavier.

A note should be made that the greatest care had been taken to insist on a personal relation · between Officers, N.C.O.s, and Men. Games and recreation of all kinds had been carefully fostered. The high fighting qualities displayed by all ranks owed much to the splendid spirit of confidence and mutual trust animating the Division.

The experiences gained by this Division in the operations around Meteren and Bailleul leave no shadow of doubt that the Machine Gun Battalion organization was adopted only just in time. From our previous experiences, the task performed by the machine guns could not possibly have been done under the old organization. The Commanding Officer reported that the enemy could not have been held except by machine guns trained and organized as a Battalion, under one control and with one centralized source of ammunition supply ; feeding with reserve personnel ; and replacement of damaged equipment

Without doubt, also, work would have been duplicated. The gaps created in the Infantry, owing to casualties, and to attacks by the enemy which from time to time drew part of the line, a thin line, to concentrate to meet them, could not have been filled except ordered by an Officer closely in touch with the whole situation and in the closest liaison with the Brigadiers and Battalion Commanders conducting the operations.

OPERATIONS BETWEEN 12TH AND 18TH APRIL, 1918.

As noted, the Division was concentrated in the Arras area on the 8th April, 1918. At 7 p.m. on 10th instant, orders were received that the Division should proceed forthwith by " tactical trains " to the Caestre area. It was, however, considerably delayed owing to the fact that the enemy had accurately ascertained the range of the railway at Doullens, and succeeded in obtaining a direct hit upon a train containing the 4th Battalion The King's (Liverpool) Regiment. Not only was serious damage done to the line itself but two coaches were derailed and forty men killed. Meanwhile the transport was making a hazardous flank movement via St. Venant and Hazebrouck.

Personnel of Machine Gun Companies with guns, tripods and eight belt boxes proceeded by train with the Brigade groups to which they were affiliated for operations, as under :—

> Battalion Headquarters and " A " and " C " Companies with 19th Infantry Brigade.
> " B " Company with 100th Infantry Brigade.
> " D " Company with 98th Infantry Brigade.

The Transport and all other material proceeding by route march.

By 5 p.m. on the 11th instant, the personnel of three groups were detrained at Caestre and were concentrated (without any transport), bivouacking in fields, as under :—

> 19th Brigade Group—Battalion Headquarters, M.G.C.   Meteren Area.
> 100th Brigade Group   Ravelsburg.
> 98th Brigade Group   Strazeele.

From this time forward the action of the Division in the operations following is necessarily divided into two separate phases :—

(1) Operations carried out by 19th and 98th Infantry Brigades under 33rd Division with " A," " C " and " D " Companies, 33rd Battalion, Machine Gun Corps.

(2) Operations carried out by 100th Infantry Brigade under 25th Division with " B " Company, 33rd Battalion, Machine Gun Corps.

OPERATIONS CARRIED OUT BY THE 19TH AND 98TH BRIGADES SOUTH AND EAST OF METEREN.

It was only known that the enemy had captured both Merville and Estaires, some seven miles South of Meteren, and had succeeded in getting further West of Doulieu. It was supposed, though not known, that his advance had been arrested in this area. Very large numbers of stragglers from the 41st, 49th and 31st Divisions were hurrying along the roads in a westerly direction, accompanied both by the wounded and by refugees. The moral of many of the British troops at this juncture in the battle cannot be said to have been high. As a measure of safety full military precautions were taken by the 33rd Division, and in conjunction with the troops of the 19th Infantry Brigade the Machine Gunners put out outposts covering the approaches East and South of Meteren.

Major-General R. J. Pinney was then put in charge of all troops West of Bailleul, whilst the 98th Brigade which had temporarily been detached, was returned to his command.

At 10.30 a.m. on the morning of the 12th, Lieutenant-Colonel G. S. Hutchison received orders from the General Staff to have a reconnaissance made South and East of Meteren Village.

At 10.45 a.m., three cyclist patrols from the Scouts were ordered to proceed ; and having located the enemy, to report to Machine Gun Battalion Headquarters, established at a farmhouse about one mile South of Meteren. Each patrol consisted of an N.C.O. and four men.

The Commanding Officer, with 2nd Lieutenant McLaren, the Intelligence Officer, proceeding in advance, reconnoitred due South of Meteren, the Windmill Ridge and to Oostersteene. Here large numbers of both wounded and unwounded men were found to be in full retreat Northwards and Westwards. Lieutenant-Colonel Hutchison pushed on with No. 2 Patrol about half a mile South of Oostersteene, where our rear guards of the 31st Division, particularly from one Battalion, were found to be in precipitate retreat without Officers and saying they had orders to retire.

The enemy was observed about 600 yards distant in groups pushing forward under covering fire.

The Infantry were rallied and lined out on a 500 yards front facing South, South of the Village, full use being made of buildings and ditches. Lieutenant-Colonel Hutchison placed 2nd Lieutenant McLaren in command, and disposed the rest of the patrol to rally the Infantry and organize the locality for defence, he himself bicycling for assistance. In twenty minutes he had reached Divisional Headquarters in Meteren, having dumped his bicycle and commandeered a Ford ambulance, and reported direct to the General Officer Commanding, suggesting that Machine Guns should be rushed up to fill the breach and Infantry sent as soon as possible.

A motor lorry was commandeered and taken to the Machine Gun Battalion Headquarters. In a few minutes it was loaded with eight guns and material, and crowded with gun teams. Orders were given to establish Battalion Headquarters at the Moulin de Hoegenmacher, and Signallers were sent forward.

Two hundred yards South of the Mill, the lorry was halted by 2nd Lieutenant McLaren and the Scouts, who, having fought in close combat with the enemy with rifles, had been forced to retire to the Windmill Ridge. Other troops shattered by the German onslaughts of the past two days, were retiring towards Meteren in complete disorder.

Between 10.30 and 11.30 a.m. the advance of the enemy was carried out with astonishing rapidity. Pressing particularly from the East, apparently trying to isolate Meteren from the troops who were supposed to be defending its Southern approaches, he even succeeded in pushing forward two light guns North of the Windmill Crest, covering a distance of about a mile and a half in less than forty minutes.

His advance from the South towards Meteren was very rapid. Stragglers which had been rallied by the Machine Gun Scouts evaporated West and North before the enemy advance, which was now only checked by the resolution of the Scouts. Both Sergeant St. Ledger and Corporal Bawn, with Private Busby in particular, displaying great heroism, ordered the defence with astonishing coolness and initiative, ably supported by a few stout-hearted stragglers.

The excursion of the motor lorry came to an abrupt end when it was halted by the last of our advance guards. It came immediately under machine gun and rifle fire. The order "Action Front" was given, and in a very few minutes eight guns were disposed on the Northern slopes of the Windmill Hill Crest, covering, in particular, the Southern and South-easterly approaches to Meteren and the Meteren Becque. Half "A" Company having been taken into action under Major Lewthwaite, and disposed in position by the Adjutant, the lorry returned to its base to collect half "C" Company under Major Judson.

This incident was probably the most thrilling in which the Machine Gunners of the Division ever took part. The rapidity of action; the extraordinary situation; the perfect discipline and drill; the setting of untouched farmhouses, copses and quietly grazing cattle; the flying civilians and retiring Infantry of other Divisions before that of the 33rd Division had come into action behind; the magnificent targets obtained; and the complete grip of the situation by, and determination of, machine gun commanders. This action, and the subsequent operations of the Battalion undoubtedly will take the highest place for all time in the history of the Machine Gun Corps, and are an epic of the tenacity and grit of the British soldier with his back to the wall fighting against great odds.

A Report Centre and Advanced Battalion Headquarters were established at the Cross Roads about 300 yards North of the Hoegenmacker Windmill. From this position, Signallers, without equipment, but with handkerchiefs on sticks, were posted in communication with Battalion Headquarters.

At 12 noon half "C" Company was brought up by lorry and disposed facing South, covering a gap of about a mile and a half South of the Meteren Becque towards Merris.

Half "A" Company was already in outpost positions, and these positions provided depth for the left of our defence. The other half of "C" Company was then brought up by road and disposed in depth behind the front occupied by the eight forward guns. About two or three full Companies of stragglers had now been collected in the vicinity of Moelenacher by Lieutenant-Colonel Hutchison, the Adjutant and the Intelligence Officer. These men, under their own officers, were then extended into two lines

88

covering a front of about a mile and a half; and were ordered to retake the whole of the Hoegenmacher Windmill-Merris Ridge. It was with the greatest difficulty that they could be persuaded to move forward. They were, however, it must be said, under threat, eventually got on the move; and a long line was disposed amongst our guns, forming a very doubtful local protection. As an extenuating circumstance for the action of these troops, it is known that they had been more or less engaged with the enemy already for two or three days, and were disorganized and partly exhausted.

Scouts and Mounted Orderlies were used during all this period to determine the situation on the flanks. It was found to be satisfactory towards Merris; but East of our line, on the Bailleul-Meteren Road, it was in a most critical condition, large numbers of the enemy being seen rapidly advancing.

After the line covering nearly three miles of front, had been held by the Machine Gun Battalion for a period of two hours with no other protection than that of about three Companies of stragglers, the 1st Battalion The Queen's (Royal West Surrey) Regiment under Lieutenant-Colonel M. Kemp-Welch, who rode fearlessly into action at the head of his men, began to come into line from the direction of Meteren, and Moelenacher. This Battalion was apparently provided with no information whatever. One Company, under Captain Avery, and another Company, under Captain Carpenter, were disposed in the line by the Machine Gunners; and Captain Avery, with great gallantry, personally led his Company forward, recapturing the Windmill Hill Crest, the Windmill and the Farms around it, under the hottest fire. He then organized posts on the Southern slopes of the Crest; three of our machine guns were pushed forward in support of these posts.

A further reconnaissance by the Commanding Officer and Adjutant of the 33rd Battalion Machine Gun Battalion, about 2 p.m. revealed the fact that the left flank of the Queen's, which had previously been reported to be in a critical condition, was entirely open, the troops who were supposed to be in position having dwindled away. The Commanding Officer therefore moved one gun up to the extreme left flank of the Queen's to cover the Windmill Ridge, whilst he disposed one of the Queen's Lewis Guns to guard the Bailleul-Meteren Road and fill the gap. Large bodies of the enemy could be seen concentrating about 1,500 yards South-east of Meteren. The enemy was again attempting that which he had attempted earlier in the day by Oostersteene, that is, to force a wedge from the East between Meteren and our troops covering its approaches from the South. A Reserve Section of "C" Company, under Second-Lieutenant Watts, was therefore moved eastwards to the high ground South-east of Meteren and about two hundred yards West of the Steam Mill; and another section, under Second-Lieutenant Cross, was thrown out to cover the right flank of the Queen's. At 7 p.m. the 1st Middlesex under Lieutenant-Colonel J. H. Hall, and the 2nd Argyll and Sutherland Highlanders under Lieutenant-Colonel the Hon. I. Campbell were moved up to Bailleul, whilst the Division was ordered to fill the gap between Strazeele and Bailleul—a tremendous task. A very full report was then sent by the Machine Gunners to the General Staff. The Commanding Officer and the Adjutant, in order to find some local protection for Second-Lieutenant Watts' section, rallied a party, which must have consisted of at least twenty different Units, under a Cyclist Officer, and disposed them to secure the East and South-east approaches to Meteren. Troops of every formation now began to arrive in our line, being rushed up in motor lorries by the IX. Corps. Cyclist orderlies from Corps Headquarters, cooks, batmen, pioneers, even, it was said, a platoon of Town Majors under an Area Commandant, in fact, anyone who could hold a rifle to stem the tide.

By dusk the 5th Scottish Rifles had been sent by the 19th Brigade to reinforce this front, whilst the Cameronians had been thrown in on the right of the Queen's, holding the line South of Moelenacher, and maintaining contact with the Australians towards Merris, which village was at this time still believed to be in our hands. By nightfall, therefore, the line, though extremely thin, was continuous and held.

As a matter of fact, it is doubtful if Merris was even at this time still held by us. One scout entered a farmyard in this village and found a foaming horse, accoutred, in the yard. He was held in conversation by the farmer, who alleged the horse to be his own. On leaving the house the horse was gone. No doubt this was one of an enemy patrol. Finding the Village unoccupied by our troops without doubt the enemy hurried to it.

Meanwhile, the commandeered motor lorry driven by Driver Sharples had made journey after journey, often through intense shell, machine gun and rifle fire, bringing ammunition, spare parts, personnel, picks and shovels to the Machine Gun Battalion Headquarters, and distributing tools round the Queen's outpost line, directed by Machine Gun Officers. During the day many targets were fired on, and, as it became more and more apparent that the enemy's concentration for attack and advance must be impeded, harassing fire was carried out with great intensity by all our machine guns. The fact that the Transport had not yet arrived and that our ammunition supply was limited to eight belt boxes per gun, necessitated sending into the line for belt filling every available man, including the "minimum reserve," No. 5 Royal Engineers Signal Section, cooks, pioneers, tailors, officers' batmen, and Company clerks. All this personnel was withdrawn at dusk and was sent up again with wire, pickets, picks, and shovels to construct a line of wire in front of the machine gun nests. Meanwhile, the motor lorry searched the countryside and back areas for Royal Engineers' dumps and wire. On his own initiative, Driver Sharples went to Reninghelst where the nearest available wire could be got. These supplies, in addition to that used by the Machine Gunners, were passed also to the Infantry, and a defensive line and wire scheme was arranged by Lieutenant-Colonel G. S. Hutchison, in conjunction with Lieutenant-Colonel M. Kemp-Welch. The working party worked with untiring energy directed by Major Andrew, Second-in-Command of the Machine Gun Battalion.

The composite force of 1,000 men collected from Corps Schools, billets and stragglers, was then sent by General Pinney to the 25th Division under Brigadier-General L. J. Wyatt to hold Dranoutre. At the same time, he arranged to hold Meteren with the 19th Brigade and the New Zealand and Canadian Entrenching Battalion ; with the 98th Brigade in Divisional Reserve.

Under cover of the mist at dawn on the 13th instant, the enemy made a very heavy attack on the centre of our line held by the 1st Queen's. The centre of this Battalion gave way, and the machine guns, having secured the richest targets, were rushed, the teams being killed almost to a man. It was possible to withdraw only one gun. Captain Avery of the 1st Queen's redisposed this line with great initiative showing perfect coolness in the hottest places. The enemy employed at least two divisions in these attacks, all of which broke down with the heaviest losses, and with practically no gain to himself. It was the opinion of the Army Commander on this day that the attacks before Bailleul were not the main Boche offensives, which he considered would be directed at Arras. The line had fallen back to the line taken up by the Machine Guns on the morning of the 12th. Two counter attacks were carried out by "A" Company of the Queen's, and the Mill passed from our hands to the hands of the enemy, and from the enemy to us, three times within an hour, after very heavy fighting, finally remaining in enemy hands. The left of the Queen's held very firm, but the centre and right were considerably shaken and began to withdraw behind the line of the guns of "C" Company of the Machine Gun Battalion, on the West of the Meteren Becque. The enemy made repeated attemps to break our line under cover of the mist during the morning of the 13th instant. With his light guns pushed well forward, he inflicted considerable casualties both on our infantry and upon our machine gunners, but all his attempts to break the line were repelled by stout-hearted Surrey riflemen and the Machine Gunners, with the heaviest losses.

The early afternoon of the 13th was most critical. The transport, whose road lay by Strazeele, now being heavily shelled, had not arrived. The question of the maintenance of our line seemed to depend upon the arrival of the Machine Gun Transport. Repeated messages by mounted orderly were sent to Divisional Headquarters asking for the arrival of the fighting limbers. At 12 noon on the 13th, the Machine Gun Transport Officer arrived, and in a style reminiscent of the Royal Horse Artillery at an Aldershot Field day, the fighting limbers with belt boxes, barrels, and small arms ammunition were galloped through a hail of shell and machine gun fire to our gun positions, depositing the ammunition and material so urgently required.

The Queen's had incurred heavy casualties. Reinforcements, however, were either in the line, or rapidly being brought up, and by the evening of the 13th the situation seemed to be quite restored. This was reported to Divisional Headquarters and to the 19th Infantry Brigade. During the night of the 13th, destructive shoots were fired at enemy positions on the Hoegenmacher Mill-Merris Ridge, and on his communications in rear. Up to this time the Artillery had been unable to fire a single shell in support of our Infantry, whilst the enemy had continually bombarded our posts and communications during the 12th and 13th with field guns, field howitzers and light trench mortars, which he brought up with extraordinary rapidity.

There is no doubt that had the enemy attacked in any strength between 12 noon and 5 p.m. on the 13th instant, he might have entirely broken through our line. During his attacks on the morning of the 13th instant, and even up to 12 noon, detachments of enemy cavalry were fired upon, one large detachment, in particular, of about 200 horsemen being cut to pieces by the fire of the Section under Second Lieutenant Watts, South-east of Meteren. By the evening of the 13th instant, the situation was again normal.

The night of the 13th, with the exception of intermittent shelling and machine gun fire, was quiet, and enabled more small arms ammunition to be brought up and the wiring of the machine gun positions to be completed ; also enabling the Infantry to redispose their positions.

The 14th was probably the most critical day of these operations, the Infantry, particularly the 1st Battalion Queen's Regiment, who had been very hotly engaged and had sustained very heavy casualties, especially amongst the Officers, were very shaken.

At dawn on the 14th, as he had done on the 13th, the enemy launched very heavy attacks against our positions from the South-east and South of Meteren. A gap was made in the centre of the Queen's line covering the Meteren Becque ; a second gap was made on the left of the 5th Scottish Rifles, covering the approach to Meteren from the East ; another gap was made between the right of the Queen's and the 1st Cameronians, North-east of Merris. The enemy exploited these gains to full advantage, pushing forward light machine guns with great rapidity. In three instances the machine gun positions were being outflanked. Major A. Andrew, who had been out during the night of the 13-14th organizing the ammunition supply, again and again redisposed the Infantry in position, or moved guns to fill the gaps, or form a defensive flank to hinder the progress of the enemy and protect our line from his enfilade fire. In this he was assisted by the Intelligence Officer. Second Lieutenant Watts and Second Lieutenant McKenzie showed splendid initiative, and on each occasion, appreciating the situation, so directed the fire of their guns that, although weakened by heavy casualties, our line was never penetrated. The splendid devotion to duty and fine initiative displayed by the Machine Gunners, undoubtedly saved the day. Most excellent targets were secured. Senior officers, gun commanders and gunners report having

BRIGADIER-GENERAL C. R. G. MAYNE, C.M.G., D.S.O.
(HIGHLAND LIGHT INFANTRY),

WHO COMMANDED THE NINETEENTH BRIGADE
FROM MAY, 1916, TO MARCH, 1919.

piled the enemy dead before their guns. Owing to the strength of the enemy bombardment and the volume of his machine gun fire, and to the fact that six Divisions were employed in the attack upon the 19th Brigade front, there is no doubt that since this attack was definitely repulsed, the heaviest losses must have been inflicted upon the enemy.

The Machine Gun Commander, after consultation with the 19th Infantry Brigade, urgently asked for one section from " D " Company, which had been attached to the 98th Brigade in Divisional Reserve. This was granted. One section, on arrival, was disposed to fill the gap on the left of the 5th Scottish Rifles covering the Eastern approaches to Meteren Village. On the afternoon of the 14th the General Staff ordered the 4th King's (Liverpool) Regiment and the Machine Gun Battalion, less one Company, to come directly under the orders of Brigadier-General C. R. G. Mayne, Commanding the 19th Brigade.

Between 6 and 7 p.m. another determined attack was made by the enemy on the front held by the 19th Infantry Brigade. The Queen's, now very much shaken, particularly on the right, South of Moelenacher, fell back, and the retirement of our troops became fairly general. All our guns remained in position covering this retirement. The Officer Commanding Battalion and the Adjutant made a further reconnaissance of the line, and they decided that it would not be possible to maintain our machine gun positions without any Infantry protection whatever.

Lieutenant-Colonel Hutchison therefore proceeded to 19th Infantry Brigade Headquarters to report the situation. The situation appeared most grave. No further reinforcements were available with the exception of two Platoons of the 2nd New Zealand Entrenching Battalion. Lieutenant-Colonel Hutchison was asked by General Mayne whether it was possible for any line to be held South and East of Meteren pending the arrival of further reinforcements, which could not be expected immediately. An answer having been given that this was possible, General Mayne directed Lieutenant-Colonel Hutchison to take up and dispose the two platoons of the 2nd New Zealand Entrenching Battalion in support of his guns, and having restored a complete line to report the situation. The line taken up was that which up to the end of the operations on the 19th instant, constituted our front line ; and this was now made our front line on the 14th instant. The Colonials undauntedly went forward with admirable energy and pluck. Orders were immediately issued for the withdrawal of our guns to this line and for them to be disposed in depth behind it, the withdrawal being carried out " Section by Section, and Gun by Gun, with covering fire." In the face of great enemy opposition, and in the teeth of heavy machine gun fire at its outset, the retirement was carried out without loss either to personnel or material. Every man and every gun was withdrawn by concealed approaches and with irreproachable discipline to the line to which the Infantry had retired, and under perfect covering fire most ably directed by the Section Officers, noteworthy amongst whom were Lieutenant Watts, Lieutenant Harris and Lieutenant Cross.

During this day a French Chasseur Division had arrived at Caestre, and the first Australian Division had reinforced the line on our West. It had been attacked and the enemy had secured a lodgment in the houses South of Strazeele. Meanwhile the 34th Division who had retired from Neuve Eglise to Ravelsberg Hill, very weak, were reinforced by the 1st Middlesex Regiment from Divisional Reserve. There is no question that the moral of many of the troops who had been suddenly thrown into the line, collected together from Corps and Army Headquarters, was very low. Probably the reason for this was that they consisted of a heterogeneous body drawn from a large number of Regiments under Officers who had little or no fighting experience, and whom they did not know. Whatever the reason may have been, and we believe it was the reason that we have stated, some of these reinforcements held their hands up when the enemy advanced. Such an action as this will in a short time spread like dry-rot through an Army, and it is one of those dire military necessities which calls for immediate and prompt action. If there does not exist on the spot a leader of sufficient courage and initiative to check it by a word, it must be necessary to check it by shooting. This was done. Of a party of forty men who thus held up their hands to the enemy, thirty-eight were shot down, with the result that this never occurred again. It is necessary to state this in order that those who were not present can properly appreciate the danger with which our line, the Channel Ports and the British Isles themselves were threatened at this time. It was not a time when either sympathy or sentiment could in any way be permitted to weigh as a consideration for anyone in battle. Neither the wounded, the exhausted, nor the afraid could be permitted either consideration or help ; for each man as long as he lived must use his weapon. Nothing else mattered.

It was at this critical time that it was decided to evacuate the Passchendaele Salient which had been won and held with so much loss during the past winter, and to straighten the line from Bailleul through Ypres up to the coast. This decision must have been a peculiarly bitter one for that veteran old fighter, General Plumer. The Belgians had been approached with a view to their lending Divisions to us to strengthen the line. This, however, they refused to do. They now, however, took over the line down to Ypres ; now that, as they said, "that obstinate man, Plumer, has consented to leave the Passchendaele Salient."

EXTRACT FROM "THE TIMES," APRIL 15TH, 1918.
"The great German thrust in the North across the plain of the Lys "has been stayed for the past forty-eight hours. For four days the "enemy had, by the use of great numbers of troops, fought their way "forward on a twenty-mile front to a depth in the centre of nine miles.

METEREN.

"On Friday they were before Bailleul, Neuve Eglise and Wulverghem,
"in the North, and were fighting towards St. Venant, Bethune, and
"Lillers, in the South. Last night they were practically in the same
"position, as the result of the most furious fighting.

"By night and day there have been battles for Wulverghem, Neuve
"Eglise, and Bailleul, on the Southern slopes of the hills of Belgian
"Flanders. During Friday night the Germans got into Neuve Eglise,
"but were thrown out in the morning. Elsewhere in this region they
"could not make any impression.

"On the Southern flank the enemy have done their utmost to
"widen their salient round Merville, on the edge of the Forest of Nieppe,
"but all their attacks here have been beaten off. Here, as elsewhere,
"the German losses in the past two days have been very heavy.

"Our correspondent at the front gives his opinion that this
"second great German thrust has for the moment spent itself, and that
"all along the line the enemy is beating against a continually stiffening
"resistance."

By dawn on the 15th, a very good line had been dug. New machine
gun positions had been dug and the reserve guns disposed in depth behind
it. Battalion Headquarters was now moved to a more central position on
the Meteren-Fletre Road, about 300 yards West of Meteren. The Infantry
had been reinforced by the 11th Field Company, Royal Engineers, disposed
on the right of the Queen's, and by the 22nd Corps Cyclists disposed on the
left of the same Battalion.

Throughout these first three days the work done by the Signallers and
Scouts had been excellent. Splendid communication had been maintained;
and the position always made clear by the energy and intelligence displayed
by the Scouts.

Two Signallers of the Machine Gun Corps greatly distinguished
themselves. With a "station" established on the top of the Hoegenmacher
Mill, they remained with full observation of the enemy on the Southern side
of the Ridge whose movements could not be seen by us; and maintained
visual communication with us. Despite the fact that the Mill was under the
hottest fire; and itself the scene of very bitter fighting, these two men
maintained their position with amazing activity. Later, after the Mill had
passed finally into the hands of the enemy, they remained there for two days
undetected by the enemy, finally fighting their way back into our lines
armed with German revolvers.

A driver acting as Mounted Orderly, on one occasion, was cheered by
men of the 1st Battalion Queen's Regiment, who rose from their trenches as
he rode through their line under a hail of fire, whilst endeavouring to locate
the direction of the enemy attack.

THE THIRTY-THIRD DIVISION.

The situation during the 15th remained unaltered, the enemy confining his activity to artillery registration and periodical shell storms. An aeroplane with British markings, but almost beyond question piloted by a Boche, again and again flew over our positions which were considerably shelled.

The night was quiet. The 19th Brigade was relieved by 98th Brigade on the left of the line, from the right of the King's who had relieved the Queen's on the night 14th/15th, up to the Steam Mill; whilst the Machine Gunners effected an internal relief.

On the early morning of the 16th, the enemy made a most determined and strong attack on our positions South-east of Meteren, our right remaining quiet. This developed chiefly against the King's, whose left was overwhelmed, whilst suffering very heavy casualties, including all those at Battalion Headquarters who were shot dead. Captain G. H. E. Warburton, M.C., who was commanding the Battalion, was treacherously murdered by prisoners who had already surrendered at Battalion Headquarters. The attack was accompanied by a very heavy bombardment, particularly of Meteren itself. By 9 a.m. the enemy had effected a very definite lodgment in the town, with his machine guns most active from the Church.

Attack and counter-attack were carried out by the 4th King's.

During this day our Artillery, which had slowly increased since the 14th, showed itself to be in some force, both 18 pounders and French ·75's combining, supported by adequate heavier pieces.

French reinforcements from the 133rd Division during all this day were streaming up the roads and disposed themselves in reserve positions and in the support lines. At 5 p.m. the 18th Middlesex (Pioneers) Regiment, under Lieutenant-Colonel McNeile, "Sapper" of literary fame, accompanied by the 11th Field Company Royal Engineers, under Major Balcombe, made a spirited counter-attack through Meteren, taking some thirty prisoners. At 6 p.m. a counter-attack by the French, was ordered to push through our troops to take over the line. The attack was not, however, carried far enough forward, and at midnight the situation was practically unaltered.

Our left by the Windmill had been bent back a little upon Meteren. The machine guns, therefore, were redisposed for the protection of the left flank and to cover the height of Fontaine Houck.

Early on 17th further attacks, chiefly by infiltration, were made by the enemy attempting to increase his hold in Meteren. These were repulsed but the situation remained most obscure. The Machine Gun Commander was sent by the General Staff to reconnoitre our line, and, if necessary, redispose our guns to fill any gaps, and to give depth to our defences on the support line running through Moelenacher, Pinchboom, Les Quatre Fils Aymon, and the reserve line running through Fletre, Les Rouklos Hill and Schaexken.

A large amount of ammunition, new belt boxes and guns were sent up during this day, and conveyed by pack animals and limbers up to the line during the night, which was quiet. In this respect the Deputy Assistant

96

Director of Ordnance Services had, during the whole action, rendered the Battalion the best support, new guns and material even being sent up in his own car at the shortest notice.

During this day the Germans attacked with extraordinary violence, but were repulsed in spite of enormous shelling. The French Chasseurs were by now well into line, but it was very difficult for our troops to distinguish the blue-grey uniforms of the French from the field grey of the German troops, and this led to a certain amount of confusion.

At 11.30 a.m. the 18th Battalion Middlesex Regiment in a very gallant sally with the French had counter-attacked through Meteren successfully, and had driven the enemy out, except for machine guns posted in the upper windows of the Church.

On the morning of the 18th it was apparent that the enemy had exhausted himself. No further attacks were made, and our lines were linked up and consolidated. The Companies in Reserve were withdrawn to good shelter behind Mont des Cats, but artillery activity on both sides remained very considerable.

Whilst in no way wishing to belittle what was subsequently performed by the French, particularly by our comrades of the 133rd French Division, at this juncture it should be noted that the German onslaught upon our positions and his attempt to break the line with the object of seizing the hills of Kemmel, Mont Noir, Mont Rouge, Parsch and the Scharpenberg had definitely failed between the 12th and 15th of April. It may probably be said with exact truth that, from every consideration, particularly that of moral, the German offensive in the Battle of the Lys crumpled up on the 15th of April, because six of their Divisions had been defeated on the front held by one British Brigade. It is true that the hill of Kemmel was subsequently captured by the enemy from our French Allies supported by British troops, but this operation was, at its best, but a local and very costly success, an attempt to shatter the moral of the Allied Line. This was unsuccessful. Von Hindenburg, in his memoirs " Out of my Life," attempts to show that the British defence was only made possible by the arrival of the French. The very detailed story, foregoing, proves him to be wrong; he knows he has lied. Von Hindenburg would do well to study the text books in common use in his own Imperial General Staff if he desires to seek the cause of his own failure. Even the capture of Kemmel Hill later did nothing more than inconvenience our mode of life in the Ypres Salient. It in no way made its tenure a tactical or strategical possiblity, whilst the Salient itself served as an admirable jumping-off place for the 2nd Army in Haig's great drive in October of the same year. During the whole period of these operations in the 19th Brigade particularly fine work was done by the 1st Queen's and 5th Scottish Rifles. Circumstances made it necessary for three platoons of this latter regiment to remain in the line to fill a gap between the 1st and 4th Australian Battalions after the Division had been relieved. These platoons were under command of

Captain John Kirkwood, M.C., and under his leadership they conducted themselves after four days of bitter fighting with the utmost gallantry to the admiration of the Australians. They fought with stubborn courage until almost annihilated.

EXTRACT FROM "THE TIMES," APRIL 17TH, 1918.

"On the twenty-mile battle front in Flanders the enemy have "transferred the weight of their attacks from South to North. With "great forces they are fighting for possession of the hills South of "Ypres, which are flanked on the East by the Messines Ridge.

"In the last two days serious inroads have been made into our "lines here. After the fall of Neuve Eglise three fresh German divisions "were flung against our trenches on the hills before Bailleul. Our troops "were forced to retire and Bailleul and Wulverghem fell into the "enemy's possession.

"On this front the battle raged throughout yesterday, and brought "fresh gains to the enemy. Already holding the Southern part of the "Messines Ridge, German troops advanced under cover of mist in the "morning, took most of the Northern half of the ridge, including "the Village of Wytschaete. On the other flank of the Northern "attack the enemy gained a footing in Meteren, where fighting continued "last night."

EXTRACT FROM "THE TIMES," 18TH APRIL.

"French troops are now taking part in the great battles on the "low hills to the South of Ypres. Fighting here yesterday was of great "intensity, and the battle line swayed considerably. At the close of "the day there was little change in the territorial positions of the "two armies.

"Our positions on Tuesday night had been considerably improved, for we "had retaken Meteren and Wytschaete and had smashed up, with heavy "losses, a German massed attack North of Bailleul. We were, however, "compelled to give up the two villages in face of continued attacks.

"The German front of attack was extended yesterday morning from "the Forest of Nieppe to Wytschaete, but at the close of the day every "onslaught had been repulsed.

"In consequence of the enemy's progress on the Lys front our troops "East of Ypres have been withdrawn to a new line. The withdrawal "was carried out without interference from the Germans. The British "reports have not yet defined the new line, but those from German "Headquarters speak of the occupation of Passchendaele, Becclaere, "Gheleuvelt, Poelcappelle, and Langemarck.

"Between Arras and Albert the parties of Germans who entered our "trenches opposite Boyelles on Tuesday have been driven out. Hostile "artillery fire has increased South of the Somme."

METEREN.

EXTRACT FROM " THE TIMES," 18TH APRIL.

" GERMAN CLAIMS."

" On the blood-soaked battlefields of last year's Flanders battle, the
" Army of General Sixt von Arnim has occupied Passchendaele and advanced
" its lines near Becelaere and Gheluvelt.

" North of the Lys, during the early morning hours, the troops under
" General Sieger stormed the Village of Wytschaete, drove the enemy from
" the heights North-east and West of the Village, in spite of vigorous
" counter-measures, and repulsed strong counter-attacks. The enemy who
" was retreating to the South-west of Wulverghem to rear lines, was pressed
" back by us across the Douve Brook.

" Bailleul and the stubbornly defended point of support of Cappelynde,
" to the North of Bailleul, and Meteren, were captured.

" By the use of strong forces, the English supported by the French
" vainly endeavoured to recapture Meteren and the lost territory on both
" sides of Merris. Their attacks broke down with the heaviest of losses.

" On the battlefield on both sides of the Somme vigorous fighting duels
" developed which during the night continued to the South of the Somme.

" EVENING.—On the battlefield of last year's Flanders battle Poel-
" cappelle and Langemarck have been taken.—Admiralty, per Wireless
" Press."

EXTRACT FROM " THE TIMES," 19TH APRIL.

" Again the enemy has sacrificed many men in vain attacks on Givenchy
" and on the Southern front of the new Allied line covering Bethune and
" Lillers. These attacks were made yesterday on a front of eleven miles,
" and were particularly severe near Givenchy, where the enemy made deter-
" mined efforts to retrieve his previous failures against the 51st Division.
" At nightfall the Germans had not given up their attempts. In addition
" to their heavy casualties, they had lost over two hundred prisoners.

" New German attacks also developed during the day South of Kemmel,
" and were repulsed.

" More detailed accounts of the fighting on Wednesday from Nieppe
" Forest to Wytschaette establish the severity of the enemy's losses. The
" fighting South-east of Kemmel Hill, where the enemy came on in three
" waves, and in the Bailleul Sector was especially heavy.

" Current German official reports of the Northern fighting contain
" little beyond accounts of the occupation of ground in the Ypres Salient,
" from which British troops have been withdrawn. Our correspondent at
" the British front says that so far the results of our retirement are that
" while we had immunity from casualties we treated the enemy very
" roughly."

THE THIRTY-THIRD DIVISION.

EXTRACT FROM A LETTER FROM LE GENERAL VALENTIN,
COMMANDANT LA 133RD DIVISION D'INF.

To GENERAL PINNEY, Commanding 33rd Division.

" MON GENERAL,

" A mon grand regret des ordres recents m'enlevent le grand
" honneur et le plaisir de combattre en liaison avec vous et avec vos
" braves troupes. Mais le regret est attendue par la cooperation de vos
" guerriers et des miens qui existe depuis deux jours devant Meteren,
" cooperation qui ma permis d'apprécier la bravoure et la tenacité de
" vos belles troupes.

" Veuillez mon Général croire à mon amitiè et à mon dévouement.

" (Signed) GENERAL VALENTIN, C.B.,
Commanding 133rd Divn. Frn."

On the night of the 18th–19th April, the Division was withdrawn into
an area around the Benedictine Monastery of Mont des Cats ; and was
relieved by the 1st Australian Division.

OPERATIONS CARRIED OUT BY THE 100TH INFANTRY BRIGADE AT NEUVE EGLISE.

Under orders of the 25th Division, at dusk on the 11th, the Brigade
took over part of " the Army Line " from Le Romarin to the East of Neuve
Eglise, with the 16th King's Royal Rifle Corps on the right and the 2nd
Worcestershires on the left, with the Glasgow Highlanders in reserve. Le
Romarin was already occupied by the enemy, but touch was gained with the
75th Infantry Brigade on the left.

At 3 p.m. on April 12th, the Army Line was subjected to very heavy
shelling, and the troops on the right of the 100th Brigade fell back, the
enemy following in pursuit and making a considerable gap on the right of
the 16th King's Royal Rifle Corps. This gap was filled by the Brigade
" Minimum Reserve."

At dawn on the 13th it was apparent that the situation on the right of
the Rifles was again most unsatisfactory, and one Company of the 9th Highland
Light Infantry was sent forward to try and gain touch with the 88th Infantry
Brigade ; whilst on the right the remains of the 75th Infantry Brigade were
at the same time extending to their left in order to gain touch. By 8 a.m.
the 25th Division had foreshadowed a general withdrawal in order to shorten
the line ; and, at the same time, information was obtained from prisoners
that the enemy would renew his onslaught upon Neuve Eglise from the
South. The 2nd Worcestershires were still holding their line intact and
were in touch on their left but not on their right. No news could be
obtained of the 16th King's Royal Rifle Corps who were forced back round
their Battalion Headquarters, where, for several hours, they put up a stubborn

fight, assisted by gun teams of " B " Company of the Machine Gun Battalion, who fought to the last man, everyone of the gun numbers being killed. The 2nd Worcestershires now discovered that the enemy had penetrated into the Neuve Eglise in rear of them in considerable numbers. He was immediately counter-attacked by the Glasgow Highlanders and driven out of the village. Fighting at close quarters of the heaviest nature followed in the village of Neuve Eglise. By the afternoon it was plain that the line of the 16th King's Royal Rifle Corps had been turned by the attack in the morning and had been taken in rear, most of the Battalion becoming casualties or being taken prisoners ; whilst the Commander, Lieutenant-Colonel A. V. Johnson, was severely wounded. By 4.30 p.m. the enemy had cleared out of Neuve Eglise, mainly owing to the counter-attacks of the Glasgow Highlanders and the Worcestershires. The Highlanders were then ordered to throw back their right and cover all approaches to Neuve Eglise, from South and South-east. Before, however, this movement could be carried out, the enemy made a further determined attack and succeeded again in entering Neuve Eglise. At the same time a strong attack, pushing North from the direction of Kortepyp, succeeded in driving a wedge between the Glasgow Highlanders and the 2nd Worcestershires, whose Headquarters were now established in the Marie, which they had put into a state of defence ; and from which, a very active defence was maintained until 2 p.m. the following day, in the course of which, heavy casualties were inflicted upon the enemy by machine gun, Lewis gun and rifle fire. Whilst the right flank of the 2nd Worcestershires was gradually being forced back, one of our machine guns opened heavy fire and succeeded in pinning the enemy, for a time, to the ground.

For a time only ; for it was discovered the left flank was being forced back, the solitary machine gun being the pivot on which two big backward movements were swinging.

The gun was swung through its traverse and deliberately exposed its rear in order to stem the tide on its left.

By 12 noon the 2nd Worcestershires, with one section of the Machine Gun Battalion, were entirely cut off, maintaining a stout all-round defence at the Marie and at the church of Neuve Eglise. This determined defence under Lieutenant-Colonel G. J. L. Stoney of the 2nd Worcestershires was a military achievement of the highest order. That day saw some of the bitterest hand-to-hand fighting ever known to British soldiers. It is impossible to describe how our men fought every inch of their retreat, pressed back by continual fresh forces and overwhelming numbers. Many gallant sorties were made by the Worcestershires, led by Second-Lieutenant J. Crowe, the Assistant Adjutant, who was awarded the V.C. for his conduct. The defence of Neuve Eglise by the Worcestershires will rank in history with those of Lucknow and of Rorkes Drift.

Riflemen and machine gunners repeatedly stemmed rushes of the enemy up the streets leading to the Square, and across its wide space poured their withering fire with murderous effect. A Lewis gun was mounted in the Mairie window and fired into the backs of the enemy as they attempted to force an entrance into the Church, stoutly defended by Lieutenant-Colonel G. J. L. Stoney, assisted by the Chaplain, the Reverend E. V. Tanner. When the enemy attempted to rush the Mairie and bomb the occupants out of it, a corporal, with rifle in hand, shot the arms of the bombers, exploding their bombs, from round the corner of the doorway; whilst his gun teams fired rifle grenades at point blank range over the wall of the Mairie garden. At 2 p.m. the 2nd Worcestershires succeeded in withdrawing from the village of Neuve Eglise, the Square of which was literally piled high with German dead. At 4 o'clock on the 14th, the 49th Division relieved the 25th Division of command of the area in which the 100th Brigade had been withdrawn from action, and were preparing a defensive position to cover Hill 70.

At dusk on this day, the Ravelsberg position was heavily bombarded, and this continued until 3 o'clock next day, when our troops began to retire from the ridge. At 7 p.m. a Composite Battalion, formed of 150 rifles 16th King's Royal Rifle Corps and 150 rifles 9th Highland Light Infantry under Major Lamberton of the latter Regiment, took up position at Keerse Boom, and the Brigade was now in touch, on the right with Brigadier-General L. J. Wyatt, "Wyatt's Force," which was on the left of the 98th Brigade; and on the left with the 103rd Infantry Brigade. Up to this point in the battle there is still much obscurity concerning the action of the various Battalions; largely owing to the fact that the Brigade on both flanks of General Baird's Brigade gave way, so that the fighting, both of Infantry and machine guns, assumed a character of desperate hand-to-hand struggles.

On the morning of the 16th a very strong attack was delivered upon the town of Bailleul. The situation was desperate, largely owing to the fact that our troops had been fighting since the morning of the 12th with little or no artillery support. On his own initiative, therefore, General Baird sent an urgent message to the 59th Regiment of French Artillery, who had just arrived at their concentration position. The French acted promptly, and were ably assisted by Captain J. W. Collins of the 9th Highland Light Infantry acting as Liaison Officer. Within a quarter of an hour thirty-eight French Field Guns were firing over the Brigade, causing heavy losses to the enemy. Undoubtedly, this action of General Baird's at this point saved the British Line from being broken. During the afternoon of this day very heavy attacks were made by the enemy, which were repulsed by machine guns, rifle and artillery fire.

During the evening two posts garrisoned by the Brigade on the right were lost, but were recovered by immediate counter-attack by the 9th Northumberland Fusiliers of 103rd Brigade. At 8.20 a.m. two prisoners captured by the 9th Highland Light Infantry reported that an attack was to be delivered immediately. The 9th Highland Light Infantry, who had suffered heavily from the bombardment, were reinforced by one Company of the 6th/7th Royal Scots Fusiliers, of the 177th Infantry Brigade, but despite our counter-attacks, the enemy succeeded in forcing a gap in our line. By 6.30 p.m. the line had again been adjusted and the enemy firmly held, whilst reinforcements, both French and British, were pouring into the line. At 2 p.m. on the 18th April, the Brigade had been relieved from the Line, having suffered in casualties 68 Officers and 1,424 other ranks.

Both the 2nd Battalion Worcestershires and the 33rd Battalion Machine Gun Corps were selected for honours by being mentioned in the Corps Special Order of the operations, as under :—

11th July, 1918.

IXth Corps Special Order No. 3.

The following " Record " is to be made of the action described below.

2nd Battalion The Worcestershire Regiment.
Neuve Eglise, 11–14th April, 1918.

On the evening of the 11th April, the 2nd Battalion the Worcestershire Regiment took over a section of the line to the East of Neuve Eglise. The night was spent in strengthening and concealing the defences of the position. The following morning two strong patrols, in charge of Lieutenants Niclin and Parry, were pushed far out, and quickly came into touch with superior enemy forces, which they fought to a standstill, inflicting heavy losses. They were withdrawn later, but not until the enemy had been obliged considerably to strengthen his patrols and to postpone his impending attack.

During the day, enemy activity greatly increased, and the battalion patrols were constantly engaged in stopping small parties who were endeavouring to work their way into the lines. At 7.30 in the evening after heavy artillery and machine gun preparation, the enemy developed an attack to both right and left of the line held, breaking through to the right. He was ejected and the position restored. Early on the morning of the 13th he again attacked to the right, reached Neuve Eglise village, and thus took the battalion line in the rear. An immediate counter-attack not only turned the enemy out of the village, but led to the annihilation of the force which had gained a footing there, and to the destruction of its machine guns.

At 6 p.m. the enemy attacked in great strength on the left, and the whole battalion withdrew fighting to a new position. The Mairie was organized as a strong point ; the garrison effectively dealt with enemy parties which had crept up to the main cross roads on the right.

During the night, attack after attack was launched against the Battalion, and eventually touch was lost with the Companies holding the left. They were last heard of holding on against overwhelming odds, fighting it out to the last.

Meanwhile, the enemy had crept nearer and nearer to the Mairie, which was held by Battalion Headquarters. At dawn on the 14th he was seen to be occupying Neuve Eglise in strength, and soon after, the Mairie was completely surounded. Second-Lieutenant Johnson at once volunteered to try and work his way through to the Brigade and report the situation. His gallant attempt was unsuccessful, and he did not return.

Clever manœuvring and well directed fire forced the enemy to relinquish his hold, and to retire to the high ground on the right, and to the church on the left. Second-Lieutenant Crowe, with a small party, worked round the flank of the former position, and surprising the enemy, forced him further up the rise. The success of this feint was completed by a very daring sortie led by the same officer and Second-Lieutenant Pointon, and supported by accurate fire from the Mairie, which compelled the Germans to withdraw to the centre of the village.

Early in the afternoon the enemy was observed to be preparing for a violent attack upon the Mairie. A withdrawal was decided upon, and in spite of heavy fire, carried out without loss, to the railway, where British troops had already taken up their positions.

By their well-planned and spirited defence under very difficult conditions, the Battalion kept the enemy at bay for three days, without rest, and in the face of greatly superior numbers. Fine patrol work delayed and harassed the preparation of attacks, rapidity of counter-attacks, coupled with skilful disposition of forces in response to every enemy move, obliged him time after time to relinquish his gains— tenacity when all seemed hopeless opened a way to safety ; while the daring and gallantry of individual officers and men did much to prevent the effective use of the larger forces at the enemy's disposal, and exacted a heavy price for every yard of ground gained.

R. L. MONTGOMERY,
(for) *Brigadier-General,*
General Staff, IXth Corps.

IXTH CORPS SPECIAL ORDER No. 2.

The following " Record " is made of the action described below.

33RD BATTALION MACHINE GUN CORPS.

12TH–19TH APRIL, 1918.

On the night of the 11th–12th April, the enemy had captured both Merville and Estaires, some seven miles South of Meteren, but the situation was somewhat obscure, and machine guns, in conjunction with the 19th Infantry Brigade, took up an outpost line covering the approaches East and South of Meteren. By 10.30 a.m. on the 12th April, the enemy had advanced very rapidly, both from the East and from the South, and had it not been for the excellent use made of an abandoned motor lorry which quickly brought up eight more guns and teams, Meteren would have undoubtedly fallen into the enemy's hands. By skilful handling of his machine guns Lieutenant-Colonel Hutchison was able to hold off the enemy and fill up all gaps that occurred in our line, so that by nightfall on the 12th April, the line, though thinly held, was continuous. On the 13th a heavy hostile attack was successfully dealt with, during which the enemy must have suffered enormous losses. In one instance, 200 horsemen were decimated by the fire of one section under Second-Lieutenant Watts. In spite of the hard fighting of the two previous days, night harassing fire was maintained during the night of 13th–14th. The 14th was probably the most critical day of these operations. At dawn the enemy launched heavy attacks against our positions and our line was penetrated in many places. The enemy exploited these gains to full advantage by pushing forward his light machine guns. On this occasion, very valuable service was rendered by Major W. C. Andrew, Second-in-Command, who handled his machine guns very skilfully, and by filling gaps and forming defensive flanks, prevented the enemy from penetrating our line to any depth. The maintenance of our line was undoubtedly due to the splendid devotion to duty and initiative displayed by the Machine Gunners, whose losses were very severe. This line was held by machine guns in face of great odds until ordered to withdraw on the evening of the 14th instant, this withdrawal being carried out in the most creditable manner, without further loss, either to personnel or material, showing the excellent state of training and efficiency within the Battalion.

On the 16th April, the enemy again made a determined attack after heavy bombardment against our positions South-east of Meteren, during which the Machine Gunners did great execution. It was during this attack that the enemy gained a footing in Meteren, where he was held, and the line handed over in this position on the night of the 18th–19th April.

Throughout the operations the action of the 33rd Battalion Machine Gun Corps very materially assisted in preventing the enemy from capturing the Meteren position and exploiting the gains made by him during the first day's fighting.

(Signed) W. MAXWELL SCOTT, *Brigadier-General,*
General Staff, IXth Corps.

In conclusion, there is no doubt whatever that had not the 33rd Division been present in Meteren early on the morning of the 12th, and actively alert with its reconnaissances and outposts, the gap which existed on a three mile front, roughly between Bailleul and Merris, would have been penetrated; and that the enemy, who showed such an extraordinary rapid advance and activity, would probably have seized Mont des Cats by the evening of the 12th. Had he done so there is no doubt that our whole position at Ypres would have been imperilled, whilst from this point of vantage and observation he might conceivably have successfully driven through to the Channel Ports.

During these operations the total casualties of the Division, less artillery, were 181 Officers and 3,760 other ranks, but with this heavy list it is not a high estimate to say that the losses to the Germans must have been at the least five times this number, probably far more. As attacks were made again and again with fresh troops upon our position, which we held always by the same unbroken posts, and as a result of which we inflicted heavy loss upon the enemy on each occasion, whilst we ourselves only suffered in comparison slight loss. It would be impossible to record all the acts of gallantry carried out in this most bitter fighting. Probably most of them will never be known.

Amongst Officers the following casualties occurred :—

ROYAL ARTILLERY.

Killed.	*Wounded.*	*Missing.*
Lieut. W. G. Bruce.	Major A. Barker.	2nd Lieut. K. R. Blackwell.
	2nd Lieut. T. G. Craig.	2nd Lieut. O. C. Clow.
	2nd Lieut. L. E. S. Groves.	
	2nd Lieut. W. H. Orchard.	
	2nd Lieut. H. E. Phil.	

ROYAL ENGINEERS.

Killed.	*Wounded.*
Lieut. T. E. Appleyard, M.C.	2nd Lieut. C. E. Drakes.
	2nd Lieut. W. G. Feary.
	Lieut. L. H. Harper.
	Lieut. A. A. Summers.
	Major G. B. P. Thompson, M.C.

19TH BRIGADE.

1ST QUEEN'S (ROYAL WEST SURREY) REGIMENT.

Killed.	*Wounded.*	*Missing.*
Lieut. J. A. Dickinson.	Capt. A. M. Allan.	Lieut. T. Crompton.
2nd Lieut. C. W. Elliot.	2nd Lieut. R. J. Brookes.	
	Capt. H. J. Carpenter.	
	2nd Lieut. H. B. Denny.	
	2nd Lieut. H. F. D. Faulkner.	
	2nd Lieut E. de W. Gre.	
	Lieut. I. T. P. Hughes.	
	2nd Lieut. W. J. C. Morgan.	
	2nd Lieut. L. D. Parker, M.C.	
	2nd Lieut. G. F. Prynor.	
	2nd Lieut. F. Russell.	
	2nd Lieut. H. G. Sweet.	

METEREN AND NEUVE EGLISE.

1st CAMERONIANS (SCOTTISH RIFLES).

Killed.

2nd Lieut. H. W. Cole.

Wounded.

2nd Lieut. W. M. Anderson.
Lieut. A. W. Butler.
Lieut. R. K. L. Craig.
2nd Lieut. R. Herbert.
2nd Lieut. T. C. Nicol.
Capt. J. J. Smith, M.C.
2nd Lieut. C. S. Spence.

Missing.

Lieut. T. G. Bruce.
2nd Lieut. L. Gunner.

5/6TH SCOTTISH RIFLES.

Killed.

Lieut. T. S. L. Loudon.
2nd Lieut. A. D. C. Pryce.
Lieut. T. O. Thorburn.

Wounded.

2nd Lieut. D. M. Ford.
2nd Lieut. D. McGregor.
Lieut. R. Wilson.
2nd Lieut. G. H. Young.

Missing.

2nd Lieut. C. G. Cheyne.

19TH TRENCH MORTAR BATTERY.

Wounded.

Lieut. W. C. Walker.

95TH BRIGADE.

4TH KING'S LIVERPOOL REGIMENT.

Killed.

2nd Lieut. G. C. Gibb.
2nd Lieut. F. Mackinson.
Capt. G. H. E. Warburton, M.C.
2nd Lieut. W. Williams.

Wounded.

2nd Lieut. H. R. Anderson.
2nd Lieut. E. Capstick.
2nd Lieut. F. H. Dawson.
2nd Lieut. W. M. Helmes.
2nd Lieut. W. H. Jones.

Missing.

2nd Lieut. A Birkumshaw.
2nd Lieut. L. Collins.
2nd Lieut. C. R. Fraser.
Lieut. H. T. Kendall.
2nd Lieut. J. F. Marrion.
2nd Lieut. C. Newman.
Lieut. D. H. Pack, M.C.
2nd Lieut. T. Spencer.
2nd Lieut. S. Thompson.
2nd Lieut. A. D. Ward, M.C.
2nd Lieut. F. Wheeler.

1ST MIDDLESEX REGIMENT.

Killed.

2nd Lieut. T. Adams.

Wounded.

2nd Lieut. G. W. Battley.
2nd Lieut. A. G. Beaumont.
2nd Lieut. T. D. Clarke.
Lieut. T. Ferguson.
2nd Lieut. H. V. Flowers.
2nd Lieut. W. W. Lodge.
2nd Lieut. D. W. Rowntree.
2nd Lieut. W. W. L. White.

THE THIRTY-THIRD DIVISION.

2ND ARGYLL AND SUTHERLAND HIGHLANDERS.
Wounded.
Lieut. T. E. Cadett.
2nd Lieut. T. H. Carmichael.
2nd Lieut. A. Wood.

100TH BRIGADE.

2ND WORCESTERSHIRE REGIMENT.

Killed.	Wounded.	Missing.
2nd Lieut. C. D. Bishop.	2nd Lieut. A. S. Abrahall.	Major E. J. Donaldson.
2nd Lieut. H. B. Green.	Capt. R. F. Barker, M.C.	Capt. F. J. Gunston.
Lieut. F. G. Hemming, M.C.	2nd Lieut. R. J. Burton.	2nd Lieut. A. Johnson.
2nd Lieut. H. T. Hicklin.	Lieut. C. S. Jagger.	Capt. C. W. V. Peake.
Lieut. W. H. Smyth.	2nd Lieut. W. Loynes.	2nd Lieut. H. O. Tredwell, M.C.
	Capt. T. F. V. Matthews, M.C.	
	2nd Lieut. F. Nickless.	
	2nd Lieut. F. G. Parry.	
	2nd Lieut. A. Rudd.	
	Capt. W. L. Smith.	
	Rev. E. V. Tanner, M.C.	
	2nd Lieut. T. Turley.	
	2nd Lieut. V. R. Vernon.	

16TH KING'S ROYAL RIFLE CORPS.

Killed.	Wounded.	Missing.
2nd Lieut. R. H. M. Lea.	Lieut. G. D. Brough.	Capt. M. K. Balshaw.
	2nd Lieut. L. W. Cheetham.	2nd Lieut. H. W. H. Considine.
	2nd Lieut. H. A. Cram.	2nd Lieut. R. W. Edwards.
	2nd Lieut. T. Gray.	Capt. L. E. Francis.
	Lieut.-Col. A. V. Johnson, D.S.O.	2nd Lieut. T. J. Goldsack.
	Capt. S. S. Scott.	2nd Lieut. B. Hodges.
	Lieut. C. H. Wilkins.	2nd Lieut. F. B. Holborow.
		Lieut. T. Honey, M.C.
		Lieut. C. Howard.
		2nd Lieut. W. H. McLean.
		2nd Lieut. T. E. Ritchie.
		Lieut. E. L. Sergeant.
		Lieut. W. Staggers.
		2nd Lieut. W. Sullivan.
		2nd Lieut. W. A. Talbot.

METEREN AND NEUVE EGLISE.

1/9TH HIGHLAND LIGHT INFANTRY.

Killed.
2nd Lieut. W. M. Beattie.
Major J. S. Chalmers.
Capt. F. J. Harris.
2nd Lieut. J. Nairne
2nd Lieut. W. Ross.

Wounded.
Lieut. W. F. Alexander.
2nd Lieut. T. Bennett.
2nd Lieut. J. W. Hendry.
2nd Lieut. J. Johnson.
Lieut. A. R. Lamberton.
2nd Lieut. T. Livingstone.
Capt. A. M. Mackay.
2nd Lieut. W. B. Metcalfe.
Lieut. P. A. Moodie.
Capt. R. C. Reid.
Lieut. G. F. Syme.
Capt. G. H. Warren.

Missing.
2nd Lieut. A. G. M. Walt.

100TH TRENCH MORTAR BATTERY.

Wounded.
Lieut. R. J. Macdonald.

18TH BATTALION MIDDLESEX REGIMENT.

Killed.
2nd Lieut. H. P. Boreham.
2nd Lieut. H. C. Bradbury.

Wounded.
Lieut. W. E. Dawson.
2nd Lieut. J. W. Goodwin.
2nd Lieut. T. F. Mawson.
2nd Lieut. T. D. Patterson.

33RD BATTALION MACHINE GUN CORPS.

Killed.
2nd Lieut. P. Barker.
Lieut. A. Heath.
Lieut. C. S. Hedgeland.
2nd Lieut. R. Nichol.

Wounded.
2nd Lieut. R. H. Goode.
Capt. H. Harrison, M.C.
Lieut.-Col. G. S. Hutchison, M.C
Major H. Judson.
2nd Lieut. T. S. Keith.
2nd Lieut. J. Mc P. Mackenzie.
2nd Lieut. C. L. Marshal.
2nd Lieut. F. Paley.

THE THIRTY-THIRD DIVISION.

ROYAL ARMY MEDICAL CORPS.

Killed.

Lieut. J. D. Arnett.
Capt. D. Mackinnon.

Wounded.

Lieut. E. P. M. Gough.
Major J. B. Lowe.
Capt. T. W. Malcolm.

DIVISIONAL HEADQUARTERS.

Killed.

Lieut. H. M. Brown, M.C.

The Machine Gun Battalion alone was awarded amongst its Officers one D.S.O. and five Military Crosses as immediate rewards; whilst among the rank and file fourteen D.C.M.'s and thirty-two Military Medals were similarly awarded. The 2nd Battalion Worcestershire Regiment was awarded one V.C., one D.S.O. and six Military Crosses amongst the Officers; and six D.C.M.'s and twenty-nine Military Medals amongst the rank and file. The total awards made to the Division for the operations between 12th–19th April, were—One V.C., two bars to D.S.O., four D.S.O.'s, two bars to M.C., forty M.C.'s, forty-two D.C.M.'s, twenty bars to Military Medal and 287 Military Medals.

The following telegram was received by the Division from the Commander-in-Chief (Sir Douglas Haig) :—

" I wish to take this opportunity to express to General Pinney, and
" to the Officers and Men of the 33rd Division. my thanks for the
" splendid fight made by troops of their Division at Neuve Eglise on
" 14th April and also for the gallant action performed by them South
" of Meteren in the earliest days of the Lys Battle when the enemy was
" still pressing his advance strongly in that direction. The determined
" resistance offered by the 33rd Division at that stage of the fight was
" of the utmost value."

30/4/18.

The following message was received :—

" To G.O.C. 33rd Division

" Wish to record my very grateful appreciation of the services of
" your 100th Brigade whilst under my command. Brigadier-General
" Baird by his ever-ready initiative and untiring energy has very
" materially assisted me in holding my line. His men were splendid
" under very strenuous circumstances. Please thank them all."

From G.O.C. 49th Division.

19th April 1918. 11.15 a.m.

CHAPTER VI.

DICKEBUSCH.

20TH APRIL, 1918, TO 1ST AUGUST, 1918.

Inspection by President Clemenceau—Actions at Dickebusch and Ridge Wood by 19th and 98th Brigades—Gallantry of the 5th Scottish Rifles—The German Offensive breaks down—Its causes—The American Invasion—The Royal Artillery.

On April 20th, the Division was relieved from the Battle of Merville after ten days incessant fighting, the area having been handed over to the 1st Australian Division and the 34th French Division. It was concentrated in the villages of Noordepeene and Saint Marie Capel, three miles West of the mount of Cassel. On the 21st, Monsieur Clemenceau, a benevolent-looking old gentleman, clad in a soft felt hat perched anyhow on his head, a long swallow-tailed Cheviot coat with great poacher pockets, baggy knee-breeches, brown and badly fitting gaiters over his black boots, a stick, and a very pleasant air, arrived, and inspected the Division. The " Tiger," as the French call him, belies his name, and is, perhaps, the more dangerous to his foes in consequence.

EXTRACT FROM " THE TIMES," OF MONDAY, APRIL 22ND, 1918.

" Of the comradeship between the two Armies nothing too much can
" be said, and a fine symbol of it was seen this morning when Monsieur
" Clemenceau, at a point not far behind the front line, reviewed the
" battle-worn men of a British Division who have borne a noble part in
" the recent fighting. Monsieur Clemenceau was visibly moved by what
" he saw and what was told him of the men's achievements, and the
" enthusiasm with which the British soldiers cheered the French Prime
" Minister, their voices hoarse with the strain of battle, was extremely
" impressive."

Between the 25th of April and 4th of May, desperate fighting between the French and the enemy took place for the possession of Montnoir, the Scharpenburg and Kemmel Hill. On the 1st of May the Division was hurried from the Cassel area to Abeele. The roads were crowded with French, and the whole area a seething mass of troops and refugees, who struggled along the roads carrying beds, mattresses, fowls, children and furniture indiscriminately on their persons, or perched upon the crazy carts which every family seemed to possess. To the East the villages and farms were wreathed in flames and smoke. To the West lay nothing but rank upon rank of British, French and American troops, who filled every village and every barn.

Before these miserable homeless refugees could obtain rest, they were forced to proceed at least one hundred kilometres behind the firing line. In those days many a British soldier went without his rations, and many a British horse was overloaded in the united effort to keep the hearts of France and Belgium from breaking.

The Divisional Artillery had meanwhile remained in the line, and after its tour of duty with the 49th Division the following message was received :—

"Please let me express to you my very warm thanks for the gallant "and efficient support given by your 156th and 162nd Royal Artillery "Brigades during their respective periods of co-operation with the 49th "(West Riding) Division in the Kemmell-Vierstraat Sector between "25th April and 5th May with special reference to the services of the "162nd Royal Field Artillery Brigade on 29th April when the enemy "attacked in strength and was repulsed.

"The Infantry are unanimous in their praise of the field artillery "barrage that day.

"The Brigadier-General Commanding 147th Infantry Brigade speaks "very warmly of the willing help given him by the 162nd Royal Field "Artillery Brigade during the period."

T. G. CAMERON,
Major-General,
Commanding 49th (W.R.) Division.
5th May, 1918.

On the 6th of May, the 33rd Division took over from the 14th Chasseurs Division East of Dickebusch Lake, the line running through Ridge Wood and Scottish Wood. Before the Division took over, the enemy, goaded on by the insatiable victory-lust of his commanders, had already captured Kemmel Hill from the French and was attempting, uselessly, to outflank our position in Ridge Wood at La Clytte. Immediately on the right of our Division was General Corvisat's 16th Corps. During this period a very heavy mist had shrouded the top of Kemmel Hill. It was this mist which helped to save the situation ; for it entirely prevented the enemy from observing the transformation of the hutments and camps of the Ypres Salient into a strongly defended line.

For more than a week the rain fell in torrents, filling the streams to such an extent that many of the guns and ammunition dumps were under water.

On the 8th of May, at 3.30 a.m., a very heavy enemy bombardment began, particularly with high explosive and gas. At 5.30 a.m. the 98th

Brigade captured some prisoners who stated it was the intention of the enemy to attack at 7.30 a.m. that morning. At the same time, General Daydrein's 32nd Division counter-attacked on our right. The French did not, apparently, get very far, and the Boche, in a further counter-attack, succeeded in effecting a lodgment behind the French left and our right, where lay the 30th Composite Brigade. At 10 a.m. the 19th Brigade reached the Vlamartinghe line to restore the situation. At the same time, the right of the Argyll and Sutherland Highlanders, under Major Colquhoun, which Regiment had fought with the greatest heroism, undergoing a gas bombardment for many hours, were driven back from Ridge Wood into the Western side of Scottish Wood, whilst the enemy succeeded in driving a wedge between the Cameronians and the former Regiment. On the right of the Cameronians, in the 30th Composite Brigade, only a few remaining men of the 2nd Bedfordshire Regiment, who had been continually in action for many days, held out. The remainder of the Brigade was thrown back and intermixed with the Cameronians, whose commanding Officer, Lieutenant-Colonel Draffin was captured. Into this breach the Argyll and Sutherland Highlanders were rushed forward with a section of the Machine Gun Corps, and not only inflicted heavy casualties on the enemy but effectively checked his advance. The Cameronians, in particular, had suffered very heavy casualties—for a time their whereabouts was a complete mystery—as had also the French on the right of the 33rd Division. A second enemy attack was delivered about 2 p.m. but broke down before our lines. The French wished to make a counter-attack at 4 p.m. but postponed this so as to join hands with us in our counter-attack at 7 p.m. Whilst the second German attack was developing, the Divisional Commander had already decided to make an immediate counter-attack and recapture Ridge Wood and restore the line, not only between the Argyll and Sutherland Highlanders and the Cameronians, but between the right of his Division and the left of the French. The 5th Scottish Rifles were moved from the extreme right of the Divisional front round the back of Dickebusch Lake, where they were well screened from observation by the trees surrounding the Lake. They were then most carefully deployed by Lieutenant-Colonel H. B. Spens, who launched a most energetic counter-attack, carried out with outstanding valour and enterprise, which rewon the whole of the ground lost.

Message from the 22nd Corps, 8th May, 1918 :—

> " The Corps Commander congratulates the 33rd Division and 30th
> " Composite Brigade on a very successful day. The stubborn defence
> " put up and successful counter-attack reflect the greatest credit on
> " all concerned."

For this Battle the following immediate rewards were made :—

One bar to D.S.O., four bars to Military Cross, thirteen Military Crosses, eleven D.C.M.'s, ten bars to Military Medal, and 110 Military Medals.

Whilst in this Sector, on the immediate left of the French, a very gallant fight was put up by the 98th Trench Mortar Battery, under Captain C. E. Paternoster, of whom the undermentioned were awarded the Croix de Guerre, as an immediate reward.

13708	Corpl. F. Smith	..	1st Middlesex Regiment.
8797	,, J. Rankin	..	2nd Argyll and Sutherland Highlanders.
9647	,, D. McCraig	..	,,
3404	Pte. J. Sinclair ..	..	,,
1744	,, J. Smith ..	..	1st Middlesex Regiment.
1338	,, W. McGreadie	..	2nd Argyll and Sutherland Highlanders.
275390	,, W. Tremble	..	,,
11013	,, R. Douglas..	..	,,
12308	,, C. Spencer ..	..	4th King's (Liverpool) Regiment.
5238	,, W. Morgan..	..	2nd Argyll and Sutherland Highlanders.

Each award was given for the following act, cited from the 46th (French) Divisional Order No. 63, 21st June, 1918, by General Levi.

" Pendant les deux rudes journées des 12 et 13 Juin, 1918, a " combattu avec un bataillon français, avec un entrain et une énergie " remarquable. Malgré les bombardements violents et l'artillerie ennemie " a tiré jusqu'à épuisement de ses munitions et a demandé ensuite à " combattre en Ière ligne à nos côtés, produisant par sa belle attitude " et la puissance de son feu le meilleur effet sur nos Chasseurs."

It was by now clear that the great German Offensive had been broken, its way being barred both on the road to Paris and on the road to the Calais Ports. But although the main force of the onslaught was broken, the German troops were still being flung into the attack in enormous numbers.

———————

By some it may be deemed a retrogression to look beyond the actual history of battles. It cannot, however, be out of place to trace those issues which led up to the point of battle. The plans of the strategist are determined by diplomacy, and where strategy ends, tactics begin. Thus statecraft, strategy and tactics carry equal weight, or nearly equal weight, in determining the results of battles. The silver thread of strategic and diplomatic purpose runs throughout a campaign, drawing in its train, not only Commanders-in-Chief, but all subordinate leaders. Statecraft and strategy go hand in hand : strategy and tactics are linked together. The firm grasp of political, strategical and tactical situations influences, in equal proportions, the success not only of a campaign but of each battle.

Therefore, in seeking those causes which influence success or failure in battle, we must probe to the bottom of the question : what directs the policy of the Commander-in-Chief ? : what influences the action of his subordinates ? : wherein lies the success or failure of their enterprise ? : and what factors stir men to desperate energy or to half-hearted and even cowardly action in battle ?—in a word, in what lies the secret of success, and in what of failure ? War, like a game of chess, is the conflict between the brains and perseverance of two Commanders, each trying to outwit the other. It is thus " pre-eminently the art of the man who dares take the " risk : of the man who thinks deeply and clearly : of the man who, when " accident intervenes, is not thereby cast down but changes his plans and " his dispositions with the readiness of a resolute and reflective mind, which, " so far as is possible, has foreseen and provided against mischance."

It is to be remembered that our Commanders were backed by the Governments for which they were directing the operations of war. If at any time there was any doubt upon this subject, and sometimes there may have been doubt, its direct result was a series of failures on the part of the troops to whom the Commanders issued their orders.

As we know, shortly after the close of 1917, the supreme command of the Allied Powers passed definitely, with the wish of Lord Haig, who so nobly and gracefully effaced himself, to Marshal Foch.

From March, 1918, we can immediately detect the change. And in August, our national army was being submitted to an unknown test which was made willingly and with deliberation, because, in the opinion of the national advisers, the time had come for striking sharp blows, which would allow the country to emerge from a doubtful position into one of complete independence. Not only Governments, but whole Nations, rich and poor alike, gave willingly and continuously of their manhood, their wealth, and their storehouses, for the common good. " The first amongst all causes of victory," says Clausewitz, " is to pursue a great object with energy and perseverance."

It is amazing that the German Nation, which had provided a military writer of the calibre of Clausewitz, whose teachings its militarists had accepted as classics, should have followed so blindly a Kaiser and his Generals, whose character was degenerate. That the Prussian Imperial Military Administration was rotten to the core, the terrible events of the campaign sufficiently showed. It is sufficient that we know that discord and revolution overtook a Nation whose State and Military leader in one, " The All-Highest," vaunted himself as greater than God himself ; whose influence, therefore, as we have shown, permeated throughout the ranks of the German national army and of the whole population. Those who believed that our defeat, at any time in the campaign, was possible, can only have been so blinded to our national virtues by their own individual vices that they thought they saw such a possibility. Those who held that our leaders were incapable, because of imagined mistakes, were themselves guilty of causing the death of more British soldiers than even the most callous and ignorant general in the Army ; for such is moral force that its possibilities for evil must always be, in the nature of man, greater than its qualities for good.

However brave men may be, Generals have no burning desire to throw away their lives, and it is surely a needless precaution to urge them not to do so. When, with due allowance for particular circumstances and difficulties, after full and fair trial, their deeds fail to justify their casualty lists, then it is time enough to call them unskilful, not because they have lost men but because they have lost them in vain.

Clausewitz says :—" Happy is the Army in which an untimely boldness manifests itself; it is an exuberant growth showing a rich soil. Even foolhardiness, that is, boldness without an object, is not to be despised." Probably Clausewitz ranks in the forefront of all writers on the art of war. In quoting Clausewitz we are quoting, therefore, the authority on whom, above all others, Moltke based his action and his teaching.

The military school of France had unquestionably studied him.

*On August 8th, 1918, Marshal Foch remarked concerning the second victory of the Marne :—" Terrible fighting that ! The Germans used up fifty-five divisions out of 180 or 190 divisions that day. Their reserves were exhausted. That had gone well. Then came the attack on the Amiens Sector on August 8th. That went well, too. The moment had arrived. I ordered General Humbert to attack in his turn. No reserves ! No matter. Allez–y ! I told Marshal Haig to attack too. He is short of men also. Attack all the same ! There we are advancing everywhere ! The whole line. En avant ! Hup ! I knew nothing could balk a victory once the Germans had accepted the final battle where they did. When the Germans came to me to ask for an armistice, I said ' I am going on to the Rhine. If you oppose me, so much the worse for you, but whether you sign an armistice or not, I do not stop till I reach the Rhine.' "

A quotation from Clausewitz is here to the point. " He who uses force unsparingly without regard to the quantity of bloodshed must obtain a superiority if his adversary does not act likewise." We will add—" If his adversary *cannot* act likewise." For it must be remembered that the Germans had already hurled their reserves into the fight, and consequently, and of greater importance, that his ranks were so torn with the spirit of revolution that his people were not prepared to make further sacrifices.

In the pomposity of Kaiserdom, and Military Imperialism, the German people had lost sight of the text upon which Clausewitz had preached. That text was *esprit de corps*. Napoleon knew it and used it. Marshal Foch had the united support of at least a dozen different nations. He embraced in himself all the great virtues of a Napoleon, a Wellington and a Moltke.

The Press of this country is to be congratulated not only in its forebearance upon subjects which were undoubtedly unmoral; but, with very few exceptions, for its wholehearted support of the Government and of those

* (Interview in Paris with Mr. WARD PRICE, April 16th, 1919.)

responsible for the conduct of operations. There was a time without doubt when our administration was so weak and vacillating, and so dangerous to the country, that the Press with a united front killed it in a fortnight and replaced it by a Government under a man whose statesmanship proved itself to be worth all the Nation's confidence.

There can be no doubt that we owe our victory to the qualities of energy, endurance and resolution, which all ranks, from General-in-Chief to Private, displayed in such a remarkable degree; and in which they were supported by the Government and the people of Great Britain, France, America and the Allies. It is in such qualities and in such support that the most certain road to victory lies. Without these qualities the best plan will fail; with them even the worst may succeed.

The much heralded entry of the Americans had begun to make itself a little more apparent by the arrival of a number of elderly gentlemen in the forward area accompanied by a large retinue of servants, in January, 1918. These we discovered afterwards were the American Generals. On one occasion our Divisional Commander met a group of American "Officers" sitting on their baggage in the Ypres square. He shook them warmly by the hand and found they were servants. It was no matter, they were equally welcome!

It is amazing to us that prior to the War the two greatest English speaking communities of Britain and America can have known each other so little, and that such a tiny "Duckpond" as is the Atlantic can have been so large a barrier between two primarily democratic Nations.

The jealousy and mistrust, at which it is no good blinking, which did exist between Great Britain and America, disappeared as rapidly as snow off a dyke, when our troops and those of America came in contact with each other in the field in the face of common danger. That the American troops were ignorant of military strategy they themselves would be the first to admit. They did admit it. Especially did they imagine that Staff work and Generalship were matters of business in the Commercial sense. Experience, however, very soon taught them that the successful business man is not necessarily equipped with all the qualifications necessary to lead an Army, or a Battalion, with success in the field. On the other hand, if he is willing to learn, his business training will be invaluable to him.

We had expected, also, that the soldier from the States would be an expert shot both with rifle and revolver, and a master of scoutcraft. This was by no means invariably so. We probably had formed this impression, not knowing the true American, from having seen the Native of the United States presented to us as an expert with the "Gun" in a Saloon bar on the "Movies"; and, as we knew the American Nation in no other way, we could only picture him as a gentleman in a wide-brimmed hat aiming sly shots at peaceful drinkers; rifling their pockets; disappearing into the fastnesses of the mountains of Arizona, and directing well-aimed rifle fire upon an army of policemen, whilst skilfully avoiding capture for many months; and eventually ending his dramatic career by marrying the daughter of the Sheriff! Undoubtedly these Americans do exist; and it was the good fortune of the 33rd Division to be in close touch with, and to fight alongside, the 30th American Division which was recruited from North and South Carolina and Tennessee, which States are supposed, so we are told, to contain the "Upper Ten" of the society to which we have alluded above. We believe, however, that this Division was unique in this respect.

Whilst the physique of the men from the mountains of Carolina was uniformly magnificent,—probably no finer specimens of the white race exist in the World than the "Tar Heels,"—the physique of those American Divisions drawn from the Cities, of which we saw a considerable amount, was indifferent. In fact, it may be generally said that the physique of the hillman of Carolina was of an average with that of our Highlanders, whilst the New Yorker averaged with the men of our Regiments drawn from the towns. After the ravages which had been wrought upon our manhood, particularly during the Somme, Arras and Ypres operations, we had expected to see an army far more virile than that of our own enter the field. It was not so. In age and maturity undoubtedly the Americans were better able, perhaps, to withstand the shock and horrors of war, but what our own troops lacked in this respect they certainly gained in experience and in boyish light-heartedness. It was not an uncommon sight to see a lad of nineteen or twenty summers, wearing one blue chevron upon his arm, surrounded by a keenly interested group of hoary old mountaineers from the heart of Texas. Between these hard-bitten men and our lads there soon sprung up an affection, in which there was no place for either mistrust or suspicion. The American Officers were enthusiastic. The American men were, if they came from the towns, exceedingly sharp and anxious to learn; if they came from the country, slow, but most anxious to get at the Boche with the bayonet.

These latter could in no way understand any reason for delay in carrying this out on a grand scale, and chafed at the weeks in which they had so rapidly to learn all that we had learned during the past three and a half years.

In many respects it was difficult for us to appreciate that the American Army was representative of a great Democracy. Certainly, when it arrived in the field such Institutions as Officers and Sergeants' Messes did not exist; but, on the other hand, saluting was even more perfunctorily carried out than in our own Army at that time. Whilst in our Army the Officer in most and best cases worked beside and with his men, and the Non-Commissioned Officer invariably so, in the American Army we were informed that it was not the custom for Sergeants to perform manual work beside the men under their Command. To us this was a most extraordinary custom in an Army

118

which had proclaimed that it was essentially democratic. Whilst it was undemocratic for a Battalion Commander to cook, let alone have cooked for him, his ration of pork and beans or to cut his bread with any knife other than that issued, it was quite democratic for him to stand and idly watch his men at work. This state of affairs, however, did not last long for we soon showed to our American brothers that we too had " figured " the problem of democracy, even if in our own insular fashion ; and whilst we culled fresh ideas and inventiveness from the mountains and prairies of the States, the " Tar Heels " gained daily in experience and in knowledge of our democracy,— founded upon Freedom, as was his own ; fashioned in the hills of India, on the burning plains of the Soudan, in the Kopjes of South Africa, or in the fastnesses of Canada and Australia ; and finally matured Imperially in the teeth of common danger, in the face of a common foe.

On the 15th of July, just two years after our first big plunge into real warfare, the Advance Guard of the 30th American Division arrived. Their advent had been announced loudly long before it came about. Rumour was at least a month ahead of them ; but when they did come it was a complete invasion. The roads, villages, such as they were, estaminets and pasture fields swarmed with men in the tightest trousers and smallest hats with which man throughout the ages has ever been fitted out. Upon their backs they carried an immense pantechnicon consisting of three blankets, a folding tent, revolver, rifle, knives, a teaset complete, half a dozen pairs of socks, shirts, underwear for winter and summer weather, masses of family photographs, and finally pictures of the Statue of Liberty and President Wilson, and ten packets of Chewing Gum. In order to lighten their equipment, or we may say with greater truth to be relieved of it, with extreme generosity many of our men not only assisted them to unburden these sky-scraping monstrosities of equipment, but relieved them of it in such a fashion that they would never again be required to carry anything but their arms and ammunition ; whilst our men then regaled themselves with Chewing Gum beneath a Californian tent !

The Plenipotentiaries arrived *en masse,* and struck one at first glance as a concourse of very grave men, probably suppressed within their extremely tight uniforms. There was much saluting, hand-shaking, and introductions, a diversion being made by the various Drum, Brass, and Pipe Bands in full war paint, which vigorously played the " Star Spangled Banner," or in the case of the pipes the nearest approach to it which could be invented by a nimble-brained Pipe Major. This latter consisted in jerkily playing the Cock of the North in rag-time with a sprinkling of air from the favourite American Melody.

The arrival of the Americans was admirably stage-managed by the Boche.

After several quiet nights heavy area shoots were put down on all approaches to the Sector. The roads forward from Ambulance Farm and Belgian Battery Corner were targets for continuous shelling.

THE THIRTY-THIRD DIVISION.

Remarkable amongst the Americans were some personalities. There was one Battalion Commander whose whimsical mannerisms and quaint humour endeared him to all ranks. Tours round the line with him were always full of interest. To all one had to say he gave a grave attention. He never lost the grim humour of the thing. The loud report at dead of night of a battery of ours would only provoke from him the caustic injunction, hardly audible " Give 'em HELL ! "

Very different was his Second-in-Command. He was as bulky and rubicund as his Commander was lean and pale, he expended so much energy in talking and laughing that he had none left for his legs (which, in any case, could never have carried his body). Accordingly, like Diogenes, he remained in his dug-out, and from its darknesses delivered oracular judgment on the War. He was a great politician. He claimed to know the price of every man's vote in North Carolina !

The real American as we had pictured him, did not arrive in our midst until a week or two later. We had decided that these quiet, thinking men of North Carolina were not at all the popular type of " Yankee." Some of them were even proud to claim English descent ! We wanted to justify our conception of the slack-jawed, keen-eyed man of quaint jargons and turns of speech that Mark Twain and others had introduced to us.

When Captain English arrived, we knew immediately that " the goods had been delivered." His first introduction was to unpeel before our eyes a cunningly twisted packet of chewing gum ; and on noticing our admiring gaze as he capaciously took it between his jaws, his hand produced sundry other packets which he proceeded to hand round. Then, while we all chewed, he narrated his complete philosophical scheme with reference to the Canal Sector and the American attachment. He had " cottoned on " to the whole thing within five minutes. He only wanted the practical experience ; he was here to learn ; we could do what we liked with him or his " mob " ; we were the right stuff ; he saw that clearly. His journey up to Smyth Farm was a series of quixotic experiences, such as had come to no other man living ; he had been blown up by a gas shell, and by a miracle had adjusted his box respirator before reaching the ground. He had seen all colours of Verey Lights in the sky, and had theories on the use of each one of them. He had floundered about in ditches and shell holes until he had completely lost direction, but with unique forethought he had measured the bearing from nowhere to Smyth Farm, and by his trusty compass (which had never failed him in all preceding campaigns) he had at last attained his objective ; despite a forty mile march that day, he was prepared to go round the Canal Sector this very night and learn what there was to learn.

And, to do him justice, he did learn it, and quickly, too. He seemed to jump into the idea of it at once. The technicalities of the science of war were to him matters of intense interest.

The rank and file were slow, even lethargic, but they had a most intense hate for the Hun and always expressed a keen desire to go over the top and at him. They took an almost childish interest in the effect of our shelling. One Sergeant, in particular, used to peer continuously over the parapet, at the same time remarking, "Say, Loo-tenant, she shure is hitting them some." This was the only remark he ever was known to pass.

Later, we heard of the doings of the 30th American Division in the fierce fighting for the Hindenburg Line, round Le Catelet and Beaurevoir. Their losses, one heard, were very heavy, but that they had achieved great things; and we pardoned ourselves for a faint glow of pride that we had been honoured with the instruction of those gallant and earnest men of North Carolina.

Whilst we learned both to respect and love our cousins from across the Atlantic, as we firmly believe that they did us, we are proud to remember that we "delivered the goods." In this respect an extract from a letter written by an American Commanding Officer to a Battalion Commander of the 33rd Division, speaks for itself.

"It appears, to our great sorrow, that our Battalion is about to be "relieved from duty with your troops, and I trust that you will permit "me to attempt to express to you and your most efficient Officers, my "deep and sincere appreciation of the most thorough and excellent "instruction which you have given us during these three short weeks, "and also to thank you for the many courtesies that you have rendered "us, and the kindest and most chivalrous hospitality which you and your "Officers have shown us.

"It is very gratifying to me to observe the marked improvement in "the Officers and Non-Commissioned Officers and Men under the guidance "and tutorship of you and your most worthy Officers and Non-Commissioned "Officers.

"I would also like to thank the rank and file of your enlisted men "for their deep interest and untiring efforts in the instruction of our men.

"I feel quite sure, from observation and what I have heard, that "no other Battalion has had such good advantages as this one while "underdoing instruction in Europe. I am sure that the American "Officers over us have observed the great improvement which has been "brought about through our instruction under your Command.

"We are to be congratulated that we were attached to your Battalion "for instruction.

"You know that most of this organization is from North Carolina.

"Yes, 'We are Tar Heels born and Tar Heels bred, and when we "die, we will be Tar Heels dead.'

"After this mighty conflict shall have ended, and our flags are flying "victoriously, we want you and your Officers and soldiers to visit us in "America, and we will show you some things that are neither in open or "trench warfare, which will give us the greatest amount of pleasure."

THE THIRTY-THIRD DIVISION.

As before the Somme operations this was a period in which the antagonists took council with their Seconds, but it is quite plain now from the German official and unofficial accounts that the Germans, even with Ludendorff and Hindenburg in their corner, were in two minds about throwing up the sponge, whilst the Allies extremely refreshed, after almost taking the count in the previous round, had the greatest confidence in their chief Seconds, General Foch, Sir Douglas Haig, Admiral Beattie and Mr. Lloyd George, and awaited the final round of the great battle in anticipation of administering the knock-out blow. This was a period in which we not only succeeded in teaching to our new Allies, the Americans, all that we had learned with so much loss and agony during the past four years, but in which we took stock of our past faults, and prepared after this brief respite, to get out of our chair, drive the enemy against the ropes and into the corner, and administer a series of smashing blows until he was down and out. Under the leadership of Field-Marshal Haig the military machine was perfected in every detail. If we suffered from any weakness it was only from lack of Field Commanders. Such an enormous drain had been made upon our Battalion and Company Commanders, through death, wounds or exhaustion that they were exceedingly difficult to replace. The Cadet system of training at Home, however, found men from the ranks, which in no other way could have been found. Warrant Officers and Non-Commissioned Officers who had shown considerable gallantry and talent of Leadership in the field were selected from every Battalion and formation in the Field Army. For the first time these men were selected for these qualities alone and were sent to the Cadet Battalions, and within a very short period came back to take their places as Officers, often as not in their old Battalions. Very often young men, as Second-Lieutenants, were selected immediately to command Companies and Battalions in the Field. It was possible that with good fighting qualities a man might be promoted from the rank of Second-Lieutenant to Lieutenant-Colonel within a few weeks, even immediately. There is no doubt whatever that our Army gained immeasureably from this new idea. It was not universal, for in our Army there were still a number of the Higher Command who were hide-bound by ancient prejudice. Where such men, as these trained young fighters, were placed in Command, it was proved over and over again that the confidence of the men, and success, went with them.

This step was the first that our Nation made into the New World. We must hold fast to this idea for in it lies the Nation's future happiness.

The Division remained in the Sector between Ypres to the North and Kemmel Hill to the South, including Dickebusch Lake, from April until the end of July, and in this area occupied itself with refitting and in training the American troops attached to it. After the strain of the past winter, and of April in particular, it was a time of welcome relief.

Notwithstanding the ravages of influenza which at this time smote our Army, its boyish lightheartedness came uppermost again, and boxing tourna-

DICKEBUSCH.

ments, sports, cricket, football, and basket ball, a new game we picked up from the Americans, immediately burst into blossom.

Special attention was paid to the rear echelon and transport lines so that there should be comfortable places in which the troops from the line could live whilst in rest. Of this Dirty Bucket Camp, why so named no one knew, and Boone Camp, were the most popular.

Our personal friends and students, the Americans, were greatly impressed with our sports. On one well-remembered occasion a typical ' Son-of-a-Gun ' spat a black stream of tobacco juice accurately through the eye of a cleaning rod at ten yards, to show us a stunt we could not do. We did not attempt to match him.

There was in these times a terrible fear gnawing the vitals of our higher command lest ' Gerry ' should take a liking to ' Pop ' and St. Omer, so various lines of defensive trenches were constructed—red, purple, brown, green, yellow and blue—in fact as many lines as had the Higher Command different colours in its paint box with which to paint the Map ; and it was " up to " the Boche to take these in turn, and for us to teach the " Boys " from the Southern States that he could not take the latter before the former.

We had received since the Battle of the Lys very large numbers of reinforcements, particularly from the young Soldiers' Battalions at home. We do not think that at any time in its history had our Army presented to the World a finer body of men, physically, mentally or indeed morally, than these splendid youths. We still had a sufficiency of trained and experienced soldiers to leaven this youth into a magnificent army. By the time that the Division was withdrawn to take part in Foch's Final great offensive, and was taken from General Jacob's Second Corps to the Fifth Corps under General Shute, we are sure that it was never in finer fettle, or more prepared for offensive action.

Unpleasant as Ypres Salient was and always must have been, it was, during brilliant weather, a scholastic and athletic paradise. A number of raids were carried out, opposite to Voormezeele and from Scottish Wood, in the latter the 1st Battalion Middlesex Regiment distinguished itself by the capture of twenty-nine prisoners. We tried a number of experiments also with gas, and for some time had the pleasure of having with the Division the General Headquarters " Frightfulness " Officer. Whilst he cheerfully discharged volumes of most poisonous gas which belched forth from specially constructed cylinders on the light railway, he read to us—for he was in pre-war days a theological student—a wonderful treatise on the immortality of the soul.

CHAPTER VII.

FINAL ALLIED OFFENSIVE.

1ST AUGUST, 1918, TO 1ST OCTOBER, 1918.

Final Offensive—Breaking of the Drocourt-Queant Line—The Cambrai-St. Quentin Battle—Assault upon the Outer Defences of the Hindenburg Line—Villers Guislain—Meath Post—Pigeon Quarry and Targelle Ravine—Passage of the Canal de St. Quentin—Clary.

ORDER OF BATTLE, JULY, 1918.

Commander	Major-General Sir R. J. Pinney, K.C.B.
Aide-de-Camp to Commander	Captain F. C. Hooper, Dorset Regiment.
Aide-de-Camp to Commander	Lieutenant A. S. G. Kennard, Hampshire Yeomanry.

GENERAL STAFF BRANCH—

General Staff Officer, 1st Grade	Lieutenant-Colonel E. A. Osborne, D.S.O., Royal Engineers.
General Staff Officer, 2nd Grade	Major F. G. Trobridge, D.S.O., General List.
General Staff Officer, 3rd Grade	Captain J. Walker, M.C., Royal Warwickshire Regiment.
Intelligence Officer	Lieutenant W. I. B. Ware, Intelligence Corps.

ADJUTANT AND QUARTERMASTER-GENERAL'S BRANCH—

Assistant Adjutant and Quartermaster-General	Lieutenant-Colonel J. G. Ramsay, D.S.O., Cameron Highlanders.
Deputy-Assistant Adjutant-General ..	Major H. C. C. Batten, D.S.O., Dorsetshire Regiment.
Deputy-Assistant Quartermaster-General ..	Major O. B. Foster, M.C., Northumberland Fusiliers.

ADMINISTRATIVE SERVICES AND DEPARTMENTS—

Assistant Director of Medical Services ..	Colonel S. de C. O'Grady, D.S.O., Royal Army Medical Corps.
Deputy-Assistant Director of Medical Services	Major J. M. R. Whigham, M.C., Royal Army Medical Corps.
Deputy-Assistant Director of Veterinary Services	Major G. H. Farrell, Army Veterinary Corps.
Deputy-Assistant Director of Ordnance Services	Major A. M. E. Beaven, Army Ordnance Department.

THE CAMBRAI—ST. QUENTIN BATTLE.

SPECIAL APPOINTMENTS—

Assistant Provost-Marshal	Major Hon. E. G. French, D.S.O., General List.
Senior Chaplain, D.C.G's Department, Church of England..	Reverend W. C. Mayne.
Senior Chaplain, P.C's Department, Non-conformist	Reverend Hugh Brown.
Officer Commanding French Mission ..	Lieutenant P. F. Girard.
Officer Commanding Belgian Mission ..	Second-Lieutenant R. G. Kreklinger.
Gas Officer	Captain H. C. Tedd, King's (Liverpool) Regiment.
Salvage Officer	Lieut. J. H. Currie, Argyll and Sutherland Highlanders.
Claims and Canteen Officer	Captain D. L. G. Pigache, Royal Fusiliers.
Baths and Amusements Officer	Lieutenant G. Prior, Middlesex Regiment.
Divisional Burial Officer	Second-Lieutenant D. M. K. McKay, Argyll and Sutherland Highlanders.

DIVISIONAL ARTILLERY—

Commander	Brigadier-General C. G. Stewart, C.M.G., D.S.O., Royal Artillery.
Brigade-Major	Major W. A. T. Barstow, Royal Field Artillery.
Staff Captain	Captain W. E. Bownass, M.C., Royal Field Artillery.
Staff Officer for Reconnaissance ..	Lieutenant T. R. Jackson, Royal Field Artillery.
Divisional Trench Mortar Officer ..	Captain C. C. W. Havell, M.C.
156th Brigade, Royal Field Artillery ..	Lieutenant-Colonel B. A. B. Butler, D.S.O.
162nd Brigade, Royal Field Artillery ..	Lieutenant-Colonel R. E. Ramsden, D.S.O.
Divisional Ammunition Column ..	Colonel L. Forde, C.M.G.
X/33 Mobile Trench Mortar Battery ..	Captain T. R. Mayler.
X/33 Mobile Trench Mortar Battery ..	Captain T. Wingate, M.C.

DIVISIONAL ENGINEERS—

Commander	Lieutenant-Colonel G. F. Evans, D.S.O., Royal Engineers.
Adjutant	Captain E. L. Gale, M.C., Royal Engineers.
11th Field Company	Major C. P. L. Balcombe, M.C.
212th Field Company	Major J. E. Anderson, M.C.
222nd Field Company	Major G. F. H. Alms.

DIVISIONAL SIGNAL COMPANY, ROYAL ENGINEERS—

Officer Commanding	Major G. W. Williams, D.S.O., M.C., Royal Engineers.

19TH INFANTRY BRIGADE—

Commander	Brigadier-General C. R. G. Mayne, D.S.O., Highland Light Infantry.
Brigade-Major	Captain A. J. Thompson, M.C., Scots Guards.
Staff Captain	Captain D. C. Robinson, Royal Lancashire Regiment.
1st Queen's Regiment, Commanding Officer	Lieutenant-Colonel G. K. Olliver, M.C.
2nd-in-Command ..	Major R. H. Philpot, M.C.
1st Cameronians, Commanding Officer	Lieutenant-Colonel J. L. Jack, D.S.O.
2nd-in-Command ..	Major Hon. H. Ritchie, D.S.O.
5/6th Scottish Rifles, Commanding Officer	Lieutenant-Colonel H. B. Spens, D.S.O.
2nd-in-Command ..	Major C. C. Scott, M.C.
19th Trench Mortar Battery, Commanding Officer	Captain W. G. Borthwick, M.C.

THE THIRTY-THIRD DIVISION.

98TH INFANTRY BRIGADE—

Commander .. .. Brigadier-General J. D. Heriot-Maitland, C.M.G., D.S.O., Rifle Brigade.

Brigade-Major .. .. Captain F. C. V. D. Caillard, M.C., Somerset Light Infantry.

Staff Captain .. .. Captain E. J. Whitson, M.C., Highland Light Infantry.

4th King's (Liverpool) Regiment,
    Commanding Officer   Lieutenant-Colonel S. E. Norris, D.S.O.
    2nd-in-Command ..   Major J. H. L. Browne.
1st Middlesex Regiment,Commanding Officer   Lieutenant-Colonel J. H. Hall, C.M.G., D.S.O.
    2nd-in-Command ..   Major L. L. Welman, M.C.
2nd Argyll and Sutherland Highlanders,
    Commanding Officer   Lieutenant-Colonel Hon. I. M. Campbell, D.S.O.
    2nd-in-Command ..   Major A. G. C. Colquhoun.
98th Trench Mortar Battery,
    Commanding Officer   Captain C. E. Paternoster.

100TH INFANTRY BRIGADE—

Commander .. .. Brigadier-General A. W. F. Baird, C.M.G., D.S.O., Gordon Highlanders.

Brigade-Major .. .. Captain J. I. Muirhead, M.C., Yorkshire Light Infantry.

Staff Captain .. .. Captain W. J. J. Coats, M.C., Highland Light Infantry.

2nd Worcestershire Regiment,
    Commanding Officer   Lieutenant-Colonel J. G. L. Stoney, D.S.O., M.C.
    2nd-in-Command ..   Major O. V. L. Symons.
16th King's Royal Rifle Corps,
    Commanding Officer   Lieutenant-Colonel B. J. Curling, D.S.O.
    2nd-in-Command ..   Major P. A. W. Laye.
1/9th Highland Light Infantry,
    Commanding Officer   Lieutenant-Colonel A. H. Menzies, D.S.O.
    2nd-in-Command ..   Major A. K. Reid, M.C.
100th Trench Mortar Battery,
    Commanding Officer   Captain B. G. T. Hawkes.

18TH BATTALION MIDDLESEX REGIMENT (PIONEERS)—

Commanding Officer .. .. Lieutenant-Colonel H. G. McNeile, M.C., Royal Engineers.

2nd-in-Command .. .. Major C. P. Hinman.

33RD BATTALION MACHINE GUN CORPS—

Commanding Officer .. .. Lieutenant-Colonel G. S. Hutchison, D.S.O., M.C., Argyll and Sutherland Highlanders.

2nd-in-Command .. .. Major W. C. Andrew, M.C.

230TH DIVISIONAL EMPLOYMENT COMPANY—

Acting Commanding Officer .. .. Lieutenant J. H. Currie.

DIVISIONAL TRAIN (ARMY SERVICE CORPS)—

Commanding Officer .. .. Lieutenant-Colonel P. G. P. Lea, C.M.G., D.S.O.
Staff Supply Officer .. .. Major A. Clifton-Shelton.

THE CAMBRAI—ST. QUENTIN BATTLE.

DIVISIONAL MOTOR TRANSPORT COMPANY (ARMY
    SERVICE CORPS)—

Commanding Officer	Major J. A. H. Waters.
2nd-in-Command	Captain H. A. G. Denyer.

DIVISIONAL MEDICAL UNITS (ROYAL ARMY
    MEDICAL CORPS)—

19th Field Ambulance	Lieutenant-Colonel W. H. L. McCarthy, M.C.
99th Field Ambulance	Lieutenant-Colonel C. R. M. Morris, D.S.O.
101st Field Ambulance	Lieutenant-Colonel L. F. K. Way.

43RD MOBILE VETERINARY SECTION (ARMY
    VETERINARY CORPS)—

Commanding Officer	Captain A. G. E. Lalor.

At the latter end of August the Division was relieved by the 50th American Division in the Canal Sector, Ypres, and proceeded by rail to the Eperlecques training area to refit for the final act of the great war drama. Brilliant sunshine and warm weather were the features of the first few days, and every advantage was taken of bathing in the canal, with rafts and boats of every description. Quite a number of people decided to try the effects, upon the system, of drowning, but were fortunately saved by their comrades.

The Division was then moved to a very scattered area West of Arras near Saulty, and was, within a few days, transferred at night in hundreds of lorries from this area, *via* Albert and Bapaume to Rocquigny, the scene of our very bitter fighting on the 2nd–5th November, 1916. It " debussed " in the early morning and occupied tents and such old Nissen huts and German stores as had not been entirely destroyed in the recent fighting. An enormous amount of material and salvage had been left behind by the retreating enemy at this point ; this included millions of bottles of soda water, of which everybody availed themselves.

About August 25th, 1918, the Battle of Bapaume was victoriously expending itself, and on the 26th of August the Commander-in-Chief launched a new attack. The first Army, advancing, swept up on both sides of the Scarpe, and the battle went on until September 1st, when a pause for breath ended the great conflict begun on August 21st. Bapaume, a name only for a few jagged walls and heaps of rubbish, had been avenged and reparation exacted. From somewhere South the peasantry dribbled back to rebuild a ruined home, to plough up the shell-torn land.

In nine or ten days most of the First Army and the whole of the Third and Fourth Armies had swept across the old Somme battle grounds of 1916 in one long continuous battle without a pause. Early in the morning of September 2nd the Infantry of the First and Third Armies drove the enemy from the famous Drocourt-Queant line, and by the 22nd September the Germans were defeated at Havrincourt, and the British forces were now faced with the formidable Hindenburg line. The losses were great on both sides, but those of the enemy, with more than twelve thousand prisoners and some five score guns, was overwhelming.

Further South, the French had reached the Crozat Canal in their advance past Noyon, of old renown, from the Oise to the River Aisne; while Pershing's Americans had won St. Mihiel, a glorious vindication of the rights of the American soldiery to stand shoulder to shoulder with the war-experienced troops of the Allies. In two days, the 12th and 13th September, the Americans had eliminated the great salient and taken many prisoners. A great wave of relief, of thanksgiving, of content and quiet joy swept over the Allied line from the coast of Flanders to the Swiss frontier, but no one saw the end, no one wanted the end yet; there was the Rhine, formidable, mysterious; and beyond—a long, long way to Berlin. Patience was there holding the Allied line in willing leash.

The seas were free as ever. Reliefs, reinforcements, supplies and ammunition poured across the English Channel. In wait for them the U boats lay hidden as a man waits for pigeons homing to the wood. Our flying boats, the famous " Spider Webb," and our destroyers were a match for them. The Convoys came up to time nothing disorganized and very little lacking.

On the 18th September, an attack upon Gouzeaucourt and the high ground East of Vaucellette Farm, with the stronghold of Vaucellette Farm inclusive, was ordered by the Third Army under the command of General Sir Julian Byng. The Divisional Artillery under Brigadier-General Nicholson, and the 33rd Battalion Machine Gun Corps were ordered to support this attack with barrage fire. The attack was most successful and the barrage Companies being out of range, after the first day, were withdrawn.

The Division was moved on the 19th up to the Equancourt area, as far East as Heudecourt.

Although enormous strides had been made to rebuild the railway it was still many miles behind, and completed work was frequently destroyed by delayed-action mines, which still further hampered progress. The roads, too, had suffered considerably, both from shell fire and neglect; and with the enormous lorry traffic upon them, were in most cases, nothing but broken tracks with a rough stone surface. Villages and farm buildings, as such, had ceased to exist, every structure having been either destroyed by shell fire, or deliberately blown up and gutted by the retreating enemy. Similarly, also, the bridges over the Canal du Nord and small streams had to be rebuilt to carry the increasing and heavy traffic demand upon them. The progress of horse transport and Infantry was confined solely to tracks across the country. After having passed over the desolation of the 1916 battlefields, except for the complete destruction of the villages as already mentioned, the countryside had not been seriously disturbed. In certain localities, where heavy fighting had occurred during the German offensive of March, 1918, the ground was much broken by shell holes, but otherwise was easily passable. Considering the

128

obstacles which it had to overcome, it seems almost incredible that the British advance could have been made so rapidly ; and that it continued after the conquest of the Hindenburg Line in October, even more rapidly.

The 33rd Division took over the front from the 21st Division between the series of trenches which had been the old front line at the end of the Cambrai Reverse. This included Poplar Trench and Beech Walk, lying West of Villers Guislain and just East of Epehy.

It was apparent from the outset that the task of the 33rd Division would be peculiarly difficult. As had always been its misfortune, the Division was thrown into battle, not when there was a chance of surprise, or when a carefully prepared artillery barrage of great strength could support it, but when the advance was held up, or had been held up, by a system of defended works of unusual strength. This may be compared to the tasks assigned to the Division at High Wood and Les Bœufs in 1916 ; at Fontaine-les-Croisilles in the Hindenburg Line, and at Polygon Wood in the Menin Road battle of 1917.

An assault was ordered upon the outer defences of the Hindenburg Line, including the network of trenches and posts commanding the approaches to the Canal de St. Quentin. For some unknown reason artillery support was very weak, neither were tanks available. Villers Guislain itself was exceptionally strong, being defended by machine guns at every point, and by concrete pill-boxes. The attack was carried out on the left by the 98th Brigade under Brigadier-General Heriot Maitland, and on the right by the 19th Brigade under Brigadier-General Mayne, the whole being closely supported by the Machine Gun Battalion. It was launched at dawn on the 21st September and in most cases succeeded in obtaining a footing in the enemy line.

The enemy on this front was the Alpine Corps, who, during the whole course of the war had gained a reputation for the possession of the highest fighting qualities. The 14th Jaeger Regiment was positioned opposite the 33rd Divisional front. A few prisoners were taken in the initial assault, but the German machine gunners tenaciously held their ground, inflicting a very heavy loss upon our troops, particularly on the 2nd Argyll and Sutherland Highlanders, the 4th King's, and the 1st and 5th Cameronians. The fighting swayed backwards and forwards between the two lines, attack being followed by counter-attack during the whole day. The crux of the position was a sunken road named " Gloucester Road " and a strong point called " Meath Post." From Villers Guislain it was possible to see our troops in the sunken road, and at another moment to see the Germans in the same position. The air was continuously filled with stick bombs, which were thrown equally by our troops as by the Boche. It was, however, apparent, that the enemy would not give up his extremely strong position. Not only was his Infantry tenacious, but his machine gunners died to a man at their posts. The work of the German snipers was also deadly. Our own men, mostly young drafts, appeared to have lost their mastery over the rifle, and whilst armed with the bomb and the bayonet, were mercilessly mown down by machine gun fire, or picked off, man by man, by snipers. " Gloucester Road " itself was choked with dead ; the Germans showing bayonet wounds, and our men in most cases having been shot stone dead through the head. Our Machine Gunners fought with the greatest gallantry, inflicting very heavy losses on the enemy counter-attacks. No losses, however, appeared too great for the enemy, who, by the evening had driven our troops completely from his lines. An attempt was made by the 5th Scottish Rifles under Major C. C. Scott to capture the enemy's line by a surprise attack during the night. It succeeded in establishing itself in Gloucester Road, and swept on carrying Meath Post at the point of the bayonet and capturing many prisoners. This position they held, despite heavy counter-attacks, until relieved by the 9th Highland Light Infantry. The time was one of the very greatest strain upon all ranks, especially the Regiments in the 19th and 100th Infantry Brigades and the Machine Gunners who had fought incessantly for five nights and days. They had suffered heavy casualties in actual assaults, and between times enemy gas and shell fire had greatly increased their losses.

Owing to the rapidity of the advance up to this point, and the mining of roads, bridges, and railways, it had not been possible to move forward the Casualty Clearing Stations. In consequence the Medical Service was taxed almost to breaking point. This was a new experience both for our wounded and for the Medical Service, who had been accustomed to the complete organization of its Casualty Clearing Stations, and main Dressing Stations, within a few thousand yards of the battle. The work, however, in this Sector of the Canadian Corps Casualty Clearing Station, particularly of its nurses, who worked at fever heat, dealing with hundreds of fresh cases daily, with practically no shelter against either shell, bomb, or weather, was beyond all praise. It does not appear to be generally known that quite a large proportion of the nursing staff of our hospitals in France were actually engaged in the Casualty Clearing Stations, and in the Operating Theatres, under shell fire, certainly at the mercy of the night-flying bombing machines, which were naturally attracted by the lights of what were Hospitals and Operating Theatres.

The enemy had experimented in April with the inclusion of gas in a bombardment of high explosive shells. All his bombardments at this period were of this nature. The pitiful sight of men struggling back to the aid posts with their limbs burned and lungs gripped as in a vice, green coloured in the face, retching and in ghastly agony can never be forgotten by those who witnessed it. The Signallers, in particular, were, from the very nature of their work, the easiest victims of gas poisoning and suffered heavily, but never was the Signal Service, considering the enormous difficulties of distance and destruction to be overcome, more efficient. The Gunners, who had little or no cover, but were lying in the open with their guns of all calibres in echelon, suffered very severe casualties, both amongst men and animals, especially from the effects of "Mustard" gas.

The enemy had put up a hitherto unmet-with resistance ; very few prisoners had been taken ; whilst both sides, after the bitterest fighting, had incurred heavy losses. The German position at Villers Guislain was in the process of being outflanked from the North whilst the 12th Division on our right had established themselves on the high ground overlooking the enemy's positions on the Canal de St. Quentin at Honnecourt.

An attack on a very wide front was ordered for the 29th September. It was intended that the German position between Villers Guislain and Venduille, should be outflanked on both flanks by the pressure of the armies on the left and right of the Third Army. The advance of the 33rd Division would consist either of a peaceful penetration into ground vacated by the enemy ; or would effect the capture of a large number of Germans whose line of retreat would be cut off by the St. Quentin Canal in their rear. On the day of the great attack, except for violent bursts of fire, no action was taken by the 33rd Division. On the evening of this day it was reported that the attack upon the passage of the canal at Venduille, and the advance of the Americans and the Fourth Army astride the Hindenburg Line, had not been carried out according to plan. In the North the attack was more successful, but although Cambrai itself was captured, our losses had been far heavier than had been anticipated, and it was necessary to reorganize the forces disposed in the attack. It was apparent also that the forces opposed to the 33rd Division had not vacated their position, and that a very large number of machine guns were still commanding the approaches—Targelle Ravine and Pigeon Valley—on the St. Quentin Canal.

EXTRACT FROM "THE TIMES," 23RD SEPTEMBER.

GERMAN REPORTS.

"Between Gouzeaucourt and the Somme there was strong artillery "activity at times. An English partial attack North-west of Bellicourt "failed before our lines. South of the Somme we withdrew our advanced "troops which had been left far in front of the position, back to this "position, thus also evacuating Essigny-le-Grand.

"EVENING.—In front of our Seigfried positions between Gouzeaucourt "and Hargicourt, large centralized attacks delivered by the English failed "with very heavy losses to the enemy.

"Under the protection of dense rolling fire, English Infantry accom-"panied by armoured cars and airmen, advanced to the attack in the early "morning between Gouzeaucourt Wood and Hargicourt.

"During the night of September 19th-20th, in anticipation of the "enemy attack, we moved our defence in the open country East of

" Epehy to the old English positions between Villers-Guislain and Bellicourt.
" When the enemy, deeply echeloned for the attack, stormed down the
" heights against out lines, he was received by the prepared defensive fire
" of our artillery, infantry and machine guns. The attack broke down
" before our lines.

   " After very strong preparatory fire, the enemy renewed the attack.
" This second attempt was also entirely without success. Although the
" English temporarily penetrated into the South-western portion of Villers-
" Guislain and into the Quennemont Farm, they were again thrown back
" by an immediate counter-attack. In the evening and during the night
" very strong artillery fire was again followed by violent attacks, which
" were repulsed."

EXTRACT FROM " THE TIMES," 23RD SEPTEMBER.

HARD-WON BRITISH ADVANCE.

   " 7.50 P.M.—In a minor operation undertaken by us this morning
" East of Epehy, English troops successfully advanced our line after heavy
" fighting. Strong opposition was encountered at all points, and later in
" the day the enemy launched a number of counter-attacks in considerable
" strength. In spite of this resistance our troops have made substantial
" progress on the whole front of their attack.

   " In conjunction with this attack, Australian troops made further
" progress in a completely successful operation in the Hargicourt Sector,
" capturing a number of prisoners.

   " 10.35 A.M.—During the night our troops East of Epehy, renewed
" their attack, and again made progress, capturing Little Priel Farm and
" other organized points of resistance. A number of prisoners have been
" taken by us in our operations yesterday and last night in this Sector.

   " South of Villers-Guislain a local attack made by the enemy yesterday
" evening was repulsed after sharp fighting. In the course of the night
" our troops advanced their line in this Sector and captured several prisoners.

   " Yesterday afternoon the enemy again attacked at Moeuvres and was
" repulsed. There, also, our troops have improved their positions and
" taken a few prisoners.

   " English troops carried out a successful local operation last night
" North of the Scarpe River in the neighbourhood of Gavrelle, advancing
" our line on a front of two miles, and capturing several prisoners.

   " A hostile raiding party was driven off last night West of Acheville
" (West of Drocourt).

   " This morning the enemy delivered a local attack against our new
" positions North-west of La Bassée. Fighting is still taking place in this
" locality.

TARGELLE RAVINE AND PIGEON QUARRY.

" 7.45 P.M.—The hostile attack North-west of La Bassée reported in this
" morning's communiqué was not pressed, and our position is unchanged.

" On the remainder of the front there is nothing to report beyond
" local encounters at different points, in the course of which we improved
" our positions slightly South of Villers-Guislain and in the neighbourhood
" of Zillebeke."

EXTRACT FROM " THE TIMES," 23RD SEPTEMBER.

HARD FIGHTING FOR STRONG POINTS.

" 10.34 A.M.—Successful minor operations were carried out by our
" troops yesterday and during the night at several points.

" In the afternoon English troops captured a German strong point
" in the neighbourhood of the Ronssey-Bony Road, which had held out
" stubbornly all day, taking eighty prisoners. Later in the afternoon a
" hostile counter-attack from the direction of Guillemont Farm was
" repulsed with heavy loss by our rifle and machine gun fire.

" During the night other English troops made progress in the
" direction of Tombois Farm, after several hours of hard fighting, and
" farther North, captured a group of strongly-held trenches and strong
" points on the Saeur North-West of Vendhuille, taking a number of
" prisoners.

" During the night, also, over 100 prisoners were captured by us in
" a successful local attack South of Villers-Guislain.

" East of Gavrelle, North-East of Arras, English troops made progress
" on a front of about three-quarters of a mile south-east of Gavrelle,
" capturing sixty prisoners.

" Early last night the enemy attacked at Berthaucourt (between
" Pontru and Pontruet, North-West of St. Quentin), under cover of a
" heavy artillery barrage, and penetrated our line at one point. An
" immediate counter attack by our troops completely re-established our
" positions.

" 7.35 P.M.—By a successful local operation carried out this morning
" North-East of Epehy we captured a German strong point which has been
" stubbornly defended by the enemy during the fighting of the last three
" days.

" To the North of this locality a hostile counter-attack this morning
" succeeded in entering our positions at one point, where a party of the
" enemy is still holding out. Elsewhere the attack was repulsed.

ENEMY REPORT.

" We captured prisoners in local raids South of Neuve Chapelle.
" The artillery activity revived between Ypres and La Bassée, on both
" sides of the Scarpe, and on the canal sector South of Marquion.

"On the sectors East and South-east of Epehy as well as between "the Omignon Brook and the Somme, the artillery duels again increased "to greater strength in the afternoon.

"Infantry attacks, which the British launched against our lines "South-east of Epehy, were repulsed. The 2nd Guard Infantry Division "especially distinguished itself yesterday, as it had done during the last "few days. Strong firing activity was kept up during the night. In "nocturnal attacks East of Epehy the enemy obtained a footing in "isolated sections of trenches.

"EVENING.—There is nothing new to report from the battle front."

On September 27th orders were received that the Division should again carry out most complicated manœuvres, regardless of the presence of the enemy and his trench systems, in order to capture the ground which we had so far fruitlessly assaulted. The Higher Command anticipated that the enemy would have vacated the ground opposite the front held by the 33rd Division. It was thought therefore that the Division should be able to take all its objectives without fighting. Meanwhile the 4th, 6th and 7th Corps had advanced well to our North, but the 4th Army had not been very successful to our South.

It was ordered by the 5th Corps, that the 33rd Division should therefore assault the enemy position with a frontal attack and capture Villers Guislain, Pigeon Trench, and the high ground commanding the Canal de St. Quentin and the Hindenburg Line from the West. From our previous experience it was obvious that this attack must be costly, and, delivered as a frontal attack, had not much chance of success ; whereas this ground could possibly have been more easily captured by an assault from the South, by leaping from one tactical point to another. The attack was launched at 5.30 a.m., with the 98th Brigade on the left, and the 100th Brigade on the right. No more gallant attack has ever been carried out. Despite the heaviest losses, the Glasgow Highlanders, under Lieutenant-Colonel A. H. Menzies, swept down the Targelle Ravine, and some even succeeded in penetrating into Pigeon Trench, where they maintained themselves in action for two whole days, completely cut off from their Battalion. The Worcestershires, under Lieutenant-Colonel G. J. L. Stoney, although enfiladed on both flanks by well posted machine guns, hurled themselves against the enemy position. Both these regiments were practically wiped out. Regular lines of dead soldiers, headed by their Officers, testified the whole way down the Valley to the valour of the troops, and to the courage of the assault. The 98th Brigade met with similar difficulties in Villers Guislain, where from the beginning of the attack they were met on all sides by murderous machine gun fire. The 4th King's, who played the difficult rôle of keeping contact with the left Division, whose task was easier, with outstanding gallantry, and despite the heaviest losses moved forward step by step from one group of shell holes to another, maintaining a perfect line of advance ; whilst the

TARGELLE RAVINE AND PIGEON QUARRY.

1st Middlesex and 2nd Argyll and Sutherland Highlanders moved through the ruins of Villers Guislain in the most bitter hand to hand fighting. Both Brigades were closely supported by Machine Gunners, who dashed forward with the foremost waves of the attack to get into action and engage the enemy machine guns who were inflicting such damage in our ranks. As far as it may be said that the attack was successful—its success lying mostly in the gallantry of the attack—Villers Guislain was captured and posts and patrols were pushed out towards Pigeon Trench. Of all battlefields in which the Division has been engaged probably none bear such hideous memories as those of High Wood, Les Bœufs and Targelle Valley. They show the same matchless gallantry, the same failure to carry out an impossible task, and the same determination to carry out the assault.

EXTRACT FROM " THE TIMES," OCTOBER 1ST.

" HARD FIGHTING ON BRITISH FRONT. GAINS AT CAMBRAI AND ST. QUENTIN.

" STRUGGLE FOR CANAL TUNNEL.

" 11 A.M.—In our operations yesterday North of St. Quentin the " 46th (North Midland) Division alone captured 4,000 prisoners and some " forty guns.

" In this sector, between Bellicourt and Gonnelieu, the enemy's " resistance yesterday was obstinate. American, Australian, and English " troops had heavy fighting until late in the evening, and, in spite of " strong opposition, gained ground and took many prisoners.

" At Bony, and at Villers Guislain, hostile counter-attacks during the " latter part of the day succeeded in pressing back our troops slightly to " the Western outskirts of these villages. Elsewhere our gains were " maintained, and, to the North of Gonnelieu, further progress was made " during the evening in the direction of Les Rue des Vignes.

" Heavy fighting took place also yesterday afternoon on the left of " the battle front, and our advanced troops, who had taken Aubencheul- " au-Bac and entered Arleux were compelled to withdraw from these villages.

" West and North-west of Cambrai the enemy was unable to prevent " the progress of our troops, whose advanced detachments have reached " the junction of the Arras-Cambrai and Bapaume-Cambrai roads, and " have entered the Northern suburbs of the town. Heavy losses were " inflicted on the enemy in the repulse of determined counter-attacks " launched by him in this sector.

" Heavy rain has fallen during the night, and the weather is still " stormy.

" 8.44 P.M.—In spite of unfavourable weather and strong hostile " resistance, important progress has been made to-day on the St. Quentin- " Cambrai battle front.

"The 1st Division, South of Bellenglise, resumed its attack this
"morning, and gained the high ground about Thorigny (North of
"St. Quentin), capturing that village and the East end of the canal
"tunnel at Le Tronquay (North-east of Thorigny), taking many prisoners.
"Here it joined with troops of the 32nd Division, who during the
"night, had carried the defences of the tunnel on the Eastern side, and
"had captured Le Tronquay village. Continuing its advance to-day, this
"latter Division has made progress on the high ground North-east of Le
"Tronquay and East of Nauroy.

"On the left of the English troops the Australian troops attacked
"Northwards along the spurs leading from Nauroy to Guoy. Pressing
"their advance with great determination astride the Hindenburg system
"they overcame the resistance of strong forces of the enemy and
"captured the greater part of the high ground South of Guoy with many
"prisoners.

"Farther North English troops recaptured Villers-Guislain, together
"with the spur to the South-east of the latter village. Before mid-day
"they had also taken Gonnelieu and reached the Scheldt Canal along
"their front from Vendhuile Northwards.

"New Zealand troops have also cleared the West bank of the canal
"as far as Crevecœur.

"English troops have had hard fighting about Rumilly and to the
"North of that village, but have made progress and established them-
"selves along the Rumilly Cambrai road.

"North of Cambrai the enemy has again resisted our advance
"strongly, employing considerable forces and counter-attacking frequently
"and violently. In spite of his efforts Canadian troops have again made
"progress in this neighbourhood, capturing prisoners and inflicting heavy
"losses on the enemy.

"In successful minor operations, carried out this morning, English
"troops advanced our line tó the West bank of the Lawes River between
"Neuve Chapelle and Picantin. At the same time progress was made
"by our troops South-west of Fleurbaix. Over fifty prisoners were
"captured by us in these enterprises."

Meanwhile, the attacks of the 4th Army, accompanied by two American
Divisions, and of the 1st Army on the left, had carried well forward, and,
at dawn on the 30th, our Division pushing forward discovered that the
enemy had evacuated Pigeon Trench, had destroyed the bridges over the
Canal, and, having retreated on a wide front, had left only rearguards
immediately East of the Canal de St. Quentin and occupying the Hindenburg
Line. The whole Division was concentrated forward on 2nd October, and
attempts were made by patrols of the Middlesex and Cameronians to cross

the Canal, but the crossings were stoutly defended by machine gunners. On the 3rd patrols succeeded in crossing the Canal but could not reach the Hindenburg Line. On the 4th bridges were constructed by the Royal Engineers, and next day the Division crossed the Canal in force and the 19th Brigade occupied the Hindenburg Line without any heavy fighting. They took Aubencheul and Bonabus before the Divisions on either side had arrived.

Before we succeeded in crossing the St. Quentin Canal, it had been necessary to carry out most careful reconnaissance, for the bridges across it were completely destroyed, neither was it certain that the enemy had retired. Lieutenant Livingstone of the Glasgow Highlanders therefore took a lonely stroll across the canal, and visited some large dug-outs in a quarry in Franqville. He was challenged by cries of " Hoch," to which he replied in similar terms, left his card in the shape of a Mill's bomb, and had to beat a very hasty retreat.

At Cambrai again, wanton and deliberate destruction was very evident. Just before the Boche retired from Cambrai he vented his anger in blowing up a large part of the town for no military purpose whatever. Fruit trees had been sawn in two when there was no possible excuse for " Cover."

On the evening of the 5th October, the 38th Division passed through the 33rd Division to follow up the retreating enemy. They got as far as Malincourt after driving the enemy from a heavily wired line at the place. The 7th and 8th October were spent in getting the Scheldt crossings doubled and in getting forward artillery and supplies of all sorts.

EXTRACT FROM " THE TIMES," 7TH OCTOBER.

RETREAT SOUTH OF CAMBRAI.—DOUAI ON FIRE.—A GERMAN PEACE NOTE.

" Under extreme pressure the German forces are withdrawing on two " more lengths of their line in France, from the Rheims district and " from the line of the Scheldt Canal between Cambrai and St. Quentin.

" For four years the enemy held the forts on the high ground to " the North and East of Rheims from which they bombarded the city. " The rapid advance of Gouraud's Army North of Somme-Py, on the " East of Rheims, and the capture by Berthelot's Army of the old " French line of the Aisne-Marne Canal on the North-west, compelled " the enemy to seek safety.

" His retreat has been rapid on a front of nearly 30 miles to the " line of the Suippe and its tributary, the Arnes. By it he has given " back to the French the Moronvillers Ridge without a fight.

" Further East, on each side of the Argonne, the enemy, heavily " reinforced, are strongly contesting the Franco-American advance towards " Grand Prè.

THE THIRTY-THIRD DIVISION.

"East of the breach in the Hindenburg Line, British troops again
"went forward on Saturday and took Montbrehain, Beaurevoir, and
"Aubencheul, with the high ground to the North. Over 1,000 prisoners
"were captured. These gains had the result of forcing the enemy to
"get away from the Scheldt Canal on a front of seven miles, and the plateau
"to the east of it."

On October 9th, at 2.30 a.m., our turn came to again take up the
pursuit. The 19th Infantry Brigade, with two companies of the Machine Gun
Battalion covered by the Artillery of 38th Division as well as our own, pushed
forward from Malincourt through Villers Ontreaux and took Clary Village.

The Machine Gun Battalion carried out the advance so rapidly and with
such perfect march discipline that Battalion Headquarters with its flag was
actually established beside Clary Village before the "mopping-up" party had
reached it. It will be remembered that this village was the first one for a
distance of some sixty kilometres Westwards which had not suffered from
shell fire, or from the destructiveness of the Germans, although it may be
noted, that it had been looted. It was also the first village in which
civilians had been met for a similar number of kilometres. The civilians
themselves turned out in the streets waving French flags, and with a
gramophone playing the "Marseillaise," as our troops entered it. Of the
village of Clary there are two incidents which are worthy of record. When a
cavalry patrol entered the village, the officer commanding the patrol was
halted by a bearded man attired in dishevelled gear. It was proved that this
man, who had been missing since the battle of Le Cateau, in 1914, was a
member of this officers' regiment. He had lived for four years in a cupboard,
sleeping in the underpart of a huge French bed, unsuspected by the enemy,
and attended and fed by an old and very poor peasant woman out of her
meagre rations. During the evening of the day of their retirement from
the Village, the enemy heavily shelled it with gas, fully knowing that the
civilians, mostly women and children, had nothing with which to protect
themselves, and inflicting many casualties amongst them.

The village of Clary was actually taken by the 5th Scottish Rifles, who
captured also three field guns East of the village. The Mayor of Clary sent
the following letter to the G.O.C., 33rd Division :—

"Thanks to their rapid and vigorous pursuit, the brave Scottish
"troops have succeeded in preventing the enemy from finishing the work
"of destruction he had commenced in our Commune."

The chief square of the town, known previously as the Place de la Mairie,
was renamed the Place des Ecossais, and a tablet has been erected to
commemorate the day and incident. When H.M. King George V. visited
Clary in November, 1918, the 5th Scottish Rifles were drawn up in this square.

CLARY.

The 5th Scottish Rifles did not stay their advance for a fight like that at Clary. Just outside Clary, assisted by machine gunners, they captured two German field guns in action at the point of the bayonet. They pressed forward and largely helped by the action of the 4th Cavalry Division on their right, captured Bertry about mid-day and Troisvilles in the evening. Here the main body of the Brigade and the Divisional Artillery concentrated for the night, covered by the Cameronians who pushed forward before dark to the line of the Selle River, where they were stopped by the enemy in considerable strength. The pursuit by the 19th Brigade group had been carried forward sixteen miles during the day. The other two Infantry Brigades followed closely behind the leaders.

EXTRACT FROM "THE TIMES," OCTOBER 10TH, 1918.

"GREAT ALLIED VICTORY. CAMBRAI WON. GERMANS IN QUICK RETREAT.
"THREE MILES FROM LE CATEAU.

"The victory of British, American, and French troops between "Cambrai and St. Quentin on Tuesday was one of the greatest in the "war. They fought and defeated twenty-three German divisions, broke "a strong defensive line, and took 11,000 prisoners and 200 guns.

"So soundly were the enemy beaten that they could not face "another battle yesterday, but retreated in haste along most of the "front leaving weak rearguards behind them. They were closely followed, "but on most of the front we did not gain touch with the main body.

"The first effects of the battle were that the enemy was compelled "to evacuate Cambrai. Canadian troops attacked to the North, and soon "after midnight and by daylight our troops had entered the city.

"Before dawn a general advance of the Allied Armies began again, "and afternoon found them far forward especially towards Le Cateau. "At two p.m. the line from North to South ran approximately as "follows :—Abancourt, Ramilles, Escadoeures (East of Cambrai), Awoignt, "thence to Bertry (three miles West of Le Cateau), South to Busigny, "Bohain, and bending back to Fresnoy. From the Western edge of "Fonsomme the line ran East of St. Quentin, direct South to Mezieres "on the Oise, an extension by the French of Tuesday's front of battle.

"Numbers of inhabitants left in the captured villages have met our "advancing troops with enthusiasm."

It would be an almost impossible task to follow the movements of each Battalion of Infantry, of the Brigades of Artillery, Field Companies of Royal Engineers and other Units of the Division in this rapidly moving and far-flung battlefield. Village after village was reached, long stretches of country passed in which were few enemy, then a fierce fight with heavy casualties on both sides. But throughout this battle nothing was more marked than the perfect co-operation of artillery, infantry and machine guns. As each new difficulty presented itself the special arm of the Service needful to deal with it effectively was on the spot and ready for action. In particular, the vigour and power of movement shown by the Artillery was astonishing.

The country was admirably suited for defence. Long open undulating country stretched for miles, the bareness being broken only by little villages and occasional clumps of trees. It suited also our cavalry, the horsemen of the 4th Cavalry Division doing very fine work on our right, until they were withdrawn before the Selle River, owing to the impossibility of crossing, and to the intensity of the enemy shell fire. They succeeded, however, in reconnoitring in advance of our Infantry, and in cutting off numerous field guns and machine guns.

To sum up, the 1st, 3rd and 4th Armies had been steadily advancing since the 10th of September, and a week later the American 1st Army in co-operation with the French commenced their great and successful attack on the Argonne positions. The Allies were reaping the great fruits of unity of command.

On October 14th, The King of the Belgians and the 2nd British Army, under Lord Plumer, attacked on a wide front in Flanders, with great success; and maintained a steady advance from that date onwards until the Armistice.

CHAPTER VIII.

FINAL ALLIED OFFENSIVE.

10TH OCTOBER, 1918, TO 1ST JANUARY, 1919.

Passage of the Selle River—Forest—Croix—Englefontaine—Passage of the Forêt de Mormal and the Sambre River—Pot de Vin and Petit Maubeuge—The Armistice, November 11th, 1918—Break-up of the 33rd Division.

On the morning of the 10th October, the 98th Brigade passed through the 19th Brigade, and carried on the advance until the rising ground about Ramboulieux Farm was reached. At this point a stout resistance was put up by the enemy, the shell fire becoming exceedingly intense.

The attack was held up. The cavalry covering our advance suffered severe casualties, and had to be withdrawn, leaving the countryside, and particularly the sunken roads, filled with mangled horses. On the late evening of the 10th, the attack was continued, supported by very effective covering fire, supplied by the whole of the Divisional Artillery and three Companies of the Machine Gun Battalion. It was, however, only partly successful; and although the line of the River Selle was reached it was not found possible to cross.

It was now obvious that the enemy had decided to defend the natural obstacle formed by the Valley of the Selle.

In the evening of the 10th, the Divisional Commander received verbal orders to hold on to the Selle crossings and ground to the East until the Corps on either flank came up into line.

It may be mentioned that the French villagers had been given four days' rations by the Germans, which shows that our arrival was not expected for four days by the enemy.

On Friday, 11th October, it was confirmed that the 98th Brigade had secured two posts across the River, but there were no regular crossings. The Royal Engineers, therefore, were set to work preparing material for crossings which at nightfall was driven down in Pontoon wagons across the open. The Worcestershire Regiment covered this movement so successfully that eleven footbridges were complete before dawn.

During the night the 100th Brigade passed through the 98th Brigade, crossed the Selle, and at 5 a.m. on the 12th October assaulted the Railway cutting and high ground to the East. The Glasgow Highlanders on the right carried a strong line of wire and seized the Railway cutting. The 16th King's Royal Rifle Corps rolled up the enemy defence, and, having no deep cutting on their front, gained the high ground beyond after short and sharp fighting. Unfortunately, the Division on our left had not got through the village of Neuvilly on the Selle, so that our left found itself a mile further East than their right. The enemy soon seized their opportunity and attacked behind the Rifles, compelling them and the Highlanders to retire with heavy casualties. The high ground and Railway line were lost, but the River crossings and posts covering them remained solidly in our hands.

The 38th Division were ordered to relieve the 33rd on the evening of the 13th and to prepare to take part in an attack on a grand scale upon the high ground to the East of the Selle on the 20th October.

EXTRACT FROM "THE MORNING POST," 14TH OCTOBER, 1918.

"NEARING DOUAI. DESPERATE FIGHTING ON THE SELLE. BRIDGE OF "LIVING MEN.

"BRITISH FRONT, *October 13th.*

"If the dead knew aught of this war there were ghosts by Le "Cateau yesterday morning rising up in joy and thankfulness from their "lonely graves at a sight which assured them of the undiminished glory "of Great Britain, and the victory for which they died—ghosts drifting "along the winding valley of the Selle, where the new army had come "at last after four long and weary years, showing its valour and "endurance in a feat that will never fade from memory. There, in the "grey dawn, the Hun, looking down from the rugged Eastern slopes, saw "his fate pursuing him as a bridge of living men.

"British sappers submerged waist high in the chilling currents, "motionless under a hail of bullets which threshed the stream, bore on "their shoulders strips of plank over which passed the infantry of the "line—Manchesters, gripping their rifles, with eyes fixed on the hills "beyond. The spirit of Le Cateau carried them on. Surely they were "buoyed and stiffened by the thoughts of the soldiers of the old army "who had died so gloriously in that sacred place. The bridge of living "men helped to carry the British Third Army of General Sir J. Byng "across the difficult, strongly defended valley of the Selle. It attacked "about five o'clock yesterday morning between Le Cateau and Solesmes "simultaneously with General Horne's 1st Army on the left, which "continues to push the enemy towards Selle between Solesmes and "Denain, in the direction of Valenciennes.

PASSAGE OF THE SELLE RIVER.

" Hun Armies Hurled Back.

" Very hard fighting was experienced, particularly by the troops of
" the 3rd Army. The result of the day's battle was to throw back the
" German 2nd and 17th Armies, their combined front hinging on positions
" just East of Le Cateau. They lost the line of the Selle valley for a
" considerable distance North of Le Cateau, and the remaining fragments
" in the vicinity of Denain, where Selle empties into the Scheldt, seemed
" untenable in view of the continued pressure North of Cambrai. The
" Selle, as I have explained, is a wandering river from four to ten feet
" deep, flanked by steep slopes. Every bridge was destroyed by the
" retreating enemy, the trees on the Eastern bank were cut down,
" trenches had been dug along the railway embankment, and a great deal
" of wire stretched by reserve troops.

" The valley of Montay, Neuvilly, and Briastre between Le Cateau
" and Solesmes, could not be put in a state of complete defence, but
" they were heavily garrisoned with machine guns. The Divisions of
" General Byng's Army, marching steadily after the vanishing Germans'
" rearguard reached the valley without much trouble. On his right the
" 66th and 25th Divisions had reached Le Cateau crossing the river
" which runs West of the town after some fighting, and experiencing more
" in the Eastern quarter, which was liberally fed by Germans from the
" high ground behind. Between Le Cateau and the Hamlet of Montay, on
" the North, English and Scottish troops gained the river by passing
" through cavalry.

" Battery Captured.

" They had taken Clary at nine o'clock on the morning of the 9th,
" after hard fighting, and captured a field battery, stopping the drivers
" just as they were about to gallop away. The priest of Clary had just
" time to cut the wires connected with shells around the base of his
" church and prevented its destruction by German pioneers. Scottish
" troops and Surreys were received with acclamations by the villagers
" and then went on to Bertry, which they occupied at one o'clock in the
" afternoon. Other troops passed through them, and took Troisvilles at
" five o'clock in the evening. At dusk the Jocks, who marched sixteen
" miles and fought twelve, pushed on to the outskirts of Neuvilly, on the
" Selle, where they found a strong German garrison. On the tenth there
" was constant ' scrapping,' between British and German Infantry on the
" opposite banks of the river.

" In the evening our troops managed to secure a footing on the East
" bank. Some got over by crawling on trees which had fallen across the
" stream, but the majority waded up to the waist even to the neck in
" water. They met very severe fire from the Germans, but stuck to their

143

"little posts on Friday, when preparations were made to get the remainder
"of the force across. During Friday night bridges were thrown over the
"Selle between Montay and Neuvilly, covered by Worcesters. At day-
"break yesterday Highlanders near Montay and Riflemen by Neuvilly
"forced the river and, after desperate fighting on the railway line,
"succeeded in getting through the wire entanglements and overcame the
"determined garrison. They gained the heights towards Amervall, were
"forced back by counter-attacks, continued to fight along the railway
"during the greater part of the day, and subsequently regained the
"ground lost.

"A Costly Obstacle.

"On the left of these troops Neuvilly proved a costly obstacle in
"the path of other English battalions, who had greater trouble in getting
"over the river. Prior to yesterday morning's attack some East
"Yorkshires rushed the stream under fire, lead by a gallant sergeant,
"who said : 'Now boys, in you go,' and in they went, some of them
"nearly submerged in the current. They floundered through mud and a
"tangle of cut trees, gained the Eastern bank, and a well camouflaged
"trench, killed the occupants, went on up a steep bank through a maze
"of wire to the railway, killed thirty Germans, and reached a trench
"where we secured forty-one prisoners and left forty of the enemy dead.
"Unfortunately the Yorkshire men were unable to retain this hard won
"position under fire from their flanks, and they came back on Friday
"night to the West bank. The Germans swarmed after them to the
"camouflaged river side trench, and swept the bank with their machine
"guns, thus preventing the construction of bridges."

The relief on the 13th October was most welcome. For four days our troops had been subjected to constant artillery and machine gun fire, and had lived in an atmosphere of gas. The rest in Bertry-Malincourt Area was short, but was thoroughly enjoyed. Tactical schemes on the ground, football and concerts were arranged until the Division moved forward, preparatory to advancing through the 38th Division again. Half the Machine Gun Battalion moved off on the 18th, and supported the 38th Division with barrage fire. The attack which they covered was successful, the high ground on the East of the Selle being captured on the 20th.

On October 21st the children of Clary village made a huge nosegay, the size of a three year old child, and sent it to the Divisional Commander, inscribed :—" Homages reconnaissants de la population Clarysienne, aux anglais morts pour la liberation du sol Francais."

Following the crossing of the Selle River, the Higher Command considered that the time was now ripe for a colossal drive which would

144

break up the German Armies and force them to retire to the line of the Meuse. The 33rd Division received orders to cross the Selle River on the night of the 22nd October, and to concentrate with its first line transport East of the river, getting into position ready to attack on the 23rd. The passage of the Selle was an exceedingly difficult and dangerous operation. The enemy was within two miles of the river. The frontage allotted to the Division was little over 1,700 yards long, so that during this night it was necessary to concentrate the whole of the infantry, with its first line transport, in an area under one square mile, and almost in the outpost line. The risk was great, but no great results can ever be achieved without the taking of great risks. This concentration was not detected by the enemy. It was an extraordinary sight to see column after column appear in sight on the skyline, creep down the slopes of a hillside, absolutely devoid of vegetation or cover and, winding their way across the foot and transport bridges constructed by the Royal Engineers, reach their positions of assembly. Such shelling as there was was intermittent and light, and the casualties sustained by the Division exceedingly few.

At 2 a.m. on the 23rd, the attack was launched with the 98th Brigade on the right and the 19th Brigade on the left. The 18th Division assaulted at the same time on the right, with the 21st Division on the left. The advance, for the first day, was divided into five objectives and covered about seven miles of ground. The bite, however, was too big to be swallowed in one gulp. The final objective of the Division was a line East of Englefontaine.

By darkness on the 23rd, the high ground between Vendegies Wood and Poix du Nord had been consolidated, the prisoners amounting to seven officers and five hundred other ranks.

Rain had fallen very heavily for over three days and constituted a considerable handicap now on our operations. The advance, however, had carried well forward, the 1st Queen's having gained the first objective, known as the Slaughter House, when the 1st Cameronians advanced through them, gaining the edge of Vendegies Wood. The Infantry advanced by Sections in easy rushes as if on the parade ground. Their advance was covered by well-directed fire from the batteries of our guns, for our own Artillery was still with us. A brief halt was now taken to rest. The enemy resistance had considerably stiffened, and his artillery had become formidable. The 19th Brigade continued the advance. Despite heavy losses the advance carried forward to the fourth objective. A halt was then called, but the attack was continued in the afternoon. A section of " D " Company of the Machine Gun Battalion, advancing well, repeatedly opened rapid fire on the machine gun nests which would have held up the Infantry. Meanwhile, " C " Company had moved well forward, giving covering fire to the Infantry for each of the first four objectives. On leaving the fourth objective, the Company proceeded independently with its guns limbered up.

A large pocket of the enemy had been left in a sunken road just North of Forest, and it opened fire upon " C " Company. The order was given to fix bayonets and charge ; and, for the second time amongst the machine gunners in this Battalion a successful bayonet charge was carried out. A large number of the enemy was killed, while thirty-four prisoners, of whom three were officers, and five non-commissioned officers were taken prisoner, whilst on our side, during this fighting only two men were wounded. The booty included two machine guns, two light trench mortars, and a very large number of field glasses and technical stores of all kinds.

The conduct of the machine guns up to this stage of the operation, had been most admirably conducted. Many very valuable reconnaissances had been carried out by both Lieutenant-Colonel J. Mood, M.C., and Captain and Adjutant G. Harrison, M.C., enabling not only our guns but the Infantry to advance without serious loss, and to inflict heavy casualties upon the enemy. Lieutenant-Colonel Mood and Sergeant Maulkin, when the Infantry was held up in front of Vendegies Wood, went forward with a patrol, into the Wood to discover the position of the hostile Machine Guns and Infantry, and returned with such an accurate knowledge of their positions that it was possible to bring fire to bear upon them, and for our Infantry to advance with very little further assistance. Similarly, also, Captain Harrison mounted to the top of a building, which was at the time under heavy shell fire, and from this position directed the fire of our guns upon the enemy retreating along the road in rear. The Royal Field Artillery with bold reconnaissance and well-directed fire, enabled the Infantry to move forward as rapidly as possible.

The 98th Brigade had made equal progress on the right of the Division. The advance of the 18th Division had not proceeded according to plan, and its advance guard was considerably further West than that of the 98th Brigade. The advance was, therefore, carried out with considerable difficulty, owing to the right flank of the Division being exposed. The enemy was found to be in considerable strength at Croix. The 98th Brigade, well supported by Machine Gunners, stormed the village, inflicting heavy casualties upon the enemy with bayonet, rifle and machine gun fire. A machine gun Section particularly distinguished itself by destroying a gun team of an enemy field gun and putting the gun out of action, and succeeded in performing a probably unique feat for small arms by bringing down an observation balloon.

The co-operation between Infantry, Royal Engineers, Artillery and the Machine Gun Corps during these operations had been splendid, showing the high state of training which had been exercised throughout the Division by its Commander. Whenever the Infantry was held up for a moment, there were the Artillery, or Machine guns, ready to assist them with fire, whilst the Royal Engineers were always up to time in bridge construction and repair of roads. It was owing to the admirable harmony which existed, through the medium of General Pinney, between all Commanders that such a state of affairs was possible, for it must be remembered that in battle everyone's nerves are on edge, and everyone wants everything for his own unit.   The system of liaison and co-operation ran as a well-oiled machine.

EXTRACT FROM " THE TIMES," OCTOBER 24TH.

" East County troops of the 18th Division, advancing to a depth of " three and a half miles, captured Bousies.   English and Scottish " Battalions of the 21st and 33rd Divisions secured the crossings of the " Harpies at Vendegies Wood, and captured Vendegies Village."

EXTRACT FROM " THE TIMES," OCTOBER 25TH.

ANOTHER GREAT ADVANCE.—RIVER CROSSINGS FORCED.—BRITISH OVERCOME STRONG RESISTANCE.

" 10.22 a.m.—Sharp fighting continued yesterday afternoon and " evening on the battle front South of Valenciennes.   Our troops drove " the enemy from Vendegies Wood, and captured the villages of Neuville, " Salesches and Beaudigines, securing the crossings of the Ecaillon River " at the latter place.

" At the close of the day, the enemy counter-attacked vigorously " opposite Vendegies, supporting his Infantry strongly with Artillery fire, " and was repulsed.

" This morning the attack was resumed on the whole front between " Sambre-et-Oise Canal and the Scheldt.   North of Valenciennes we " cleared the enemy from the Forêt-de-Raismes and captured the villages " of Thiers-Haute-Rive and Thun.

" Determined local fighting took place also West of Tournai without " material change in the situation.

" 8.20 p.m.—This morning our battle front was extended Northwards " as far as the Scheldt at Thiant.

" Along the whole of the battle front between the Sambre Canal and " the Scheldt, the enemy's resistance has been overcome and our advance " has continued.   Hard fighting has taken place at a number of points.

" On the right, the 6th Division have fought their way forward to " the Eastern edge of the Bois l'Eveque and have taken Ors.   North " of this point, our troops are approaching the Western outskirts of the " Forêt de Mormal, and have captured Robesart.

" In the right centre of our attack our troops have continued their " advance successfully to the neighbourhood of Le Quesnoy.   We have " taken the villages of Poix-du-Nord and Les Tuileries, and made " progress beyond them towards Englefontaine.   The village of

THE THIRTY-THIRD DIVISION.

" Ghissignies was taken by the 37th Division after a sharp struggle, the
" enemy defending with determination the crossing of the Ecaillon in
" that vicinity. North-west of Ghissignies we have secured the river
" crossings at Beaudignies, which is in our hands. Here, also, vigorous
" resistance was encountered by New Zealand troops, who in this locality have
" captured a number of batteries, including guns of heavy calibre."

During the night the Brigadiers reformed their units ; and, at 4 a.m.
on the 24th, the 19th and 98th Brigades carried a strongly wired trench
line by a fine charge and continued the advance till Poix du Nord was in
our hands. The Machine Gunners took full advantage of the targets
presented by the retiring enemy. Our advance was checked by German
positions about Englefontaine, and by a strong artillery support to cover
these positions.

It could now be seen that a determined stand was to be made West of
the Forêt de Mormal. The country had become very closely wooded and
thickly dotted with villages. To add to the difficulties from the artillery
point of view, the villages were occupied by civilians. A common sight was
that of a cart drawn by an ox, bearing away civilian corpses wrapt in white
sheets. The civilians, however, soon learnt to remain in their cellars during
the fighting.

In spite of the exhaustion of all ranks, and the very heavy enemy fire,
it was decided that the attack would be continued until Englefontaine was
in our hands. In the early morning of October 25th the Divisional and
100th Brigade Staffs made reconnaissances towards Englefontaine and reported
it and the high ground on both flanks very strongly held by the enemy.
The 5th Corps, however, insisted that there was nothing but a weak rearguard, perhaps a Company, in our front and that we could advance without
further difficulty.

At 10 a.m. the Divisional Commander collected the Commanders of Units
in the front and held a conference in a cellar in Poix du Nord, and gave
orders and instructions for a night attack. The plan was, briefly, this :
the 19th Infantry Brigade were to work round the North of the Village, the
98th Brigade round the South and to join each other on the main road on
the East ; when the retreat of the enemy was thus cut off the 100th Brigade
was to move through the Village to " mop up." The rather complicated
barrage of artillery and machine guns was most skilfully worked out by
Brigadier-General Nicholson, who had relieved General Stewart as the
Commander of the Divisional Artillery. The Commanders rejoined their
Units and made the plan so well understood by all ranks that the attack
went through like clockwork and the Village, with the whole enemy position
and over 500 prisoners and much material, was in our hands by daylight on
the 26th October.

Where practically the whole Division was engaged it is difficult to

148

ENGLEFONTAINE.

mention Units—the complicated outflanking movements North and South were led by the 1st Queen's and 4th King's (Liverpool) Regiments respectively.

There were extraordinary scenes in Englefontaine immediately the enemy were driven out. While the prisoners were being collected the inhabitants came out of their cellars and literally fell round the necks of the British troops. Coffee was very freely distributed, and general rejoicing took place, whilst hundreds of French flags appeared as from a conjuring hat.

During the 26th the line was consolidated and harassing fire directed on the village of Hecq, and Western side of the Forest. In the evening the Division was relieved by the 38th Division, and moved back to Troisvilles to refit and rest.

In the actions described the casualties in horses and mules were enormous, and the drivers suffered heavily also, but the rapidity of the advance could not have been achieved had it not been for the admirable handling of the transport, particularly that of the Artillery and Machine Gun Corps.

To show how keen a spirit permeated the Army it may be mentioned that the Departmental Officers, such as the Ordnance, Train and Supply, were all anxious to join the most advanced centres of the Divisional Headquarters however "unhealthy" they might be.

As the result of these operations the following messages were received :—

"*To* G.O.C., 33rd Division.
"G. 434. "26/10/18.
"Please convey to all ranks under your command my congratulations "on the gallantry and endurance they have shown during the recent "hard fighting.

"They may well be proud of the advance from Malincourt to the "River Selle, where all resistance was overcome until the final objective "was gained, and the assault and capture of Englefontaine, with 500 "prisoners, after fifty-six hours of continuous heavy fighting and hard "marching over most difficult country, was a magnificent piece of work "well organized and most gallantly carried out.

"The present nature of fighting was a little new to the Division, "which made their task harder and more costly, yet in spite of heavy "casualties, their plucky determination to win, and splendid soldierlike "spirit, carried them through to success.

"Please convey to them my personal thanks for all they have done.
"*From* G.O.C., Vth Corps."

and
"*To* G.O.C., 33rd Division. "26/10/18.
"The Mairie of Englefontaine, which met this afternoon in a cellar "of this village, begs to express to you in name of the 1,200 inhabitants "freed by the British Army its deepest feelings of hearty gratitude.
"*From* O.C., French Mission, 33rd Division."

149

Before its destruction by the Boche, the village of Englefontaine must have been one of the most picturesque in France. It lies on the Western outskirts of the Forêt de Mormal. The Western outskirts of these woods had been largely destroyed by shell fire, and the groups of trees remaining were literally choked with German dead, who apparently had been trying to escape from the village into the Forest, but had been held up by its thick undergrowth. Many of them also had obviously come into their own gun barrage. The village itself was devastated beyond description. The anger and horror of the civilians at all they had undergone at the hands of this barbarous Nation cannot be exaggerated.

The task of the 5th Corps included the penetration and capture of the Forêt de Mormal, an immense and very thickly-planted forest of dense undergrowth, extending from West to East for over seven miles ; the passage of the River Sambre ; and the capture of the important town of Aulnoye.

The plan of operation was that the 38th Division should assault and capture the village of Hecq and the Western edges of the Forest, which were known to be held in great strength by the enemy ; and that the 33rd Division, passing rapidly through the 38th Division should continue the 5th Corps programme.

Many difficulties presented themselves. For the passage of the Wood one road only was available for transport, and this had been at many points already destroyed by mines and rendered impassable. It was impossible for the Infantry to pass through the greater portion of the Wood owing to the heavy undergrowth, whilst the clearings in the centre of the Forest afforded excellent fields of fire for the enemy defence. The bridges over the Sambre River, with the exception of one, had also been blown up by the enemy. It was decided at the outset, in order to avoid the probable heavy gas bombardment of the Forest, that the whole of the Machine Gun Battalion, with its transport, should follow immediately in the wake of the leading Infantry Battalion of the leading Brigade ; and in this position, should advance at least as far as the Eastern edge of the Forêt de Mormal. This bold plan of advance, which it is probable had never been entertained by any other similar Unit, and might have been regarded as foolhardy, as will be seen, proved to have been most wisely decided upon.

On the 3rd November, the 38th Division attacked the strong enemy position on the West of the Forêt de Mormal and with the utmost gallantry attacked and killed a very large number of the enemy. This Division captured all its objectives including the village of Locquignol as it swept forward, the 33rd Division being concentrated closely behind its advance ; and, on the evening of the fourth, the whole of our Division was bivouacked amongst the trees of the Forest. Considerable shelling took place, but the fire of the German gunners showed only the inaccuracy and wildness of exasperation, and inflicted very few casualties amongst our troops. The enemy himself had suffered very heavy casualties, both in the village of

Hecq and in the Forest, where rows and rows of enemy dead were found piled behind the fallen tree trunks or slit-trenches, for the most part bayoneted. On the morning of the 5th November, the 33rd Division passed on to the attack and made very rapid progress. Despite the congestion of traffic on the road and in the drives, the enormous craters which had been blown, and the obstacles formed by fallen trees across them, rapid progress was made. Little active opposition checked the advance of the Division until Sart Bara and Berlaimont were reached. These villages were attacked and captured by the 100th Brigade ably supported by two Companies of the Machine Gun Battalion. By the afternoon all the West bank of the Sambre was in our hands.

The following address is possibly appropriately here set out :—

ADDRESS FROM INHABITANTS OF SART BARA, FORÊT DE MORMAL.

" Commandant la [⚃ domino] Division.

" A Monsieur le Général,

" MONSIEUR LE GÉNÉRAL,

" Permettez à une population éprouvée par le joug le plus odieux " que l'histoire ait connu de venir déposer à vos pieds l'expression de sa " reconnaissance la plus sincère et de son dévouement le plus absolu. " Pendant plus de quatre ans, nons avons gémi sous la botte teutonne, " nons avons connu toutes les humiliations, toutes les injustices, toutes " les violences.

" Nous avons vu élever à la hauteur d'une institution nationale le " vol, le délation, la courtisanerie. Et nos coeurs et nos ames se sont " répliés comme des fleurs trop délicates sous un souffle glacé.

" Mais un jour s'est levé, Monsieur le Général, ou grâce à votre " Science militaire, grâce à l'incomparable valeur de l'armée Britannique, " nos malheurs se sont évanouis comme au soleil-levant s'envolent les " fantômes de la nuit.

" Monsieur le Général, nous vous disons le merci le plus profond que " nos coeurs puissent ressentir.

" Vive à jamais, Monsieur le Général, Vive à jamais la belle et " vaillante Armée Britannique !

" Que Dieu donne longue vie à son Roi, à sa gracieuse Souveraine " et prospérité à tout le peuple Anglais."

The 98th Brigade now pushed through the 100th Brigade and took up the pursuit. The enemy had retired to the high ground on the Eastern side of the Sambre River, destroying, after his passage of the River, the only bridge remaining. The river itself was unfordable ; and the enemy directed upon it, and in particular upon the ruined bridge-heads, a very intense fire from machine guns, field guns and howitzers. Despite this fact, however, it was decided that the 98th Brigade should force the passage of the Sambre River at Berlaimont ; and that the 100th Brigade should cross by an extemporized bridge of rafts about one mile to the right of the 98th Brigade.

Both these crossings were successfully carried out. At the former, buildings were on either side of the river and the piers of the old bridge remained. The Sambre, dark and swollen from the recent rains, would have been a serious obstacle at manœuvres, but when the surface and banks were spattered by machine gun bullets, and there were frequent howitzer shell-bursts in the river and the adjacent houses, the task demanded all the qualities of soldiers. Our machine gunners kept down the fire of the enemy from the opposite bank. The Middlesex Regiment under Lieutenant-Colonel D. C. Owen, D.S.O., and Captain Booth, V.C., D.C.M., worked doggedly carrying beams and planks selected by Major Anderson, M.C., and his Sappers of 212th Company, Royal Engineers, who by nightfall had made a bridge to carry wheeled traffic. At the same time the Machine Gun Battalion under Lieutenant-Colonel G. S. Hutchison, D.S.O., M.C., improvised a very temporary bridge from limbers and ropes, and carried two sections of guns and some of the 98th Brigade across the river at a point further to the right, and less exposed to the shelling. The whole 98th Brigade group were on the Eastern bank by daylight on the 6th.

The crossing of the 100th Infantry Brigade was only opposed by Infantry and machine guns, whose fire was kept down by our machine gunners. The 222nd Company, Royal Engineers, helped by the Infantry made a foot-bridge of rafts from materials collected on the spot. General Baird's Brigade was also on the Eastern bank by daylight on the 6th, and by 8 a.m. the Argyll and Sutherland Highlanders had taken Aulnoye, the 100th Infantry Brigade had taken Petit Maubeuge and Leval, thus giving us space to manœuvre on the slopes East of the river. The 162nd Artillery Brigade crossed the river during the day and came into action close up to the Infantry. The Royal Engineers were working without respite at doubling the bridges.

In the evening the 19th Infantry Brigade took up the pursuit, having followed the 100th Brigade across the raft bridge. At one time this bridge became impassable, and the Signallers of the Queen's Regiment greatly distinguished themselves by swimming the river and taking forward ammunition to the Worcestershire Regiment, who were temporarily isolated.

By the morning of November 7th, the 19th Brigade had taken Pot de Vin, and with the 4th King's Regiment of the 98th Brigade, pressed the enemy rearguards Eastwards till night-fall, when they had reached the Maubeuge-Avesnes Road. Here the 38th Division relieved us for the last time.

POT DE VIN AND PETIT MAUBEUGE.

Probably owing to the insanitary conditions and the strain, both physical and mental, put upon all ranks the Division was smitten at this time with the influenza scourge. At one time the bulk of the Divisional Staff and many Commanding Officers were all temporarily *hors de combat*, whilst a good many of them were evacuated to hospital.

The 19th Brigade, with a Company of the Machine Gun Battalion, reinforced the 98th Brigade at Aulnoye and carried forward the advance to the Avesnes-Maubeuge high road, where the 38th Division again took up the pursuit.

EXTRACT FROM " THE TIMES," 6TH NOVEMBER, 1918.

" 8.50 P.M.—In the great battle opened by us yesterday between the " Sambre and the Scheldt the troops of the Fourth, Third and First " British Armies, composed chiefly of men from English towns and " counties, engaged and heavily defeated, with severe loss in killed, " wounded, prisoners, guns and material, no less than twenty-five German " divisions. The German defence was thus broken on a front of thirty " miles.

" Owing to this brilliant success, the enemy to-day is in retreat on " the whole battle front.

" In spite of heavy and continuous rain, our troops have pressed his " retiring forces closely throughout the day, driving in his rearguards " wherever they have sought to oppose our advance and taking a number " of prisoners.

" In the haste of his enforced withdrawal yesterday and to-day, " the enemy has abandoned complete batteries and large quantities of " material of every description.

" Our troops have passed through the Forest of Mormal and reached " the general line Barzy-Le-Grand Fayt-Berlaimont West of Bavai-Roisin- " Fresnes.

EXTRACT FROM " THE DAILY MAIL," 7TH NOVEMBER, 1918.

" WHOLE BATTLE LINE ADVANCING.

" Main Railway Crossed.

" British Official Report.

" During the day we have progressed along the whole battle front in " spite of heavy and continuous rain. Sharp fighting has taken place at " a number of points with German rearguards, and some hundreds of " prisoners have been taken by us.

" On our right our troops pushing forward, have captured Cartignies " and Marbaix. In the centre driving the enemy from his hastily " constructed defences on the East bank of the Sambre, we have crossed

" the river about Berlaimont, and have captured Leval and Aulnoye,
" where we have taken prisoners. The important railway junction at
" Aulnoye is in our possession. (This is the Northern part of the lateral
" railway from Ghent to Hirson, Mezieres and Metz.)

" Farther North we have crossed the Avesnes-Bavai Road, East of
" Mormal Forest, and have reached the railway South and West of Bavai,
" where sharp fighting is taking place within a short distance of the
" town. We have cleared the West bank of the Honnelle as far North as
" Angre, where there has been stiff fighting all day. In this locality the
" enemy is resisting our advance with determination, and has delivered
" two counter-attacks, both of which were repulsed.

" On the left Canadian troops are continuing their progress East of
" the Scheldt, and have captured Baisieux and Quievrechain."

The Casualties during the operations described, from 20th September until
the Armistice amounted to

Killed	..	65	Officers and	866	Other Ranks.
Wounded	..	171	,,	,, 5,834	,,	,,
Missing	..	11	,,	,, 629	,,	,,

The Division suffered great loss in the death of Lieutenant-Colonel the
Hon. H. Ritchie, D.S.O., commanding the 1st Cameronians, who had been
wounded three times during the past three weeks, and was now finally killed ;
and in the death through shell fire of Lieutenant-Colonel B. A. B. Butler, of the
Divisional Artillery. Lieutenant-Colonel Butler will always live in history as
the author of the B.A.B. code, universally used throughout our Army during
the war as the official secret trench code, and thus named from his own
initials. He had served in the field from Mons until the end, a very gallant
and brilliant officer. Further serious and deeply regretted losses were those
of Major C. P. L. Balcombe, M.C. and bar, commanding the 11th Field
Company, Royal Engineers, who was killed at Poix du Nord,—he had served
for a long time and with great distinction with the Division— ; and of
Captain E. McCosh, M.C., of the Glasgow Highlanders, an equally distinguished,
gallant and popular officer.

Our casualties in these operations included the following Officers :—

33RD DIVISIONAL ARTILLERY.

Killed.	*Wounded.*
Lt.-Col. B. A. B. Butler, D.S.O.	Lieut.-Col. A. K. Barker, D.S.O., M.C.
	Capt. G. Coleman.
	Major H. C. Cory, M.C.
	Major G. Fetherston.
	2nd Lieut. C. J. Fuller.
	Lieut. H. L. R. Gough.
	2nd Lieut. P. A. S. Hadley.

THE FINAL OFFENSIVE.

33RD DIVISIONAL ARTILLERY (*continued*).
Wounded (contd.).
2nd Lieut. E. P. R. Martin.
2nd Lieut. J. C. Mitcheson.
Capt. F. C. Packham.
Lieut. D. S. M. Paterson.
Capt. R. H. Pavitt, M.C.
2nd Lieut. M. H. Rollason.
2nd Lieut. G. F. Taylor.
2nd Lieut. T. E. Wimshurst.

ROYAL ENGINEERS.

Killed.

Major C. P. L. Balcombe, M.C.

Wounded.

2nd Lieut. M. C. Ashworth.
Lieut. F. D. Frank.
2nd Lieut. R. Love.
2nd Lieut. B. McKendrick.
2nd Lieut. W. T. Malcolmson.
Lieut. P. Russell.
2nd Lieut. J. H. Simson.

1ST QUEEN'S (ROYAL WEST SURREY) REGIMENT.

Killed.

Capt. E. W. Bethell.
2nd Lieut. M. B. Blagden.
2nd Lieut. R. F. Higgs.
2nd Lieut. O. Jackman, M.M.
Capt. & Qmr. G. H. Wallis, D.C.M.
Lieut. H. C. L. Whittaker.

Wounded.

Capt. A. R. Abercrombie, D.S.O., M.C.
Capt. E. S. Bingham.
2nd Lieut. L. T. Brooker, D.C.M., M.M.
Capt. C. A. B. Brown.
Lieut.-Col. H. W. Green, D.S.O.
Lieut. A. J. R. Haggard.
2nd Lieut. J. G. Harker.
2nd Lieut. P. J. Jakes, M.M.
2nd Lieut. J. H. Mayland.
2nd Lieut. W. J. C. Morgan.
2nd Lieut. H. Nallett.
Capt. R. H. Nevins, M.C.
2nd Lieut. W. A. North.
Lieut. F. W. Pelling.
2nd Lieut. E. L. Phillips.
2nd Lieut. S. H. Pierssene.
2nd Lieut. W. J. Pratt.
2nd Lieut. S. F. Prior.
2nd Lieut. J. E. Shipton.
2nd Lieut. J. A. Talbot.
Lieut. R. O. V. Thomas.
2nd Lieut. F. H. E. Whittaker.

THE THIRTY-THIRD DIVISION.

1ST CAMERONIANS (SCOTTISH RIFLES).

Killed.

Capt. J. E. Baker.
2nd Lieut. J. G. Cathro.
2nd Lieut. A. G. Clark.
Capt. W. T. Craig.
2nd Lieut. J. F. Garrity.
2nd Lieut. D. R. Macarthur.
2nd Lieut. H. S. McDonald.
2nd Lieut. D. Maclean.
Lieut.-Col. Hon. H. Ritchie, D.S.O.
2nd Lieut. H. F. Wells.
Lieut. A. J. Wyatt.

Wounded.

2nd Lieut. J. B. F. Brown.
2nd Lieut. W. Brownlie.
2nd Lieut. N. G. Dobson.
2nd Lieut. C. Gemmell.
2nd Lieut. A. Henderson.
2nd Lieut. R. Herbert.
Lieut.-Col. H. H. Lee, D.S.O.
Lieut. M. Lindsay.
2nd Lieut. J. McDonald.
2nd Lieut. B. G. McKerracher.
2nd Lieut. J. McMillan.
2nd Lieut. A. D. Manson.
Lieut. R. G. Nicol.
2nd Lieut. J. T. Whitson.

1/5TH/6TH SCOTTISH RIFLES.

Killed.

Lieut. A. G. Kerr.
Lieut. A. B. McRae, M.C.
Lieut. J. P. Miller.
2nd Lieut. J. S. White.

Wounded.

2nd Lieut. A. Anderson.
Lieut. N. Clark, M.M.
Lieut. R. Dick.
2nd Lieut. D. M. Ford.
2nd Lieut. G. Hibbert.
2nd Lieut. C. S. McDonald.
Lieut. J. H. McPherson, M.C.
2nd Lieut. W. McG. Patience.
Capt. N. M. R. Smith.
2nd Lieut. W. McC. Smith.
2nd Lieut. J. Young.

Missing.

2nd Lieut. A. Anderson.

4TH KING'S (LIVERPOOL) REGIMENT.

Killed.

2nd Lieut. G. B. Harper.
2nd Lieut. W. C. Marshall.
Capt. A. R. Nicholls.

Wounded.

2nd Lieut. F. P. Arthur.
2nd Lieut. F. J. Baughen.
2nd Lieut. E. W. Bell.
Lieut. A. Boardman, M.C.
Lieut. A. P. Dixon.
Lieut. D. H. Parker.
Lieut. I. Rothfield.

THE FINAL OFFENSIVE.

2ND ARGYLL AND SUTHERLAND HIGHLANDERS.

Killed.	*Wounded.*	*Missing.*
Capt. D. McGregor.	Lieut. K.W. D. Campbell, M.C.	2nd Lieut. W. H. Duncan.
Lieut. J. Milne.	2nd Lieut. W. C. Clark.	Lieut. W. W. McLean, M.C.
Capt. D. Ross, D.S.O., M.C.	Capt. G. Fraser.	
Lieut. J. M. Taylor.	2nd Lieut. J. Greenshields.	
	2nd Lieut. C. W. Hadwen.	
	2nd Lieut. J. L. Johnston.	
	2nd Lieut. J. A. Kelly.	
	2nd Lieut. D. S. Kerr.	
	2nd Lieut. J. McAustin.	
	Lieut. E. C. Maskelyne, M.C.	
	Lieut. D. Matthews.	
	2nd Lieut. J. H. Paterson.	
	Lieut. J. W. Pinckney.	
	Lieut. T. Prentice.	
	2nd Lieut. C. Ross.	
	Lieut. W. F. B. Shaw.	
	Lieut. M. E. Squirl.	
	2nd Lieut. R. Stewart.	
	Lieut. J. M. Taylor.	
	Lieut. J. McC. Thompson.	
	Lieut. H. Todd, M.C., D.C.M., M.M.	
	Lieut. N. D. M. Torrey.	
	2nd Lieut. C. D. Vint.	
	Lieut. J. S. Watson, M.C.	

1ST MIDDLESEX REGIMENT.

Killed.	*Wounded.*	*Missing.*
Lieut. J. N. Beeman.	2nd Lieut. H. de B. Askew.	2nd Lieut. C. E. Cade.
Capt. F. B. Broad, M.C.	Lieut. A. Atkinson.	
2nd Lieut. J. C. B. Brown.	2nd Lieut. A. H. Greene.	
Lieut. J. Gray.	2nd Lieut. H. G. Jackson.	
Lieut. D. W. Hay.	2nd Lieut. E. F. Johnson.	
2nd Lieut. R. E. Holland.	Lieut. A. A. T. Morris, M.C.	
Lieut. W. L. Hoospith.	Lieut. F. J. Smith, D.C.M.	
Lieut. A. C. T. Kroenig-Ryan.	Lieut. F. T. Sobey.	
Lieut. E. S. Matthews.		

THE THIRTY-THIRD DIVISION.

2ND WORCESTERSHIRE REGIMENT.

Killed.
2nd Lieut. S. Benbow.
2nd Lieut. A. E. Bullock.
2nd Lieut. H. Croydon-Fowler.
2nd Lieut. G. Lambert.
2nd Lieut. C. E. Neale.
Lieut. L. E. Ransom.
2nd Lieut. J. A. Sudbury.
2nd Lieut. G. E. Woodward.
Lieut. R. K. Wright, M.C.

Wounded.
2nd Lieut. F. D. Barnard.
2nd Lieut. C. Devereux.
2nd Lieut. B. W. Dudley.
2nd Lieut. H. Garratt.
Lieut. H. G. Hill.
Lieut. H. H. S. Laughton.
2nd Lieut. J. A. Starkey.
2nd Lieut. H. J. Walford.
2nd Lieut. H. J. Walths.
2nd Lieut. J. Watkin-Jones.
2nd Lieut. V. G. S. Wickham.

16TH KING'S ROYAL RIFLE CORPS.

Killed.
Capt. G. S. Hogan.
2nd Lieut. P. Knight.
2nd Lieut. S. N. Levitt.
2nd Lieut. N. F. Surry.
2nd Lieut. A. H. Villiers.
Capt. G. M. Warner.
2nd Lieut. D. R. Wilson.

Wounded.
2nd Lieut. F. G. Budd.
2nd Lieut. G. H. Coe.
Capt. G. B. de Courcy-Ireland, M.V.O., M.C.
2nd Lieut. C. V. T. Everett.
Major P. A. W. Laye.
2nd Lieut. F. J. North.
Lieut.-Col. F. L. Pardoe, D.S.O.
2nd Lieut. A. H. Pinnington.

1/9TH HIGHLAND LIGHT INFANTRY.

Killed.
Lieut. R. T. Anderson, M.C.
Lieut. C. A. Baird.
2nd Lieut. A. McK. Bruce.
Lieut. A. H. Donaldson.
Lieut. A. Hill.
Capt. E. McCosh, M.C.
2nd Lieut. J. J. A. Ritchie.
Lieut. G. G. Taylor.

Wounded.
Lieut. J. C. Dewar.
2nd Lieut. J. S. Dunlop.
Lieut. H. S. Hall.
2nd Lieut. F. H. A. Hendry.
Lieut. T. Lewis.
2nd Lieut. R. M. McPhail.
Capt. W. B. Metcalfe.
Capt. F. B. Thomson.

Missing.
Lieut. W. F. Alexander.
Lieut. D. F. Brodie, M.C.
Lieut. T. A. Dickie.
2nd Lieut. R. Menzies.
Lieut. J. R. Patterson.

18TH MIDDLESEX REGIMENT (PIONEERS).

Killed.
2nd Lieut. A. M. Drage, M.M.

Wounded.
Lieut. B. L. Fish.
2nd Lieut. A. Poynton.

THE ARMISTICE.

33RD BATTALION MACHINE GUN CORPS.

Killed.
Lieut. T. Cullen.

Wounded.
Lieut. B. Bedson.
Lieut.-Col. G. S. Hutchison, D.S.O., M.C.
2nd Lieut. R. W. Kallend.
Major W. Lewthwaite, M.C.
2nd Lieut. J. M. McKenzie, M.C.
Major A. McPherson, M.C., D.C.M.
Lieut. J. McQueen.
2nd Lieut. F. H. Marshall.
2nd Lieut. P. D. Mathie.
2nd Lieut. A. B. Parsons.
2nd Lieut. C. H. Rogers.

Missing.
2nd Lieut. A. S. Hunt.

TRENCH MORTAR BATTERIES.

Killed.
Lieut. J. M. Martin.

Wounded.
Lieut. J. M. Humphrey.
2nd Lieut. W. C. Whitehouse.

ROYAL ARMY MEDICAL CORPS.

Killed.
Lieut. J. A. McQuillan. (U.S.A., M.O.R.C, attd).

Wounded.
Capt. R. McCowan Hill, D.S.O.
Lieut. A. C. Paterson.

ROYAL ARMY SERVICE CORPS.

Wounded.
2nd Lieut. H. G. Kelsey.

On the 9th November the Division was withdrawn from the battle to the Berlaimont-Aulnoye area. Early on this day, it was strongly rumoured that the enemy had sent over plenipotentiaries to Marshal Foch pleading for an armistice. This was officially confirmed at 12 noon, stating that Marshal Foch had agreed to an armistice under very severe conditions to the enemy, and that he must accept or continue the fighting by 12 noon on the 11th. The excitement, both amongst the British soldiers and the civilians, was intense. It was immediately decided to open an immense one franc sweepstake on the result; and a deserted shop was taken over for this purpose. Subscriptions poured in, both from our own men, and those of the Welsh Division ; and shortly before 11 o'clock on the 11th it was announced that the enemy had accepted the terms, and as the result of the sweep takings a very large sum was paid out to a lucky private.

With characteristic promptness it was, again, immediately decided to celebrate the event in an equally characteristic and original manner. At 12 noon, the hour of the Armistice, the Machine Gun Band turned out in the streets of Aulnoye in full war paint, and, after a peal of bells from the Church, marched through the streets of the town playing three soul-stirring marches, and ending in the square with " La Marseillaise " and the National Anthem.

An enormous crowd of soldiers and civilians thronged the streets and hung from the windows, cheering and waving flags, whilst the Maire of the town presented a bouquet of flowers to the Bandmaster and hung a garland of roses round the neck of the Commanding Officer. At 7 o'clock the same evening, a torchlight procession, forty torches on 12 foot poles having been provided at a moment's notice by energetic pioneers, was organized through the town, ending at the old German Officers' Club in the Square, in front of which an enormous bonfire had been built and a stage for an impromptu concert erected. The progress of the Band, through even greater crowds than during the morning, was preceded by volleys of Verey Lights of every known colour, being fired into the air.

On December 10th, the Division began its long march back across the old battlefields to the Hornoy Area, West of Amiens.

The curtain was rung down upon the Division as such, by the first allotment for the demobilization of the Veterans of the Division, whilst it was split up and proceeded to march to the Base Camps at Rouen, Dieppe, Havre and Abancourt, where its personnel was speedily demobilized, or retained,—filling in time the while guarding German prisoners.

CHAPTER IX.

RETROSPECT.

Weather as a Mnemonic—The Royal Regiment of Artillery—The Royal Engineers— The Royal Army Service Corps—The Royal Army Medical Corps and Auxiliary Services—Marshal Foch on the British Army—The Divisional Commander— The Divisional Staff—Divisional Characteristics—The End.

Casting the mind's eye back across the memories of war, the incidents which stand out most clearly in memory are those with which we can connect, it may be subconsciously, the state of the weather. This is a curious fact, but it may be common to the British only. We do not remember in detail the little incidents, or indeed, the big facts connected with our greatest achievements, as we do the seemingly petty incidents,—the grey evening clouds hovering like vultures ready to swoop down with outspread wings and devour the landscape; a bright and sunny day; or a night upon which the flying clouds brushed past the cold rays of the moon, sometimes lifting their train to allow a shaft of silver to steal down upon mortal man enshrined in a watery waste of shell holes.

We are sitting in the cornfields, lazily leaning against the little stooks, whose long purple shadows lie stretched upon the ground, sleeping or smoking, a snatch of melody from several voices floats through the still evening air; equipment and rifles are lying here and there. Against the homestead farm a group of officers sit chatting and studying a map. It is a peaceful scene. A loud crack, a sheet of flame, a column of smoke and a cloud of brickdust. It is the trumpet call of war! The Eastern end of the farmhouse is rent by a huge hole. The air is filled with sound,—the boom of guns, the clanking of equipment, sharp orders, and hurrying feet across the stubble. The skyline of the meadow and orchard in the offing is crowned with little figures in grey darting hither and thither. A rattle of musketry; some sleepers will sleep on for ever. The Battalion retires. From a window high up in the farmhouse a machine gun spits out its withering fire upon the hordes rushing like grey rats through the orchard.

A cloud of pink dust;—the window has disappeared, but from its ruins emerges a little man, as coated in white as a miller, and bearing on his shoulders a Maxim gun and tripod. He is pursued, but cheerfully drags his way across the stubble field. The enemy is upon him; but, as he reaches the little pond beside the church, he hurls his precious burden into it, and thus defeats his enemy.

Four years afterwards this same little man, old as a yew tree and wiry as its roots, would gaze across the parapet and await the day when he would go forth and retrieve his weapon. For that day he did not wait in vain; for that same gun was brought into action once more from the same ruin, but upon a very different target.

The sun glares down upon the trenches. It is the first day of summer after many rains. In the front line men are washing; here one with his periscope perched on the parados shaves off his three weeks' growth; another naked to the waist, stretches his fine young limbs in the morning air. Red-haired Jock, "Ginger," is busy with his chanter crooning a little group to slumber and to happy memories of burn and glen. Only the sentry, with his one eye glued to the canvas-covered look-out hole in the parapet, appears to take interest in the life beyond the meshes of the barbed wire. The jagged tower of the Ypres Cloth Hall keeps silent watch.

A green and yellow cloud belches forth from the enemy's line. It wends its way, sometimes snakelike and sinuous, sometimes unrolling itself in wide ethereal fronds, or in massed blossom opening like the petals of a flower.

A mighty uproar, crash and noise. Rifles are seized. The trench is filled with dust and smoke,—red, green, black, yellow. The rifle spits here and there. A machine gun fitfully opens fire. And all the time slowly creeps on a great green cloud. It seems to roll over the edge of the parapet. Wild-eyed men, who feverishly work the bolts of rifles, are gripped in its octopus embrace. What was once "Oxford Street" is now a shambles: some dead; others choked with gas fumes; others heaped with tattered clothing and mangled bodies lie gasping in the wreckage of a strong point. With a final wail of agony the chanter falls from the hand of Jock. His red hair will never glisten in the sun again; his face is grey,—his hair clotted and matted in a dull crimson. It is war—deadly war.

The front line has gone. The enemy pours across "No Man's Land," and with shrill cries enters our line and proceeds to rush through the Communication Trench to our support line. But resolute men are here. Headed by their officer, they strike across the open space between the support and the front line. It seems to be suicide, but the party attains its end. "On vous aura"! They have them in the back! The enemy is trapped; he turns, but it is too late. Men sway backwards and forwards in the yellow clay soil. It is war to the knife;—an eye for an eye and a tooth for a tooth;—bayonet and bludgeon and bomb.

A second wave of the enemy pours down upon the trench, but its saviours are there. A Feldweber is left jerking on a strand of wire, his stomach blown through his back by a rocket from a "Verey light" pistol at ten yards range. The machine gun speaks again. The line is held. The Tower of Ypres still keeps its Eastern watch. Just a little incident of war. Only a passing Show, all on a summer's day.

And so on ; for if we give to our memory full play, it will summon up many such little cameos of war, centring around a particularly glorious day which burst through February's murky skies ; the torrents of rain which bucketed down our dug-out steps at Les Bœufs ; or the sheet of lightning in September, 1918, which lit up the phantom shapes amidst the ruins of Gouzeaucourt.

* * * * * *

It always seemed to us singularly unfortunate that our Artillery so rarely supported its own division.

To the lay mind, the statement that the 33rd Divisional Artillery seldom operated with the 33rd Division, requires brief explanation.

It will be generally admitted that the work required of all arms of the service was equally onerous, but the privations from weather conditions, and casualties suffered by the Infantry, were, in ratio of time, greater than those of other arms of the service. The strain, however, of the other arms of the service was unquestionably in the same ratio, equal to that of the Infantry.

For instance a brigade of Infantry would be ordered to assault a certain position, supported by its affiliated brigade of Artillery. Possibly, the visibility might be low. The enemy only cared about saving his position at a minimum loss to himself, and with a maximum loss to us. He would, therefore, as in fact was usually the case, for most of our attacks were precipitated at dawn in low visibility, direct his fire, that is of his protective artillery barrage, upon the advancing waves of infantry, and restrain himself from firing at our artillery positions. It followed that such heavy casualties were exacted from, and strain put upon, our Infantry, in a short period of time, that they had to be withdrawn from the line ; whilst, in the same period of time the Artillery had only suffered slightly in casualties, and was in no sense exhausted. Whilst the Infantry was withdrawn from the line to rest, the Artillery remained to cover assaults of another division.

Technically, also, it was important that the Artillery should be maintained in the same area for as long a period as possible compatible with the strain which it was fair to inflict upon its personnel and guns.

Such things as making ammunition dumps, establishment of horse lines and divisional ammunition columns, laying of telephone lines, establishing of observation posts, and all the concomitants of an Artillery war cannot be done in a night. Whereas, the Infantry of a Division can be deployed for action during the night, carry its objective, be completely disorganized and worn out as the result; and be relieved the following night without dislocation of its supply services, or of those arms attendant upon it.

In view of these considerations it will be found, therefore, that the movement of troops in a comparatively immobile war, was for the reasons stated, bound to dissociate the Artillery from its Infantry within the formation of the tactical unit of a Division.

From the examination of the war diaries of the Infantry, the Artillery, the Army Service Corps, and the other arms of the Service, it will be found that the strain of war upon each arm was in ratio of time equal; or so nearly equal as not to be a bone of contention; as it so often was between the various arms, each of which considered that they, and they alone, were responsible for victory. When the Somme Battle started on July 1st, 1916, Lord Rawlinson tells us that 13,000 tons of artillery ammunition were fired into the German lines, and that in September, 1918, when the British attacked the Hindenburg Line, 65,000 tons of shells were projected upon the enemy's battle front. General Rawlinson's army alone fired, in forty-eight hours, the enormous amount of 3,000 tons of rounds of artillery ammunition, which in money is nearly 5,000,000 pounds sterling.

Whilst the Infantry was withdrawn from the line at Passchendaele, and enjoyed the fruits of its labours in the estaminets and picture houses of Poperinghe, the Artillery maintained its positions in the dark and muddy fastnesses of Zonnebeke. The Royal Army Service Corps, whilst still responsible to feed that Infantry, entailing long night drives across the wasted fields and macadamless roads of Abele, in bitter wind and driving rain, was also responsible nightly, to ration that same Artillery amidst the fœtid fields of Potijze, with no other light to brighten their journey into the Unknown than that of the fog-veiled starshell, or the quick-cut flash of bursting cordite.

Whilst those in warm and brightly-lit billets were charmed and transported by band and ragtime, they who remained in battle formed the audience of a sublime orchestra, whose crescendo of shrieking shell, and thunder of gun, intermittently thrilled and appalled; or, whose pianissimo of distant cry coming over the skyline at dawn, lulled them to fitful slumber.

Sometimes we have gone; and many weeks later returned to the same area, still finding there our trusty friends, the Royal Field Artillery, their guns axle-deep in mud, but still speaking; their pile of shells seemingly undiminished, were it not for the thousand empty cases around the gun emplacements; their horses, hairy as Highland cattle; and one day, they too have gone to Poperinghe and the estaminet lights for their well-earned rest; whilst we, with their Relief, have remained in audience to the chill music of Mars, who, with rude hands, has snatched the pipes from Pan, and with discord, blows his strident note.

THE ROYAL REGIMENT OF ARTILLERY.

Very little has been said about the work of the Artillery for the reasons already stated. Although always protected as if by a sure screen by the Artillery curtain of fire, except as we passed backwards and forwards to the battery positions we saw little of the intimate side of their work, and had little personal touch with their personnel. While we drifted on from one Sector to another, the supporting batteries remained in their positions to maintain their protective barrage across the front. The relief of one Division by another was complex, but this arrangement was nothing more than a simple advance to battle and a rear guard action, which had to be covered by artillery fire. In relief, as we drifted by platoons in long snakelike curves, by tracks upon the Passchendaele Salient or across the dusty soil of Arras and the Somme, the boom and roar of 60 pounders, and rattling field guns kept up an unsubdued fire, which much reduced the precision of the enemy batteries, technically known as counter battery work. When we advanced to attack, the air was filled with the screams of shells thrown from the batteries. Very few outside the ranks of the Royal Regiment of Artillery ever realized the organization required to prepare even one six-gun battery to take part in the big offensive, in which the battery must be maintained for many weeks. The re-calibration of guns, adjustment of sights—the work of the Ordnance service; little corrections to carriage mountings and final adjustments of wheels to ensure the perfect spring—the work of the wheelwrights; weeding out of animals in poor condition, replacements by similar species, height and colour, rest and better feeding for a well-tried wheeler, and the thousand little touches of the medical side of horsemanship—the whole of this the work of the Remount and Veterinary services; the collection of ammunition from rail heads, its transport forward by lorry and by pack mule into gun positions, its camouflaging from enemy observations and protection against bombardment and fire—the work of the ammunition columns; repairs to saddlery and harness as well as to signal and telephone apparatus—the work of the batteries' technical experts; and, finally, the preparation of map and plan, of charts and air photographs, the laying out of lines and switch points for day and night firing—the work of the junior officers and non-commissioned officers of the battery; and the whole to be supervised by a Major, probably of not more than 25 years of age, with the whole responsibility resting on his shoulders. If sometimes our relations and friends, not to say our tailors and other creditors, were a little amazed that we had no time to reply to their letters, when all these things are borne in mind, perhaps the fact that there are only twenty-four hours in each day will be appreciated. It must not be thought, however, that the Artillery always remained in fixed positions. In the operations of March and April, 1918, we have seen guns of the heaviest calibre, which travel in three pieces, towed by motor lorries, ambling along the roads as nimbly as the little field guns do at a military tournament. In September of the same year, after the breaking of the Hindenburg Line, guns and ammunition were transported across the rotten, shattered bridge over the St. Quentin Canal, the sure-footed mule, trotting as lightly as a Blondin across the swinging planks, the battery limbered up the other side and preceding the infantry into battle. In action, the field batteries kept well to their positions by skilled, hard-riding drivers, their knees well in, heads down, and whips soothing the willing off-side leader, whose repeated efforts urge the slacker to exert himself; unlimbered, action front, the air some 3,000 yards ahead filled with little white puffs of smoke beneath which the great masses break and run, leaving some of their numbers stretched in death; a counter battery searches it out, first a long, then a short, then a direct hit; the drivers are called into action amidst the burst of shells, with a horse down here and a badly wounded man there; stretcher bearers; and the battery has disappeared into the valley to emerge again in another position in action to the support of the thin line, and little group of Infantry, which are always pressing on.

It is not only dangerous, but a difficult game, this one of keeping a mobile battery in action. All the same questions which were raised by its commander over the immobile offensive, and pondered over, must now flash through his brain as his battery moves from point to point. There is no rest for the leader of a battery.

In the 33rd Divisional Artillery Lieutenant-Colonel B. A. B. Butler, D.S.O., killed almost at the end of the war, after having served continuously since Mons, Lieutenant-Colonels H. C. Rochfort Boyd, D.S.O., also killed, O. M. Harris, D.S.O., Lieutenant-Colonels Skinner, D.S.O., and R. E. Ramsden, D.S.O., have in particular helped to make, by their fine fighting qualities, the Division what it was; under the leadership primarily of Brigadier-General C. G. Stewart, C.M.G., D.S.O., an officer who has spent nearly the whole of his thirty odd years of service in fighting in many lands.

Of the Royal Regiment of Artillery perhaps too little has been written. But the thunder of their guns re-echoes in our ears—listen and you hear it. As we rest, as we sleep, as we march and counter march; as wave after wave of gallant Infantry sweep over bog, morass, and devastated shell-torn waste; as we die, as we live! " *Ubique* "—" *Quo fas et gloria ducunt.*"

* * * * * *

Our Royal Engineer Companies, the 19th of the Old and the 212th and 222nd of the New Army, were a very strong factor in the Division, especially to their respective Infantry Brigades with whom they habitually worked. In the stationary trench warfare the material for defences and dug-outs and all the most important strong points, was designed and fashioned by the Sappers. In the violent defensive battles the Sappers often handled their infantry weapons as well as any rifleman. In the final advances they were always at hand to make the way easy for the other Arms. These material duties were much, but the high character, efficiency and bravery of officers and men had a great moral effect on other Units. The personality of Major H. A. S. Pressy, M.C., Captain G. E. Sim, D.S.O., M.C., Captain C. la T. Turner-Jones, D.S.O., M.C., Major H. T. Morshead, D.S.O., Captain Thompson, M.C., Major J. E. Anderson, M.C., Major C. P. L. Balcombe, M.C., and Captain E. L. Gale, M.C., will always have a high place in our memory.

The Signal branch of the Royal Engineers were like the nerves of the human body which transfer thoughts in the brain to action in the limbs. So the Signallers by night and day, in quiet times and in stress of battle, conveyed the orders and messages from Headquarters to Units with methods swift and sure.

Major G. W. Williams, D.S.O., M.C., and Captain Louth, especially, organized and carried through the complex system with great success.

* * * * * *

The work of the Royal Army Service Corps is always difficult to explain; and is, therefore, little understood. A moment's reflection upon it is not sufficient; the fighting troops owe a little more than that.

An Army Service Corps driver may not often be seen wearing his tin hat. As the song says "Sailors don't care" nor do the Army Service Corps drivers; not a tinker's curse for anything—except the rain—*then* the shell hat goes on, and the only part of the driver that's dry is his head. They seldom catch cold, or if they do they do not know it, they are so really uncomfortable that they wallow in it:—rain, mud, sleet, snow, chill, fatigue or dust: heat, dust-colds, sore eyes, fatigue rations, sleep and dirt.

The Mechanical Transport grew from a small nucleus of nineteen Motor Transport Companies existing in July, 1914, till the number of lorries on its establishment had been multiplied five hundred times by the end of the War. On the cessation of hostilities, in France alone there were over thirty thousand lorries, while the personnel had swelled to some hundred and sixty thousand men; and the training, mobilization, equipment, and embarkation of the whole proceeded throughout the War with astonishing smoothness. One Branch, the Road Construction Companies, covered weekly in their duties, fourteen million kilometres of French roads ($8\frac{1}{2}$ million miles).

The Horse Transport, originally consisting of some fifty-one Companies stationed at home and in the Colonies, had been expanded beyond count. While the establishment and formation of supply services all over the world can only be imagined when it is realized that the feeding strength of the British Armies in France alone was over two million, seven hundred thousand men and four hundred thousand animals; and a Division in weight alone required some two hundred tons of supplies a day. The necessary introduction of a higher standard of comfort, in order to maintain the great strain on the health of the troops under the abnormal circumstances consistent with the

War, threw a great additional strain on the Army Service Corps, in addition to the difficulties involved by the by-no-means gradual increase in the Ration strength itself.

Sir Douglas Haig wrote in his despatch, March 21st, 1919 :—

"Unless our Supply Services had been fully efficient, the great "advance carried out by our Armies during the Autumn of last year "could not have been achieved. Wars may be won or lost by the "standard of health and moral of the opposing Forces. Moral depends "to a very large extent upon the feeding and general well-being of our "troops. Badly supplied troops will invariably be low in moral, and "an army ravaged by disease ceases to be a fighting force. The "feeding and health of the fighting forces are dependent on the rearward "Services, and so it may be agreed that with the rearward Services "rests Victory or Defeat. In our case we can justly say that our "Supply System has been developed into one of the most perfect in the "world."

The trains ran so slowly because in his retreat the enemy blew up all the bridges. The festoons of wiring lay along the line, the telegraph poles pulled down and cut in half where there was time. Coaches had been blown up where they stood, and the permanent way twisted as though the rails had been made of rope. Gangs of Chinks jibbered and grinned as they worked in the slow Oriental fashion, their filthy bundles piled by the railroad sides, and farther down the Hun prisoners were sullenly at work repairing the very destruction they had wrought. The signal posts were gone, adding to the danger of all trains.

Railheads for supplies were very often necessarily a long way off, and usually we "drew" very early in the morning so as to get supplies up as soon as possible in the day. The Mechanical Transport Company (33rd Division Mechanical Transport Company) never let us down ; though, heaven knows, they had difficulties enough to contend with from time to time.

Few soldiers have any idea of the difficulty of maintaining and running a supply railhead, and few have any idea of the wonderful way in which even at the worst times, accuracy and promptness in accounting and issuing was carried out. Besieged by half a dozen Senior Supply Officers of as many divisions, all utterly selfish to a great extent in the interests of their particular division, to satisfy all, and yet maintain friendly and sound relationships with each, between themselves, was a task calling for the utmost patience and tact.

The mule, and all connected therewith, is, we fear, a hobby which has been ridden to death ; but since our animals' strength was very great, it will be seen that keeping them shod was no child's play ; but shoeing

LIEUTENANT-COLONEL P. G. P. LEA,
C.M.G., D.S.O.,
Royal Army Service Corps.

LIEUTENANT-COLONEL W. B. GARNETT,
D.S.O.,
2nd Battalion Royal Welsh Fusiliers.

LIEUTENANT-COLONEL H. B. SPENS,
D.S.O.,
1st 5/6th (T) Battalion The Cameronians
(Scottish Rifles).

LIEUTENANT-COLONEL T. K. PARDOE,
D.S.O.,
2nd Battalion The Worcestershire Regiment.

LIEUTENANT-COLONEL H. DE B. PURVIS,
M.C.,
2nd Battalion Argyll & Sutherland Highlanders.
(Killed in Action.)

SOME COMMANDING OFFICERS.

smiths and our mules thoroughly understood one another, for we have seen many a time the affirmative and the negative of their arguments wax equally hot. Most shoeing smiths have, we believe, spent some time in India, and without doubt, habitually addressed the mules in " Urdu." Anyhow, we find our vocabulary lacking in most of their terms of endearment. He is a man with great equanimity of mind who can shoe a mule with 9.2's bursting in the vicinity !

*   *   *   *   *   *

In the Royal Army Medical Corps the Division was equally fortunate. Under the watchful eye of the late Colonel S. de C. O'Grady, C.M.G., D.S.O., the Division possessed a medical staff unequalled in skill and that quality which perhaps is more invaluable to the doctor—" the bedside manner "— in this case happily adapted to field conditions. The courage and fortitude of the personnel of the Field Ambulances has been illustrated in the Brickstacks at Cuinchy, on the Somme Battlefields, at the Battle of Arras, where the Medical Officer attached to the 1st Queen's Regiment for hours sat in the open with a grenade box as his operating table, under heavy shell fire, tending his cases with unshaken nerve and hand ; on the Menin Road, where stretcher bearers fell by the score, whilst others in simple duty fell in to take their places unflinching ; and in the final offensive when the work of the medical services was strained to its utmost limit. In sport, too, the Royal Army Medical Corps excelled, aided and abetted by Major Daly. And so with unbroken good cheer, kindly help, firmness and skill the Royal Army Medical Corps did much not only to alleviate suffering, but to maintain the moral of the Division at a high level. With them must equally be included many American medical officers who served with the Division, in permanent attachment.

Nor can any History of the Great European War be complete without some mention of that abominable and enduring scourge of lice which afflicted our troops in the line without interruption and without regard as to person from 1914 until 1919. Few verminous insects are more foul and unsightly than the body louse. It is a proved disease carrier. Yet, even under most adverse conditions so efficiently did the Divisional laundry, sometimes operated by men of the Divisions, at others by Flemish peasant girls, deal with this plague, that on leaving the line for even one or two days' respite we could almost always be sure of a clean and pure change of garments to give us a fresh start in the unceasing warfare upon this nerve-wracking, sleep-destroying, uncomfortable and unhealthy plague. We can well remember often seeing a young Highlander, fresh as the dew upon his native hills, blushing all over like his September heather, standing, clad only in his clean shirt, hosetops and boots, whilst a buxom Flemish woman, laughingly and quickly, singed out the lice and eggs from the pleats of his kilt and completed the work by hammering the remains to pulp with the back of a large brush.

THE THIRTY-THIRD DIVISION.

A danger to the well-being of our lads has been the gypsy life they have led,—continually taking over ground hurriedly evacuated by the enemy whose casualties are well known. Frequently, the only possible strategic object has been grossly insanitary, and, therefore, conducive to all kinds of maladies. The Royal Army Medical Corps and especially the sanitary men of battalions and other formations have been indispensable for the thoroughness with which they always attacked these spots; and thanks to them our second day on new ground always found us replete with every hygienic contrivance.

It is all the more meritorious when one considers the difficulties of obtaining material, and the fact that a less energetic discharge of these disagreeable duties might conceivably have passed muster.

Some idea of the routine work of the Royal Army Medical Corps may be gauged from the following statistics :—

CASUALTIES—1918.

	KILLED.		WOUNDED.		MISSING.		SICK.		TOTAL.	
	Officers.	Other Ranks.	Officers.	Other Ranks.	Officers.	Other Ranks.	Officers.	Other Ranks.	Officers.	Other Ranks.
January	3	36	12	190	—	12	8	319	20	557
February ..	—	9	2	73	—	12	11	139	13	233
March	4	99	21	498	1	3	12	286	38	886
April	30	468	92	1,519	39	1,393	20	380	181	3,760
May	7	89	30	644	2	88	35	423	74	1,244
June	3	47	16	417	—	1	29	418	48	883
July	2	52	15	336	1	4	15	289	33	681
August	—	21	5	117	—	5	7	330	12	473
September ..	22	215	59	1,179	2	240	20	328	103	1,962
October	38	607	92	2,551	9	362	—	—	137	3,536
November ..	5	44	20	258	—	27	39	831	64	1,190

* * * * * *

Major G. J. S. Lloyd, M.C., and Captain the Honourable E. G. French, D.S.O., each served a considerable time with the Division as Provost Marshal. They and the Military Police did not have much provost work, thanks to the fine spirit in the Division, but they were familiar figures and always ready and willing to keep things going even outside their special province.

It would be an impossible task to recall to our mind all those officers and other ranks who from one cause and another made themselves notable or notorious, and who served with such gallantry and distinction, within the Division. By their deeds they are known. Perhaps, also, we have given

170

LIEUTENANT-COLONEL G. S. HUTCHISON,
D.S.O., M.C.,
33rd Battalion Machine Gun Corps.

LIEUTENANT-COLONEL L. M. CROFTS,
D.S.O.,
1st Battalion The Queens (Royal West Surrey Regiment).

LIEUTENANT-COLONEL H. C. COPEMAN,
C.M.G., D.S.O.,
4th (T) Battalion, The Suffolk Regiment.

LIEUTENANT-COLONEL A. H. MENZIES,
D.S.O., T.D.,
9th (T) (Glasgow Highland) Battalion,
The Highland Light Infantry.

LIEUTENANT-COLONEL E. M. BEALL,
C.M.G., D.S.O.,
4th (Extra Reserve) Battalion,
The King's (Liverpool Regiment).

SOME COMMANDING OFFICERS.

undue notice to some Battalions over others. This is for no reason of prejudice, but rather ignorance, and the great difficulty of obtaining fuller personal information from those who have been demobilized and who still serve with their old Battalion. Little has been said, also, with regard to the work of the Royal Army Ordnance Corps, the chaplains, and all those auxiliary services who attended to the efficiency and comfort of the troops in the field. It would require a far more comprehensive volume than this to do so.

* * * * * *

The most astonishing thing is the way the New Armies took to all the various problems of War. We used to say it took two years to make a gunner; and a gentleman cadet spent from one to one and a half years at Sandhurst before he could win his first commission; and then, by a clause in the King's Regulations, was on probation for three years; captains were men who waited anything up to fourteen years for the rank; and elderly majors, cut off from hope of command, consulted the Pay Warrant regarding their pensions, and drifted to Bath and to Cheltenham.

Out came these old warriors at the first sound of the bugle, scenting action, after years of inaction; "dug-outs" indeed! and why? To them, how much we owe, while the young blood of our standing army was poured out like water on the Road from Mons and upon the vile mud of Flanders. There were as many new, as old, army officers on the staffs of commands as the war dragged on. Once the primary need of discipline was over, the "amateurs" were second to none. The untrammelled lay mind brought fresh power to a sorely-tried machine, and the great business of war became a fertile field for the brains and dispassionate energies of the countless business . men and technical experts, who gave up everything, except their honour, to win through to a high success.

* * * * * *

The Division was fortunate in being able to see H.M. the King during the Somme operations when he passed beside the Division, whilst visiting the battlefields at Fricourt and Mametz. Later, His Majesty visited the Division at Lorie Château, near Ypres in August, 1918, an inspection carried out very near to the front; so near, indeed, that His Majesty's car had only just passed the cross roads at Waton, when they were heavily shelled. H.M. King George V., accompanied by General Plumer, lunched with the Divisional Commander, who afterwards presented the officers of his staff and commanding the formations of the Division. It will remain a matter of justifiable pride to those thus presented to their Sovereign on the field of battle—the highest of all honours. Those so presented are shown in the Order of Battle, July, 1918. His Majesty again honoured us with a visit in November, 1918, very shortly after the Armistice.

* * * * * *

Then we have had Marshal Foch's views upon the British Army. "Ah, I know them well. I have lived in very pleasant intimacy with them. There are three stages in the development of the British Army. The first was the old regular forces—a most excellent army—but very small. They suffered most heavily and fought most magnificently in the first battle of Ypres. Then came Kitchener's Army and the Dominion troops. They were very gallant, and, like all young troops, very confident, but very inexperienced. They thought that bravery by itself was a match for the bullets. They bought their experience dear on the Somme: 1917 was a year lost on both sides. Then came the third stage in 1918. The German attack began badly for the British. General Byng's army pulled itself together very quickly. The British lost 15,000 men. Things were going very ill with them. The fighting round Villers-Bretonneux was most terrible. Amiens and Abbeville were the crucial points for us. My first step when I was made Commander-in-Chief of the Allied Armies was to knit the British and French closer together. Otherwise they would have been forced apart. The British would have fallen back on to their bases on the coast. The French would have fallen back on to the Seine. The Germans would have been through." Clasping the fingers of both hands tightly together, the Marshal went on. "They needed to be joined like that. Once that was done it did not matter how hard the Germans battered. The line was solid. I helped the British as much as I could. I made them work very hard. Dig trenches! If you have four lines, dig six; if you have six lines, dig eight so that you will always have positions to fall back upon. So, thanks to the fact that the Germans left us alone in May and June, we were able to re-organize; and when I started my offensive in July, the British troops were as fresh and as full of fighting as ever; the whole line thrusting, elbowing its way forward. No stop! No rest! That was the supreme test of the British Army. And they came through it splendidly. No attack in the history of the world was better carried out than the one made on the Hindenburg Line, near St. Quentin and Cambrai, by your fourth, third, and first Armies. The enemy positions were most formidable. They swept right over them. It was a glorious day for the British Army." From these words from the lips of Foch himself, we can see how the great principle of unity of command, acquiesced in nobly by our own Commander-in-Chief, ran its strong course to certain victory; and how the workings of the directing mind were reflected in the minds of our own Commanders. We know how the 33rd Division, which played its glorious part on the road to victory, was guided as surely and as unhesitatingly by Sir Reginald Pinney, as the master minds guided the whole. We knew, inversely, by the calls that were made on the 33rd Division where we stood, and we were proud: we knew that we were reckoned with, and we knew that it was relied on always with certain and unfailing trust that our general had, "by the labour of preparation done beforehand," so fitted his Division, that time after time, from one battle it could be thrown into another again, anywhere, to decide an issue.

* * * * * *

And of the Leader of our Division, Major-General Sir Reginald Pinney, K.C.B., his character stands out. His cheerfulness and courage and great sense of proportion; his decision, his tireless systemization; and his great spirit. He was a soldier's general. No château could tempt him, no security decoy him; where the men were, there he was; how they lived, so did he. As temperate in his living as he was in tempering justice with mercy, as stern as he was kind, he could win a battle in the morning and help Belgian farmers stack their corn in the evening. He came not of a race of courtiers, nor had his way been made smooth by wealth. He won his position by sheer hard work—he passed into the Staff College at the age of twenty-five.—His stock was that of the Yeomen of England, his forefathers farmers and squires of the Dorset Downs, whence he acquired his birthright—his rugged frame, his unwearying patience; his kindliness, trained by his military life to a sure sense of justice; his eye for country—one of the greatest military gifts; and his love for his fellow men and for horses. Prior to the War he had had ample experience both as a Regimental and as a Staff Officer. He had commanded his own battalion of the Royal Fusiliers, of which he made not only fine soldiers but fine cricketers. He had tasted of war in South Africa. And he had never ceased to profit from his varied experience of military life and of men. Tireless, his set face ever ready to break into a smile of encouragement when his quick eye saw it was needed, he was everywhere— yet nowhere was he absent. He had the great gift of generalship; he was the right force in the right place at the right moment; his honour was our honour; his name our name; his disappointments ours, and his victories ours. His K.C.B. came late, so that we could honour it the more; the true knight whose spurs indeed were won in battle.

"The glory of great men ought always to be rated according to the means used to acquire it."
LA ROCHEFOUCAULT.

Spare and straight in workmanlike kit,—no spit and polish in the field; nothing unnecessary, but stripped as an ironclad for action; typical of his race, his firm mouth set and his keen eyes lit with just the smile and light that the sight of a friend a long way off will bring.

Yet who can tell the burden that must weigh at times on the mind of a general of division as he returns from the slaughter of his men, when he loves those men? Yet, the light of optimism lest the living should be depressed,—the look of Victory when the heart was heaviest!

* * * * * *

THE THIRTY-THIRD DIVISION.

The Divisional Staff is readily remembered. A line of General Staff Officers who served the Division with distinction, gallantry and extreme devotion—Lieutenant-Colonel A. Symons, C.M.G., D.S.O., 13th Hussars, who was with us during the early stages of the Division; Lieutenant-Colonel D. Forster, C.M.G., D.S.O., R.E., a man of unqualified energy, bravery and rare military gifts; Lieutenant-Colonel E. C. Gepp, D.S.O., D.C.L.I., of great and merry heart and singular fortitude, who ably helped to carry the Division through the arduous operations at Meteren and Dickebusch; Lieutenant-Colonel E. A. Osborne, D.S.O., R.E., also of great good cheer, popular, with the right word at the right moment for officer or private, abundant energy, and whose foresight and bravery helped us much in the great bounds of the final offensive. A long list of more junior staff officers, in whom the Division was fortunate in having—those who combined all those qualities necessary, not only to the successful carrying out of major or minor operations, but in the prevention of friction. With sorely tried nerves and overwork, both amongst the Staffs and Commanding Officers, the Division was indeed happy in that Major-General Sir Reginald Pinney organized his officers into so perfect a team. In the Adjutant-General and Quartermaster-General's Branch, too, the Division was equally fortunate. Mention has already been made of Lieutenant-Colonel P. R. C. Commings, C.M.G., D.S.O. In Lieutenant-Colonel T. G. Ramsay, D.S.O., Cameron Highlanders, Major O. B. Foster, M.C., Northumberland Fusiliers, and Major H. C. C. Batten, D.S.O., Dorset Regiment, the Division possessed Staff Officers of singular experience, bonhomie, unwearying and unfailing energy and resource. When we recollect the enormous field covered by their work, including the supply of clean clothing, bathing arrangements, washing, supply of ammunition and bombs, supply of reinforcements, promotion of officers, supply of horses, cinemas, concert parties; equipment, canteens, rations for both men and animals, heating and lighting appliances, and a thousand other services, some conception of the work entailed can be realized. When we remember also that the numbers of all things are limited, the demands unceasing, and priority of delivery expected immediately by every arm and every unit of that arm, a further idea of the tact and energy required in this Department can be conceived. Mention must also be made of Captain D. L. G. Pigache, Royal Fusiliers, who as the officer in charge of canteens was always accessible, unwearying in energy, and gave to us a canteen anywhere and everywhere.

Attention has been drawn to the fact that for almost all their period of active operations, the Infantry Brigades and the Divisional Artillery were commanded by the same men. With such a happy command from the Divisional Commander downwards the machine was bound to work smoothly, whilst confidence was assured.

Brigadier-General C. R. G. Mayne, C.M.G., D.S.O., of the 19th Brigade, will always remain a familiar figure in his great height and rugged strength, striding over the battlefield, possessed of that quality which he so happily shared with his General, unwearying patience and good cheer; Brigadier-General H. D. Heriot Maitland, C.M.G., D.S.O., of the 98th Brigade, remains constant in our memory at the head of his victorious Brigade, quiet in manner, thoughtful, every move in our own or the enemy's game carefully considered, and of final, invincible decision; whilst Brigadier-General A. W. F. Baird, C.B., C.M.G., D.S.O., of the 100th Brigade, stands out as a master mind in battle and in organization, of enduring physical and mental energy, possessed always of the most comprehensive knowledge both of his front with its network of shell craters and trench systems, and of his officers and men. A man never defeated. The Brigade Staffs were examples of hard work, courage, and unselfishness.

Nor must be forgotten the staff-sergeants and clerks at Divisional and Brigade Headquarters. Much of the success and comfort of the Division depended upon their unstinted work, day and night.

* * * * * *

It was a noteworthy fact that the 33rd Division was representative of not only a country side and nearly every town in Great Britain, but was a combination of all the special qualities of the old Regular, Territorial, Special Reserve and the New Armies. We had six regular battalions, three territorial battalions, one special reserve battalion, and three battalions of the new army; whilst the Divisional Artillery and the Royal Engineers were also of the new army. Of these battalions, the 1st and 5th–6th Scottish Rifles and 9th Highland Light Infantry represented Glasgow, the Lowlands of Scotland and the great centre of industry of the Vales of Leven and Clyde. The 93rd, 2nd Battalion Argyll and Sutherland Highlanders represented the Highlands and the countryside of Scotland; the 2nd Battalion Worcestershire Regiment, the 4th Battalion Suffolk Regiment, the 1st Battalion Queen's (Royal West Surrey) Regiment represented the counties and towns of rural England; the 1st and 18th Battalions Middlesex Regiment and the 20th Battalion Royal Fusiliers represented London; the 2nd Battalion Royal Welch Fusiliers represented the hills and mines of Wales; and the 16th Battalion King's Royal Rifle Corps and the 4th Battalion King's (Liverpool) Regiment, the only Special Reserve Battalion which went to France, came from the Midlands and the Northern industrial centre of England. This composition is remarkable, and to it may probably be traced the singular success and astonishing fighting qualities of the Division in every circumstance of war.

General Lawrence, Chief of the Staff at General Headquarters, in bidding farewell to General Pinney, said, " The 33rd Division has always been stout, other Divisions were sure when you were alongside."

* * * * * *

We must not forget how great a thing Britain has done. It does not seem to us that we as a race yet realize that this country has achieved the greatest feat that it has yet accomplished. Never in her history has Britain been so near destruction, and never has she risen so triumphantly to the occasion. When the Germans wrote their "Hymn of Hate" and emphasized England as its object, they directly diagnosed the situation.

The Great War has been won by Britain, and without her, success would have been impossible. The feat which our Fleet has accomplished is without parallel in the world's history. The second greatest Navy of the world was, from the first day of the war, confined to its ports; and from the first day of the war was unable to put a single merchant ship on the sea. We all know the fact, but it is worth emphasizing, that it is without parallel in the world's history. Further, Great Britain, has often sent victorious armies to the Continent, but never in the world's history has she ended a war with the largest and best army in the world.

At Waterloo we had scarcely 40,000 British troops under arms, and that was about the average size of our Army up to that date. The Prussian army in that campaign numbered about 120,000 and the French Army about the same. With that compare the relative numbers of the armies when the Armistice was signed. One hundred years ago, it is true, we financed the armies that were allied against Napoleon. In this war we have not only financed them, but have, to a great extent, supplied them with munitions, so that our victory has been achieved by the united effort not only of the men and women of these islands, and our colonies and dependencies, but by the sacrifice of all the treasure from our storehouse.

*   *   *   *   *   *

WE must finally reflect upon those qualities which gave birth to the spirit which animated and inspired our Navy, our Armies and our Airmen, alike in defeat as in victory. There was only one quality—the quality of equality and comradeship.

Even as the Old Contemptibles, as a lion at bay, turned on their tormentors at the Battle of the Marne on September 7th, 1914, and hurled them back in most bitter fighting from a line which, to the end of the campaign, the enemy never succeeded in recrossing; and as the New Armies, in April, 1918, animated by the same indomitable spirit, struck back that enemy, who, with blood-seared eye, and lustful heart, longed once more to rape Paris as he had raped her in 1870, so will it be that same quality, the quality of comradeship, which will direct our Nation into that New World, of which all fighters and workers during the Great War have had a very true vision.

During the War an appeal was made to men, as it was to women, through the spirit of Patriotism and National endeavour, even to the test of National unity in death; the finest thing in life was the act of dying for one's country. There is, however, a thing equally as fine as this for those of us who have been tempered in the white-hot furnace of war—this is to live for one's country and our countrymen!

Through the ranks of the Service, the Nation in arms has passed tens of thousands of young men, who if they have gained nothing else have certainly gained in vitality and in vision. Some of those men have shown themselves to be pre-eminently leaders, not merely leaders in the military sense, but leaders of the hearts, lives and ambitions of men; in short, the select pilots of the ship of State. We wonder, in the absorption of these men once more or possibly for the first time, into our civic life, if those who now direct our destinies have realized that these are the men who should be chosen to lead the Nation into the " New World " of which these men alone have had a vision.

When our men went forth in their millions, aided by their women each one of them went with a vision of green fields, and waving corn, soft lapping seas and shingled coves, the cottage and the stook, rolling hills, glen and moorland stream, love of family and pride of race, no thought of the drudgery of life. Their thoughts were of boyhood days, when Youth stepped forth from his cities to find his God in the smell of the loam, the music of the stream, the tang of the myrtle berry, the caress of the upland breeze, and the sight of the rolling hills, mounting higher and higher, boulder upon boulder, and crag upon crag, even as a ladder unto Heaven. Some of our Generals were not blind to this fact. We well remember Lieutenant-General Sir Thomas Snow when he addressed the 100th Brigade prior to an attack upon the Hindenburg Line, in May, 1917, recalling to their minds the pleasant vales and cottages of Worcestershire, shrouded in a blue film of wood smoke and haze; the shady glens, the purple hillsides, and triumphant peaks of the Highlands; the red-roofed villages of Surrey; and then, dramatically turning, he pointed to the jagged, torn remains of the villages of Ayette and Hamelincourt. He knew what appeal to make. He knew what lay at the root of every man's heart. As men have surged to battle, or stood in the trenches knee-deep in freezing mud, their constant thought has been of their home, the country of their boyhood, a free country. They have seen the vision of a Promised Land. We stand on its threshold now. The lads have returned. The War Correspondents and Official Reporters were right when, throughout the War, they drew public attention to this fact, namely, our insatiable cheerfulness. We went through Hell with a song upon our lips. The song may yet be choked in our throats by the strangle-hold of self-interest. How true is it that the Age of Competition culminated in the most furious output of man's created works that ever disgraced the history of human progress—the creation of guns, munitions, tanks, machine guns, bombs and Zeppelins, poisonous gas, and every conceivable device for the wholesale slaughter of mankind; the destruction of his works and of the beauty of God. What a monument, indeed, to Civilization!

THE THIRTY-THIRD DIVISION.

The fact of the matter seems to be this, that throughout history men have been struggling with each other instead of for each other.

Even as a burbling brook tumbles headlong from the snow-capped peaks of the mountains, stretching their white fingers to Heaven, and rolls onwards in a great stream, carrying upon its troubled waters the obstacles which would impede its progress, and ever swelling into a mighty river, belches forth into the ocean, so is the stream of human progress ; it sprang from Heaven on high ; it has tumbled and cascaded through the dim ages ; it has swelled in the stream of mediævalism ; it has driven on, dashing its sure course through barriers of repression ; it has passed through the maelstrom of conflicting civilizations and now is surely rolling on into the open sea of the boundless brotherhood of man.

Nothing shall stay its torrent. Its destiny is sure. Man's life is physical, moral and spiritual. He has passed through the physical ; he has entered the moral ; and goes surely on to the spiritual, for the destiny of man is in God.

" For, I dip't into the future, far as human eye could see,
" Saw the Vision of the world, and all the wonder that would be ;
" Saw the heavens fill with Commerce, argosies of magic sails,
" Pilots of the purple twilight, dropping down with golden bales.

*   *   *   *   *   *

" Till the war drum throbbed no longer, and the battle flag was furled,
" In the Parliament of man, the Federation of the world."

ALFRED TENNYSON.